MAKING
A HABIT OF
SUCCESS

MAKING A HABIT OF SUCCESS

TWO BESTSELLING WORKS
COMPLETE IN ONE VOLUME

How to Make a Habit of Succeeding

How to Win with High Self-Esteem

MACK R. DOUGLAS

BARNES
&NOBLE
BOOKS
NEW YORK

TABLE OF CONTENTS

How to Make a Habit

of Succeeding

1

How to Win

with High Self-Esteem

233

How to Make a Habit of Succeeding

DEDICATED
TO

Aline, Linda, Don, Laura and Elaine who now understand why those hundreds of hours late at night in the home study.

Nell Seaver and Eunice Pitcher for excellence in manuscript preparation.

Napoleon Hill, Dale Carnegie and Earl Nightingale for their influence on me and this book.

The Fort Lauderdale Sales and Marketing Executives Club for encouragement and challenge.

Walter Dunn and the staff of WFTL *in Fort Lauderdale, Florida, for both the name of this book and for daring with Bob Watson and* KGNC *of Amarillo, Texas, to pioneer in my radio program, "How to Make a Habit of Succeeding."*

CONTENTS

PART ONE: THE POWER OF PURPOSE

1. Dynamic Purpose 11
2. Limitations of Purpose 16
3. Finding the Power of Purpose 19
   Exercise: The Power of Purpose 26
4. Developing Purpose 27
5. Purpose Grounded in Achievement 33
   Exercise: How to Develop Purpose 38

PART TWO: GOALS CAN CHANGE YOUR LIFE

6. Establishing a Goal 43
7. The Discipline of Goals 49
8. Examples of Goals 52
9. Benefits of Goals 58
   Exercise: Goals Can Change Your Life 63

PART THREE: IMAGINATION

10. Vivid Imagination 67
11. Imagination Defined 71
12. Brainstorming 74
13. Creative Leisure 77
14. Hindrances of Imagination 81
15. Developing Imagination 85
    Exercise: Imagination 89

PART FOUR: BUILD CONFIDENCE AND SUCCEED

16. Whip Worry 93
17. Fight Fear 99
18. Dominate Doubts 102
19. Act Aggressively 105
20. Possess Your Mind 109

Exercise: Build Confidence and Succeed   111

PART FIVE: THE POWER OF PERSISTENCE

21. Persistence Produces Power   115
22. Persistence Empowers Purpose   122
Exercise: The Power of Persistence   129
23. Persistence Pays High Profits   131
24. Persistence Is Education   137
25. Persistence Produces Results   141
Exercise: Persistence Pays High Profits   145

PART SIX: MOTIVATION

26. What Motivates Men?   149
27. How to Develop Energy   154
28. Motivation's Source   160
29. Excitement   164
30. Motivating Yourself and Others   169
Exercise: Motivation   172

PART SEVEN: BUILD BURNING DESIRE AND SUCCEED

31. Burning Desire Is Power   177
32. Burning Desire for Recognition   190
Exercise: Build Burning Desire and Succeed . .   195
33. How to Achieve Burning Desire   196
34. Burning Desire Develops Competition and
     Pride   204
35. Producing Burning Desire   211
Exercise: How to Achieve Burning Desire   215

PART EIGHT: NOW—ACTION!

36. Planning   219
37. Proper Attitude   222
38. Action Develops Courage   224
39. Action Produces Achievement   228
Exercise: Now — Action!   229

FOREWORD

Success has an evasive nature that does not permit its easy acquisition by the majority of those who pursue its rewards. But success, when realized, is sweeter because of its very nature—its constant elusiveness.

Success is a montage of exceptional effort, formative planning, consistent study and circumstances over which we often have little or no control. Throughout the ages man has attempted to determine the proper combination of these factors—to assure for himself the rewards that success represents. If, perchance, one individual could create this magic combination of factors, there would be no success possible—except for those who deviated from that pattern.

Success is not made for the masses, but rather for that select few who diligently combine and recombine an endless flow of patterns into one productive process that accomplishes successful results, yet whose composition is everchanging.

Mack Douglas does not attempt to provide a format for success, but rather he gives us avenues of pursuit, elements of thinking, actions and formulas derived from experience so that we can, in our finite ability, search out, combine and develop our own design of accomplishment.

Thus, Mack Douglas can never take credit for the success of anyone who reads this book—and he does not desire to claim the credit—but he can, and will, materially contribute to the ingredients of your success. Having fortified your determination with the contents of this book, you can accomplish that success in its fullest dimension with justified pride in personal accolades.

W. HEARTSILL WILSON

PART ONE
THE POWER OF PURPOSE

CHAPTER 1

Dynamic Purpose

Your key to personal success is building a dynamic purpose. Purpose differs from goals, for purpose is like the pot of gold at the end of the rainbow—the ideal that we seek. As soon as we attain one mountain peak of purpose we see another, and another is still ahead of us. Disraeli has said that "the secret of success is constancy to purpose."

Your key for personal success today is having a high purpose.

> If you can't be a pine on the top of the hill
> Be a shrub in the valley but be
> The best little shrub by the side of the hill;
> Be a bush if you can't be a tree.
>
> If you can't be a bush be a bit of grass
> And some highway happier make;
> If you can't be a muskie then just be a bass,
> But be the liveliest bass in the lake.
>
> We can't all be captains, we've got to be crew,
> There is something for all of us. There
> Is big work to do and there's lesser to do
> And the task we must do is the near.
>
> If you can't be a highway then just be a trail;
> If you can't be the sun be a star;
> It isn't by size that you win or you fail.
> Be the best of whatever you are.
>
> —Douglas Malloch[1]

---

[1]Douglas Malloch, "Be the Best of Whatever You Are," from *The Best Loved Poems of the American People* (Garden City, N.Y.: Garden City Publishing Company, 1936), page 102.

When Moses stood at the burning bush God said to him, "Draw not nigh hither: put off thy shoes from off thy feet for the place whereon thou standest is holy ground." Challenged by the burning bush experience Moses not only set free 2,000,000 of his kin and countrymen but led them through miraculous experiences for forty years to make a nation of dedicated people out of former slaves. Today Christians and Jews alike claim Moses to be one of the greatest men who ever lived. He had high purpose.

Presidential Purpose

Several years ago it was my privilege to have a forty-five minute interview with former President Harry S. Truman. I asked him what we can do today to combat juvenile delinquency. His answer was firm, forthright and forceful: "Pick out their grandparents." Mr. Truman turned to the pictures of his two grandfathers on the wall behind the desk and related his warmhearted conviction of what those pioneer settlers meant to his life. "I could not be untrue to my parents and grandparents, to my family tradition." Mr. Truman went on further to say that parents should stay out of taverns, and should take their children to Sunday school and church and lead them in constructive play.

Later I had the privilege of taking eighty young people to visit Mr. Truman's library in Independence, Missouri, to hear Mr. Truman lecture on government. Those young people saw firsthand an excellent example of a man of high purpose. That's the best formula I know to rid our nation of juvenile delinquency. Give them family loyalty. This will make a tremendous difference in their lives.

Hitler's Selfish Purpose

High purpose of course deals in the value of human life, in the happiness of others, in lifting up the downtrodden, bringing courage to the disheartened. Earl Nightingale

12

tells in one of his radio addresses of the German Sixth Army at Stalingrad, composed of twenty-six divisions, 300,000 well-trained, experienced troops. They were surrounded in November of 1942 by the Russians. Instead of allowing them to retreat from the terrible Russian winter Hitler demanded that they stay and fight. Without adequate supplies, without adequate ammunition and support and certainly without adequate clothing and food, by February 200,000, or two-thirds, of these troops had been killed, wounded or captured. More than 100,000 were killed. Of the 90,000 survivors captured by the Russians only 6,000 ever reached Germany alive. There was no high purpose in Hitler's dreams—only selfish, sordid, sick, personal ambition.

In sharp contrast look what the British army did at Dunkirk. Every possible ship, boat, raft—anything that would float—at tremendous sacrifice, was not only offered to the British General Staff but volunteered, and some even piloted by women and children. They shuttled back and forth across the channel under constant air attack until by June 3, three-fourths of the British army had been safely evacuated to Britain, living to fight again. That's the difference. The British General Staff valued human life.

In establishing high purpose you must find a great human need, find the answer to fill that need, and burn all your bridges behind you taking the answer of that need through a channel of service to the people who need it.

Purpose Comes from Within

One of the real fallacies of our day is the popular notion that happiness depends on external circumstances and surroundings. There is no question that our internal moods are colored by external situations, but real personal joy comes from internal conviction, determined by character that is the direct result of high purpose.

13

Success is his who is consistently progressing toward a worthy purpose. Carlyle has said, "A man with a half volition goes backwards and forwards, and makes no way on the smoothest road; a man with a whole volition advances on the roughest, and will reach his purpose, if there be even a little worthiness in it. The man without a purpose is like a ship without a rudder—a waif, a nothing, a no man. Have a purpose in life and having it, throw such strength of mind and muscle into your work as God has given you."

Peace Corps Purpose

In the spring of 1963 I saw firsthand in Northern Luzon in the Philippines some of America's most outstanding young people giving of themselves in every possible and imaginable difficult task. These were Peace Corps members, nearly 700 of them in the Philippines in all, living in thatched-roof barrios, eating the food of the Philippines, working for $2.00 a day. What drove them?

It was the high purpose expressed in the inaugural address of President John F. Kennedy when he said, "Ask not what your country can do for you, but what you can do for your country."

The man with purpose does not sit back waiting for Dame Fortune to appear, but rather, he will take every opportunity and use it to the good of others and to his own advancement.

The Path of Purpose

In accomplishing the life-long majestic adventure of high purpose you must take time to map this glorious journey. Remember when you were a child and played the games of make-believe? There were no limitations of criticism. You could do or be whatever your imagination created.

14

Believe it or not, steadfast dreams do come true. I dare you to be different, to leave mediocrity, one of America's greatest menaces, and travel on the high road of glorious adventure.

"See yourself as you want to be; know you can reach the level to which you aspire and, through the 'I will' spirit build upon the premise yet to be described, take the simple steps necessary to bring your plans into fruition."

—Ben Sweetland[2]

Ben Sweetland has also suggested some of the objectives you might have in your life. Under the category "Material Possessions" there might be: a new home, fine furniture, new automobile, big wardrobe, and financial security. Under "Physical Being" you might have: better health, loss of or more weight, better memory, concentration, the ability to relax, the master of habit, happiness and peace of mind. In "Public Affairs" you dream of: respect of all, leadership, a prestige job, and the love and respect of your family.

To those we would add "Spiritual Goals": a personal relationship with the Lord, the assurance of inward peace, freedom from guilt, fear and worry, strong self-confidence, the joy of service where you worship, and the happiness of being a worthy example to your children, friends, and associates.

How is your life? Are you on the high road of magical purpose? Then start right now. Establish a high and lofty purpose. You can be successful.

---

[2]Ben Sweetland, *I Will* (Englewood Cliffs, N.J.: Prentice-Hall, Inc., 1960), page 12.

CHAPTER 2

Limitations of Purpose

Your key to personal success for today is purpose.

There are two limitations of purpose: (1) The tendency to change your purpose short of its realization, and (2) the dangers of uncontrolled ambition—uncontrolled and unguided purpose.

Changed Purpose

Have you ever seen a salesman become tremendously successful in a certain venture? Then as he gets into a larger income bracket he suddenly finds he wants to be in management or he wants to change products or he wants to go into a different field. In the process he nullifies or violates the principles and practices that brought him his success. Thus purpose is short-circuited by change in plans. The unfamiliarity of the new responsibility can often destroy the very principles that made him successful.

A singer may become successful and have a gold record in recording and nationwide fame. Suddenly she decides to become an actress. In the emotional confusion and frustration that comes by seeking to learn a new field she destroys the very principles and practices that brought her success.

A friend of mine is an electronics expert, a genius in the laboratory, an outstanding creator. Opportunity came

16

along for him to organize his own company so he took his life savings and established a stock company in the very field in which he was successful. But he failed. He was unfamiliar with management. He did not know accounting. He did not know buying and selling, and he became so frustrated that he actually contemplated suicide. He was out of his depth, and his mind, in the principles that had led him to achieve. He went bankrupt. Now he is back in engineering and creating, where he belongs, but the experience has marked him for life.

Purpose and Uncontrolled Ambition

Remember the terrible story told by Albert Camus of a young man who had been gone from home for twenty-five years. He married, became wealthy and decided to return to the home of his childhood to visit his mother and sister. He arrived unannounced at the little inn his mother and sister operated. They did not recognize him so just for a joke he carried them on and did not reveal who he was. When he retired for the evening he was still pretending that he was just another traveler. That night his mother and sister robbed and killed him and threw his body into the river. They had been murdering travelers for years. To them he was no different from anyone else. When his wife, searching for him, came to the inn and told them her story they, from the shock of what they had done, killed themselves.

Can you find a more graphic illustration of the tragic luring that uncontrolled ambition brings? The only ones I can think of that are even more graphic are Hitler and Stalin and the other communist masters.

It is better to be a nobody, so to speak, and live a life of mediocrity than to let the evil of uncontrolled ambition make you its slave.

17

Purpose is our tool for success. Purpose is our instrument. It is enslaved to our will as the servant to the master but, oh, what a wonderful slave and servant controlled purpose is. Your key for success today is to learn to control your purpose. Make it a tremendous helper.

CHAPTER 3

Finding the Power of Purpose

Your key for personal success is to find the power of purpose. What is the difference in one man and another? Here's a man who is dynamically, enthusiastically, vibrantly alive. Everything he does is charged with power. Here's another who droops, drags, and meanders through a mere existence. That difference is purpose. There is amazing power in purpose.

Do you realize that nearly 80 per cent of all high school and college students do not know what they are going to do? They are like the horses used during the threshing season on the farm. They go around and around and around every day, eating, sleeping and then back to the same old grind; or like the elevator operator, spending as much time going down as he is going up and never getting anywhere.

But you can't keep a purposeful man down. Take Clarence E. Birdseye for example. In 1924 he lost all of his money—everything he had, even the money borrowed on his life insurance—when his frozen food business failed. However he believed there was a market in frozen food. He started over with $7.00 and borrowed a corner of a friend's ice plant for his experiments. Then five years later he sold out his frozen food company for $22,000,000. Retire? Not Birdseye. He went on to secure more than two-hundred-fifty United States and foreign patents. In 1945 he came out with still another tremendous discovery in the food processing field.

H V. Kaltenborn quit high school after one year, moved from one job to another—lumber camp, war correspondent, door-to-door salesman—then went to school at Harvard, with only one year of high school, and graduated cum laude. He was the best known voice of broadcasting in America during World War II. He was a man with a powerful purpose.

One of the greatest achievements of purpose as well as one of the greatest joys is recognition. "Those who live nobly, even if in their life they live obscurely, need not fear that they will have lived in vain. Something radiates from their lives, some light that shows the way to their friends, their neighbors, perhaps to long future ages. I find many men nowadays oppressed with a sense of impotence, with a feeling that in the fastness of modern society there is nothing of importance that the individual can do."

—Bertrand Russell

Margaret Culkin Banning relates an interesting discussion. One man said to another that the lifetime savings of a certain friend had been swept away. A lady who overheard it said, "You mean that he lost his money." "Yes," the friend replied, "that's what I said." "No," said the lady, "you didn't say that. You told us that the savings of his lifetime were gone, which is not true. They're not gone. He has a mind stored full of knowledge and experience. He has made large investments in charity which haven't depreciated in yielding a return to society today. He saved his simple habits in his pleasure in living. You don't have to worry about him. He lives on."[1]

---

[1]Margaret Culkin Banning, *Indestructible Wealth*. Quoted by Earl Nightingale, *Our Changing World* No. 734 (Chicago: Nightingale-Conant Corporation).

The man with a dynamic purpose doesn't jump out of a hotel window when depression comes. He realizes that the loss of money is simply a temporary detour on the road to success. When the crash in 1929 came a friend of mine went to his wife and said, "Well, honey, today we lost $160,000." Imagine the shock many women would have had if they had lost all that they possessed. However she was a woman of high purpose and deep spiritual insight. She smiled at her husband and said, "But, sweetheart, it is only money." That's the last thing they ever said about it.

Sir Thomas Buxton has said, "The longer I live the more I'm certain that the great difference between men, between the feeble and the powerful, between the great and the insignificant, is energy, *invincible determination of purpose once fixed and then death or victory*. This quality will do anything that can be done in this world; and without it no circumstances, no talents, no opportunities will make a two-legged creature a man."

Purpose Finds a Success Formula

"The important thing is not where you were or where you are but where you want to get," states Dr. Schwartz.[2] He suggests that you write out an image of yourself ten years from now:

A. The Work Department ten years from now:
    1. What income level do I want to attain?
    2. What level of responsibility do I seek?
    3. How much authority do I want to command?
    4. What prestige do I expect to gain from my work?

---

[2]David J. Schwartz, *The Magic of Thinking Big* (Englewood Cliffs, N.J.: Prentice-Hall, Inc., 1959), pages 188-189.

B. The Home Department ten years from now:
   1. What kind of standard of living do I want to provide for my family and myself?
   2. What kind of house do I want to live in?
   3. What kinds of vacations do I want to take?
   4. What financial support do I want to give my children in their early adult years?

C. Social Department ten years from now:
   1. What kind of friends do I want to have?
   2. What social groups do I want to join?
   3. What community leadership positions would I like to hold?
   4. What worthwhile causes do I want to champion?

There is power in such purpose as this.

If you really want something and want it bad enough and bring the intensity of all of your mind, your soul, your heart, your being to bear upon it you will achieve it. How many people will take something as it comes floating by but haven't the vision or the courage to make their utopia by applying the power of purpose that does achieve!

Dr. William C. Menninger, the world famous psychiatrist from Topeka, Kansas, in an article in *This Week Magazine* said: "Do you know whether you are going in the right direction and most of all where you want to go? Not just in your business alone but in the important personal areas: the atmosphere in your home, your relations with the members of your family, your own feeling of status and worthwhileness in life, your own dignity and your own integrity."[3] Check up on yourself. How do you measure up?

Have you ever had the fuel line in your automobile freeze up in the winter? Sometimes water will get in the gas tank and then freeze in the fuel line. It is impossible to

---

[3]Quoted by Earl Nightingale, *Our Changing World*, No. 930.

start a car without gas. I remember one cold night when the temperature was in the teens having a friend push me for several miles through the crowded streets of St. Louis, not knowing that my fuel line was frozen. I finally had to leave the car and come back the next day. When the weather had risen to a warmer temperature the gasoline flowed.

Earl Nightingale says that there are four reasons why people fail. In other words, there are four frozen points in the fuel line that keep the power of the fuel from getting to the motor of achievement. They are:

"(1) We don't have to.
"(2) We are doing about as well as the next guy.
"(3) We are using averages as standards to satisfactory performance.
"(4) We don't know we have so much reserve power and ability. We take ourselves for granted."[4]

Put the heat of excitement, enthusiasm to your frozen power lines. You can be successful.

The person who dares to dedicate himself to high and lofty purpose will have power. The power is there. It is inborn. We always have the energy to do the things that we enjoy doing. Have you ever seen a teenage boy come in from school, from football practice or from exercise and flop down on the couch and claim he was too tired to study? No energy, exhausted, worn out, but let his girl friend drive by and toot the horn. He bounds off the couch, runs through the house, leaving the front door ajar, and rushes out to the car, not taking the time to recall that he's exhausted. He comes back after an hour's drive exhilarated. You see he had energy for doing what he wanted to do.

---

[4] *Our Changing World,* No. 811.

So like the husband who has no energy on his day off to finish mowing the grass, or to paint the shutter, or to haul out the garbage, but has plenty of energy to go fishing, or to play golf. The power comes with the intensity of purpose.

No Purpose in the Home

One of the problems of family life in America today is the tragedy of men with no purpose, men who simply, under the pressures of finance or the home or whatever, walked away and left the wife and children to struggle for themselves. Many, many times have I had to assist in such circumstances. You see these men were trying to escape from life's responsibilities. They had no purpose. However, the power to provide for a family is there for a purposeful man.

In one of his radio addresses. Earl Nightingale gives three things to do to become rich[5]:

1. Make up your mind that there is no good reason why you can't get the money you and your family want. If other people can get rich so can you. The largest industrial empires in this country were started by the idea of a single individual and they all started as small businesses.
2. Decide on the exact amount you want to earn and set a time limit for yourself. Be realistic and sensible. Ask yourself what your qualifications are and set up a reasonable amount in a reasonable length of time. At the same time make up your mind that you are going to concentrate on this exclusively until you reach your goal.
3. The magic formula for financial success has never changed since the first coins were minted in Asia Mi-

[5] *Our Changing World*, No. 769.

nor. It is six words: "Find a need and fill it." That's
your part of the bargain. Don't go afield into areas in
which you have no experience. Is it easy? No, but it
works. The power is available for a man who has high
purpose.

The Cleveland, Ohio, manufacturing firm of Warner
and Swasey recently in an ad said, "It wasn't the Goths that
defeated Rome. It was the free circuses . . . Luxuries,
power, indulgence had made the once tough Roman people soft. To stay popular their Emperors gave them more
and more of the ease they craved—free bread, free circuses, easy living, so the Romans softened up themselves
for the ambitious, hard-working barbarians and in A.D.
410 the greatest nation the world had ever seen was in-
vaded and destroyed." Half of all the people in the then
known world were slaves, working for the other half. The
majority of the people living in Rome were on relief. The
government had become their benefactor. Their will to
live was destroyed. They had lost their purpose. And never
forget it could happen in America today.

A ten-year study of men in various occupations conducted by General Motors Research Institute showed that
as men advanced in their responsibilities and positions
their mental and emotional capacity increased markedly as
well as their ability to withstand strain. In other words men
with high purpose not only live longer they have the power
to produce more!

The Power of Purpose

How purpose can help you make a habit of succeeding:

1. Write out below the most important objective you could achieve in your lifetime.

2. State the benefits of this life-long achievement:

    A. To family

    B. To business or professional associates

    C. Religious and social

    D. National

3. Are you willing to alter the pattern of your life to achieve this purpose?

4. State how you will alter your life.

    William James said, "The greatest discovery of my generation is that human beings can alter their lives by altering their attitudes of mind."

CHAPTER 4

Developing Purpose

Your key to personal success is to build a dynamic purpose. How do we develop purpose?

According to Charles B. Roth there are seven motives of life:

1. Health. Everyone wants it and seeks it.
2. Wealth. (Some think the most dominant drive in many people's lives.)
3. Gratification of appetite—hunger and thirst for physical things but for mental and emotional as well.
4. Amusement—entertainment, games, recreation, all forms of diversion.
5. Security. This is important.
6. Vanity—the desire to be admired. This motive is always important in influencing others.
7. Self-improvement.[1]

Study these motives. You will find that they will help develop dynamic purpose in your life.

Making money will not necessarily make you happy. You must have a stronger, greater goal than that of just financial security. Jesus of Nazareth established a new standard when He gave us the rule that service is greatness.

---

[1]Charles B. Roth, *Winning Personal Recognition* (Englewood Cliffs, N.J.: Prentice-Hall, Inc., 1954), pages 30-31.

A Cause Greater Than Self

Remember the Biblical truth that he who would exalt himself shall be humble and he who humbles himself shall be exalted. This paradox is surprising to some. Have you ever noticed the persons who exalted themselves, living only for the purpose of satisfying their own desires—the Hitlers, the Mussolinis, the Napoleons, the Capones? Lincoln and Ghandi stand in sharp contrast. When a person dedicates his life and time and effort and energy to a cause greater than himself he develops a dynamic purpose that truly makes life a romance and glorious adventure. One of my mottoes is, "The greatest use of life is to so live your life that the use of your life will outlive your life." Finding this cause is the first step in developing purpose. Now you are really beginning to live.

Dr. Chester A. Swor said, "An opportunity grasped and used produces at least one other opportunity."

Let's say that your motto or your purpose, your goal, your objective is to make other people happy. Now look at its long-range aspect. It will affect your insurance program. You will not be selfish enough to spend your entire income on yourself. You will provide for the possibility of your death by meeting the needs of others through an adequate insurance program. You will establish a long-range effectiveness by saving. Every week lay aside something for the inevitable rainy day. This will affect you in your personal health, pay off in the enrichment of your life. Expanding your life over a longer period of time will enable you to make others happy longer.

But also look at the short-range aspect of it. Everything you do will seek to lift those others round about you. Remember those lines, "When I met him I was looking down; when I left him I was looking up." The taxi driver, the bus driver, the doorman, the elevator operator, the clerk in the store, the waitress at lunch, the secretary at the office, the client, the customer—nearly everyone else has more problems than you have. Why don't you set your purpose to making other people happy?

Commit Yourself

To develop an effective purpose it must be written out. It must be stamped indelibly upon your mind by repetition. Write it out and put it over the dashboard of your car, above the mirror in the morning, over the sink and certainly in your billfold. Never forget that we develop a purpose by making it become a steadfast habit of our life.

Your Seeking Mind

The next step in developing your purpose is to make real in your life the words of Aristotle when he said, "All men desire by nature to know." Yes, we have some people in America who have been educated beyond their intelligence. But they are the rare exception. Isn't the ceaseless desire for knowledge one of the most outstanding contributions that an education can give a person? Remember that old story of a boy who was on his way home from college and had all of his college notes for four years catalogued very carefully in his trunk but in a train wreck the trunk was destroyed by the ensuing fire. He was not injured but he had to go back for four more years to gain more notes.

Equally tragic is the person who files away in his Fibber McGee closet all of the information and inspiration that he had in college, never to desire further knowledge.

Recall the times you have gone into your favorite drug store and asked the druggist for a particular item. He knew immediately where it was. He also knew about further developments in that field. For example there may be a competitive product that has recently come out that is better than the one you are accustomed to, and he may make this observation and suggest its use to you. Here is a man who has knowledge of the product and a knowledge of his store. But most important of all he knows you and your needs. That's why you keep going back. Here is a man who is successful. He is persistently increasing his knowledge in order to serve you better.

Make No Little Plans

For the further development of your purpose you must make big plans. For many years I have been quoting Daniel Burnham of the Chicago Plan Commission. I believe Mr. Burnham was the first man to develop one of America's shopping centers. The whole structure of our city and urban life has been changed by this man's vision. Remember his words, "Make no little plans. There is nothing in little plans to stir men's blood. Make big plans. Once a big idea is recorded it can never die."

You have never known a little man to come up with a big idea. This is true in this life and in the next, for Jesus said: "Thou hast been faithful over a few things, I will make thee ruler over many things."

No janitor ever immediately became president but some of America's industrial giants began as janitors. In the process they were painstakingly successful in accomplishing the first plan, then they raised their goal—their purpose, vision, aspirations, intentions—to another and then another and on until they achieved the pinnacle of their goal of success. How big are your plans? How long has it been since you analyzed them? Are they big enough to stir your blood and other men's blood as well?

Earl Nightingale has discussed some of the things people want to gain in life, what they want to be and what they want to save.[2]

They want to gain: (1) Health. (2) Time. (3) Money. (4) Popularity. (5) Improved appearance. (6) Security in old age. (7) Praise from others. (8) Comfort. (9) Leisure. (10) Pride of accomplishment. (11) Advancement, business and social. (12) Increased enjoyment. (13) Self-confidence. (14) Personal prestige.

What people want to be: (1) Good parents. (2) Sociable. (3) Up to date. (4) Creative. (5) Proud of their possessions. (6) Influential over others. (7) Gregarious. (8) Efficient. (9) First in things. (10) Recognized as authority.

What people want to save: (1) Time. (2) Money. (3) Work. (4) Discomfort. (5) Worry. (6) Doubts. (7) Risk. (8) Personal embarrassment. But none of these things can be yours without first developing a dynamic purpose.

Let me suggest that you get the book *TNT, The Power Within You* by Claude M. Bristol and Harold Sherman and by all means major on the chapter "How to Build Mind Pictures." There is an ancient saying, "Look within. Within is the fountain of good and let it bubble up if thou would ever dig." Now as you think in mind pictures, picture yourself as you want to be, accomplishing the things you desire, achieving the goals you have set for yourself. You will find that this is the most magnetized picture you have ever imagined. You will draw the strength, knowledge and power to accomplish it because you have established it as a visual picture.

This picture will become the pattern of your success. It will be mental television. You will see yourself accomplish-

<hr>

[2] *Our Changing World*, Nos. 720, 820.

ing all that you desire. Never forget the words from the Bible in Mark 11:24: "Therefore I say unto you, What things soever ye desire, when ye pray, believe that ye receive them and ye shall have them." The minute you establish this dynamic purpose and begin the persistent achievement of this challenging, worthy goal you become successful that very moment; for so often the achieving, the accomplishing, the realizing, the journey itself means far more than the privilege of having arrived.

This then will be your success insurance. You will be a dynamic, dedicated man whom nothing can stop. And never forget that those who are following you will take strength, inspiration and challenge from you—your children, your associates, your employees and employers and all of your social, church and community friends.

CHAPTER 5

Purpose Grounded in Achievement

Your key for personal success is dynamic, invigorating purpose.

For purpose to be all consuming, powerful and challenging it must be grounded in success and achievement in little endeavors. Persistent achievement brings the challenge for greater purpose. Achievement comes from seeing and recognizing a need, and from purposeful action resulting in the solution of that need.

A need is a gap between a stimulus aroused and that stimulus achieved. This achievement comes when the task is completed and well done. The vast majority of us have the joy of achievement in the present. Johann Sebastian Bach had been dead twenty-five years before the musical public was willing to accept his compositions. It was still another quarter of a century before his true greatness was acknowledged around the world. He was buried in a pauper's field; but today he is accepted as one of the most outstanding musicians the world has ever known. Here's the tragedy of achievement coming too late. However, this need not be so in your life. You can know the joy of achievement as a result of your purpose now.

Don't Sell Yourself Short

"I'm a practicing psychologist," said Randall B. Hamrack.[1] "In twenty years I've talked with, tested and given vocational counsel to at least 10,000 young men and women. One characteristic that almost all had was the tendency to sell themselves short. We need not worry about the bright educated. His kind is not very common. But we do need to worry about the legions of young people who underestimate themselves. When at least three out of four sell themselves short we are suffering a community tragedy that is compounded by the individual tragedy of each unfulfilled life." Did you catch the scope of that? Three-fourths of all the young people in America sell themselves short; they are not measuring up to their total personality, therefore they are living mediocre, meaningless existences. America can't reach her heights unless our young people are dynamically motivated to purposeful action.

You're Responsible for Your Face

The story is told that one of Lincoln's advisors urgently recommended a candidate for appointment to Lincoln's cabinet and Lincoln declined to follow his suggestion. So he was asked to give his reason. "I don't like the man's face," Lincoln explained. "But the poor man is not responsible for his face," insisted his supporter. "Every man over forty is responsible for his face," Lincoln replied, and turned away to resume discussion of other matters.

I believe Lincoln was right. Medical scientists tell us that the will to live is one of the most important, if not the most important factor in a sick person's getting well. I have talked with patients who had decided to die. I've seen some take my challenge and as they responded dynami-

---

[1] Quoted in *Our Changing World*, No. 633.

cally and enthusiastically their medical case history immediately reversed itself.

If this is true with a sick person how much more true is it with a well person. Therefore your purpose actually will affect your looks. A person with dynamic purpose is a person who is on fire—a person living for new goals, a person living for the fullest in life. The excitement and vigorous life will show on his face.

Life Purpose

Let me suggest three purposes of your life and, if you will practice them, I can assure you that you will enjoy the true results of dynamic purpose.

1. One is service. Jesus taught us to serve. Rome had ruled the minds and will of others with its might. To the Romans, "might was right." You and I know that he who would be great must be the greatest servant. You can have a dynamic life but it is necessary that you seize every opportunity to serve.

Would you like to know God's will for your life in service? The following will help you find it: (A) Do you see a needed task? Maybe it's a Boy Scout troop that needs a leader. Maybe it's the establishment of a Boy's Club. Maybe it's a P.T.A. responsibility, or a Sunday school class. Maybe it's an invalid who needs a visit or a person in jail who needs a friend. Maybe it's a family that needs food. See the opportunity. (B) Say to yourself, "By the grace of God I can do that." (C) Start doing it. Get right at it. (D) If God doesn't stop you, that's His plan for your life.

"The secret of success in life is for a man to be ready for his opportunity when it comes."   —Benjamin Disraeli

Remember that serving takes effort. "When God wanted sponges and oysters He made them and put one on a rock and the other in the mud. When He made man he did not make him to be a sponge or an oyster; He made him with feet and hands, and head and heart, and vital blood, and a place to use them and He said to him, 'Go work.' "

—Henry Ward Beecher

2. Leadership that you give to others is a true result of purpose. Everyone is looking for someone to say, "Well done." How well I remember my high school and college days when my coaches in athletic events would say a word of commendation after a particularly hard effort, whether in practice or in the game. In high school I would have done anything for Joe Robert Gouldman's words of appreciation. I wanted above everything else, seemingly, to satisfy my coach. The same was true of Stanley Robinson in college. This is the power of purposeful leadership.

Never forget you are the leader someone is looking to. Every boy wants to be like his dad. Every girl wants to be like her mother. One of the greatest things a man can do is to leave a purposeful heritage, to leave an example of dynamic purposeful leadership.

When Lee Scarborough returned from Harvard Law School and Baylor University to his West Texas town the crowds came to hear him preach his first sermon. Some of the men who heard it were weighing the difference between his country preacher father, limited in education, and the well-trained son. One said, "Well, he can out-preach his dad." They were shocked when the man in front of them turned, and they recognized Lee's father. He sparkled with their words, smiled broadly and said, "That's the finest compliment you could give me, for you see he's standing on my shoulders." That is that result of purpose, a leadership that others seek to follow.

3. A third result of purpose is impact. What you do for good, what you do in purposeful success will be a part of

the total triumph of democracy. Andrew Carnegie has so well said, "No man can become rich himself without in turn enriching others." If you come to the end of life's journey and can honestly look back and see in the trail of your years many people wonderfully blessed, lifted up from their discouragement because you passed their way, people whose livelihood, happiness, achievement were accomplished as a result of your encouragement, then you have made a definite contribution to the way of life that we believe is the best ever known or achieved on the face of this planet.

As Dale Carnegie so well said, "Instead of worrying about what people say of you why not spend your time trying to accomplish something they will admire." And do it honestly.

Don't forget those words from Jeremiah 17:11: "As the partridge sitteth on eggs, and hatcheth them not; so he that getteth riches, and not by right, shall leave them in the midst of his days, and at his end shall be a fool." Honesty—strict and uncompromising—is still the best way to run a business or to get wealthy in this world.

Back before the turn of the century a Christian business merchant in Philadelphia by the name of John Wanamaker decided that his convictions demanded that he practice the golden rule in business. He sought to satisfy the customer. He was laughed at. People said it would never work. Do you know what happened? Today his desire to satisfy the customer is one of the prevailing principles of business in America. "The customer is always right." There isn't room to list all the large, successful business firms in America built upon this principle.

Yes, Wanamaker made a contribution, a lasting, effective, dynamic contribution to all that western men believe in. He was a part of the total triumph of democracy and of righteousness.

How to Develop Purpose

The habit of a developed purpose equals success:

1. Restate your life-long purpose.

2. Is this purpose a cause greater than yourself?

    A. Are other people happier?

    B. Are all others enriched?

3. What habit of personal improvement have you developed?

    A. Dale Carnegie Leadership Course?

    B. Dale Carnegie Sales Course?

    C. The Science of Personal Achievement Course?

    D. A Professional Course?

    E. Others?

4. List the twelve things people want in life in order of importance according to you:

    A.

    B.

    C.

    D.

    E.

    F.

    G.

    H.

    I.

    J.

    K.

    L.

5. Are you producing greater service?

6. Are you producing greater leadership?

7. Is our nation stronger for having experienced you?

8. Is the torch of your purpose worth handing on to the succeeding generations?

PART TWO
GOALS CAN CHANGE
YOUR LIFE

CHAPTER 6

Establishing a Goal

Your key for personal success is to establish a goal. Goals and purpose are different. Purpose is the long range—the pot of gold at the end of the rainbow. When you reach out for it it is still ahead of you. Goals may be long range but they are more clearly defined.

What Goals Are

Notice three things about goals.
1. Goals are concrete. They are concrete actions we can and intend to do.
2. Goals are measurable. They afford measures so we can judge our progress. They may be quantitative—how much we intend to do and how often. They may be in terms of time—how soon we plan to accomplish them.
3. Goals are related to a definite period. They are definite time targets—an intent to accomplish a result for that particular period. While objectives may be pursued for indefinite times in the future, goals are what we determine to do within our planning period to move toward the objective.

The Dynamics of Setting Goals

Frank Bettger, one of America's outstanding salesmen and lecturer on sales and author of three popular books for salesmen, spends Friday afternoon setting up next week's work. Frank even schedules his haircut. On the weekend he developed an intensity of purpose, a dynamic desire. He went to work on Monday morning vibrantly alive. You see, there are dynamics in setting goals.

Know Where You're Going

Thomas A. Edison said, "The most important factors of invention can be described in a few words. They consist first of definite knowledge as to what one wishes to achieve. One must fix his mind on that purpose with persistence and begin searching for that which he seeks, making use of all of the accumulated knowledge of the subject which he has or can acquire from others. He must keep on searching no matter how many times he may meet with disappointment. He must refuse to be influenced by the fact that somebody else may have tried the same idea without success. He must keep himself sold on the idea that the solution of his problem exists somewhere and that he will find it . . .

"When a man makes up his mind to solve any problem he may at first meet with dogged opposition, but if he holds on and keeps on searching he will be sure to find some sort of solution. The trouble with most people is that they quit before they start."

Dr. Alexander Graham Bell said, "I had made up my mind to find that for which I was searching even if it required the remainder of my life. After innumerable failures I finally uncovered the principle for which I was searching, and I was astounded at its simplicity. I was still more astounded to discover the principle I had revealed was not only beneficial in the construction of a mechanical hearing aid but it served as well as a means of sending the sound of the voice over a wire. Another discovery which came out of my investigation was the fact that when a man gives his order to produce a definite result and stands by that order it seems to have the effect of giving him what might be termed a second sight which enables him to see right through ordinary problems. What this power is I cannot say; all I know is that it exists and it becomes available only when a man is in that state of mind in which he knows exactly what he wants and is fully determined not to quit until he finds it."

Team Power

An excellent example of the dynamics of setting goals is the intensity of purpose, the strength of discipline that's involved in an athletic team, particularly a high school group. The hardest work I ever did in my life was getting in shape for football, both in high school and college. While tearing around the field at the end of practice as darkness was spreading across the stadium I used to say to myself, "This is the hardest work you have ever done. Why do you continue to do it?" Why? I did it to make the team. I did it to help win the game. I did it for the recognition of the school. I did it for my teammates. The goal was there and the dynamics resulted.

Have you ever thought about the dynamics of riding a bicycle? You have to get up a certain amount of speed before you can hold the bicycle on course. A man is like riding a bicycle. When we have the dynamics of a goal it develops the equilibrium necessary to move the bicycle forward. But when we slow down, the bicycle wobbles and will finally fall.

Dr. Maxwell Maltz in his book *Psycho-cybernetics* says: "We are engineered as goal-seeking mechanisms. We are built that way. When we have no personal goal which we are interested in and means something in us, we have to go around in circles, feel lost and find life itself aimless and purposeless. We are built to conquer environment, solve problems, achieve goals and we find no real satisfaction or happiness in life without obstacles to conquer and goals to achieve. People who say that life is not worthwhile are really saying that they themselves have no personal goals which are worthwhile. Get yourself a goal worth working for. Better still, get yourself a project. Decide what you want out of a situation. Always have something ahead to look forward to."[1]

Find out what you really want to do in life above everything else. Determine your goal. Visualize it in your mind. Picture what you want to be, the kind of person you want to become.

Then get all the facts about it. Get everything that is possible from the public library, from your personal rating and experience of others, from every bit of information you can gather. Analyze, discuss and test these facts. Put them in logical order. Determine how you are going to accomplish your goal.

The next thing to do is to set a time schedule. Don't let anything divert you to chasing rabbits. Stay on the path. Finally don't just talk about it, get at it. Start out this very moment. Remember that a journey of a thousand miles begins with one step. So start in. You can be successful.

A little goal soon reaches its realization. The same intensity of effort brought to bear upon a large goal will inevitably result in the same accomplishment. If your wife wants a new dress or a new hat, she will find a way to get it—out of the grocery money, out of savings, put it on the bill— somehow she will get it. Plato said, "A work well begun is half ended." And of course the best way to begin a work is to have faith that inevitably it will be successfully completed. Remember the words of Paul J. Meyer, "What you

---

[1]Maxwell Maltz, *Psycho-cybernetics* (Englewood Cliffs, N.J.: Prentice-Hall, Inc., 1960), pages 57-58.

ardently desire, sincerely believe in, vividly imagine, enthusiastically act on must inevitably come to pass."

Energy Unlimited

Often people ask me, "Where do you get your energy?" Arnold Bennett has given us the best answer to this question: "Perhaps you've been hoping to create energy in yourself. Now you cannot create energy in yourself or elsewhere. Nobody can. You can only set energy free, loosen it, transform it, direct it. An individual is born with a certain amount of energy, no more. And what is more important you cannot put additional qualities into it. You may sometimes seem to be putting energy into him but you are not; you are simply setting this original energy free—applying a match to the coal or fanning the fire. Some people seem to lack energy when as a fact they are full of energy which is merely dormant, waiting for the match or waiting for direction. The usual idea of the amount of energy possessed by an individual is the intensity of the desire of that person. It is desire that uses energy. Strong desires generally betoken much energy—and they are definite desires. Without desire energy is rendered futile. Nobody will consume energy in action unless he desires to perform the action, either for itself or as a means to a desired end.

"You must not confuse vague, general aspiration with desire. A real desire is definite, concrete. The desire which indicates great energy is always there, worrying. It is an obsession—a whip, it has no mercy."

I have goals in life. I have purposes to perform; I've written out these purposes and they make my life wonderfully and joyfully worth living. You see, goals set our innate energies free.

Check Points

The greatest dynamics come during the setting of the goal and the process of reaching it. Once the goal is reached there is a natural letdown. Far too many people rest on their oars and drift into some secluded cove never to establish another goal. They literally deteriorate with inactivity. Some people die at thirty and are buried at seventy. In fact, I know some who have been embalmed but haven't been laid away yet! So is the one who has reached a goal but stops there. Goals are temporary rest points on the journey to a fulness in life. We pause to reflect—to look back and examine. We pause to get our breath and energy and to set our direction for the next height to scale. The climb itself is far more invigorating, stimulating and dynamically enthusiastic than reaching the height itself.

This truth is so well described in the words of a philosopher who said, "There is not much to do but bury a man when the last of his dreams is dead." Henry J. Kaiser turned over his huge business interest to his son and went to Hawaii to retire. But a man with dynamic goals can't rest and can't retire. So he set out to build first one hotel, then others, then a beautiful office building with a revolving restaurant on top. Today Waikiki is a fabulous development, all because of the dream and the goals of one man. As Earl Nightingale has said, "A person is as young as his dreams—or as old as his doubts." Let each goal be a temporary pause on the road to greater achievement.

CHAPTER 7

The Discipline of Goals

Your key for personal success for today is the discipline of goals. Every person should read Napoleon Hill's *Think and Grow Rich*. In it he has listed ten causes for failure in leadership. They are: "(1) Inability to organize details. (2) Unwillingness to render humble service. (3) Expectation of pay for what they know instead of what they do with that which they know. (4) Fear of competition from followers. (5) Lack of imagination. (6) Selfishness. (7) Intemperance. (8) Disloyalty. (9) Emphasis of the authority of leadership. (10) Emphasis of title."[1]

Each of these qualities of failure is the result of a lack of goals. For goals intensely established, regularly checked on, ardently desired, bring wonderful discipline of action.

Harry Emerson Fosdick once wrote, "No horse gets anywhere till he's harnessed, no steam or gas drives anything until it's confined, no Niagara ever turned anything into light or power until it's tunneled, no life ever grows great until focused, dedicated and disciplined."

Ninety-five Per Cent Fail

Take a hundred men at age twenty-five all expecting to be successful. If you will trace these men through forty years of business life, you will find, as they face retirement, one is rich, four are independently wealthy, five are still

---

[1] Napoleon Hill, *Think and Grow Rich*, rev. ed. (Chicago: Combined Registry Company, 1960), pages 107-109.

working, thirty-six have died and fifty-four are dead broke. Now if each one of those men would only save 10 per cent of what he makes and if he never made more than $6,000 a year he would have set aside $24,000 during that forty years of business experience. Now at normal interest rates this $24,000 would have grown to $58,000. Certainly that's an adequate figure to keep the wolf away from the door. But why is it that so many men don't do it? They simply have no goal. They have no purpose. They do not have the discipline of a purpose out ahead. They do not write down their goal and bring all their energy to bear upon it.

Alexander Maclaren said, "The man who has not learned to say *no* will be a weak if not a wretched man as long as he lives." He will have no goals, no discipline, no joy, no achievement, no provision for family, no nest egg for a rainy day, no investment for that opportunity of financial growth.

The Apostle Paul became the greatest follower of his Master the world has ever known by the impact of his life and by the dedication of his efforts. You see he had a goal. It is recorded in Philippians 3:13: "This one thing I do, forgetting those things which are behind, and reaching forth unto those things which are before, I press toward the mark."

Would you go hunting a Rocky Mountain bear with a shotgun full of bird shot? No. The bird shot is so diffused by the shotgun that even if it hits the target, which is possible but unlikely, it will not accomplish the purpose of killing the game. No, you take a high-powered rifle for big game—one that will reach the goal and can kill when it reaches. This is the secret of a goal. Instead of scattering our efforts in diffused activity a goal brings the single-mindedness of purpose.

A One-Eyed Man

Be a one-eyed man. That's what Jesus was saying when he said, "When thine eye is single, thy whole body also is full of light." Be then a one-eyed man. That's what Andrew Carnegie was when he said, "Put all your eggs in one basket and watch that basket." Concentrate on one purpose and then you will be successful.

"A shockingly large number of our worries and our hidden tensions stem from the fact that millions of people have never found themselves, and never discovered the kind of work they could love and do well. Instead they seeth with inner rebellion because they spend their lives doing work they despise."   —Dale Carnegie

Can you find a better definition of the diffused life with no purpose, no plan, no goal?

"The educated man is the man who has learned how to get every thing he needs without violating the rights of his fellow men. Education comes from within; you get it by struggle and effort and thought."   —Napoleon Hill

Your key for personal success is to establish a definite goal, for in the dynamics of its purpose there will be the discipline that will lead you to personal success. Remember that the definition of success is the persistent achievement of a challenging, worthy goal. I dare you to be different. I dare you to be personally, dynamically successful. You can be. Establish your goal and you will. It is inevitable. You will!

CHAPTER 8

Examples of Goals

Your key for personal success is goals. In this section there are examples of goals that have made men's lives dynamic. Sallust said, "Every man is the architect of his own fortune." Do you believe that?

A Formula for Goal Success

Framed in my office is the motto of another dynamic individual who owes his success to the setting of goals. His is called the million dollar personal success plan. Paul J. Meyer was a millionaire at twenty-six. Here is his formula:

"1. Crystallize your thinking. Determine what specific goal you want to achieve. Then dedicate yourself to its attainment with unswerving singleness of purpose, the trenchant zeal of a crusader.

"2. Develop a plan for achieving your goal and a deadline for its attainment. Plan your projects carefully—hour by hour, day by day, month by month. Organize activity and maintain enthusiasm of the well springs of your power.

"3. Develop a sincere desire for the things you want in life. A burning desire is the greatest motivator of every human action. The desire for success implants success consciousness which in turn creates a vigorous and ever-increasing habit of success.

"4. Develop supreme confidence in yourself and your own abilities. Enter every activity without giving

52

mental recognition to the possibility of defeat. Concentrate on your strengths instead of your weaknesses; on your powers instead of your problems.

"5. Develop a dogged determination to follow through on your plan regardless of obstacles, criticisms or circumstances. Construct your determination with sustained effort—controlled attention and concentrated energy. Opportunities never come to those who wait—they are captured by those who dare to attack."[1]

Paul Meyer left his native California and headed for the Eastern Seaboard expecting to learn life insurance. His first stop was in Columbus, Georgia, where he nearly starved to death for the first six months because some agent simply threw a rate book at him and said, "Here, poor sucker, root hog or die." But in that six-month period he learned some principles of life insurance. By the time he was twenty-three he was vice-president of the insurance company and had the largest volume of business for any man his age in America. He was called upon to be the speaker at the Million Dollar Round Table. Today he is the president of Success Motivation Institute of Waco, Texas, a living, dynamic example that goals do pay off.

Two Hundred Success Stories

In the book *You Are Better Than You Think* by Albert, Dr. Charlotte Buhler of the Psychological Institute in Vienna reports the study of lives of 200 famous men and women. They discovered that in every case there was a self-selected goal that directed all the energies of the individual.[2] "Write down what you want to achieve. Then frame the

[1]Conversation with Paul J. Meyer.
[2]Dora Albert, *You Are Better Than You Think* (Englewood Cliffs, N.J.: Prentice-Hall, Inc., 1957), page 193.

paper on which you have written it and hang it on the wall," said Johnson O'Conner.

Lawrence Gould, the psychologist commented, "Many a man has been puzzled at the lack of results from his grim determination to succeed when his real unconscious desire was to have a good time and to take life easy—a picture that often comes in my mind is the scene in the old-fashioned melodrama when the heroine pretends to yield to the villain's embraces, but behind her back waves a white handkerchief to call the hero to the rescue."

To achieve any goal there must be the conscious and the unconscious commitment of all that you are to the dedication of the effort of that goal. There must be harmony. There must be energy. There must be oneness in purpose if you are to reach your goal. Dora Albert gives a simple plan for achieving your goals:

"1. Find out what your unconscious goal is by studying what you have accomplished so far.

"2. Figure out where your conscious goal corresponds with what you do. For instance, if your goal is success and you are drinking your way to failure whom are you kidding?

"3. Visualize yourself succesfully realizing and achieving your goal.

"4. Write a summary to yourself, telling yourself exactly what specific steps are needed to achieve it. If you need additional educational training write down what kind of training. Then plan to get it.

"5. Write a letter or make a phone call that will help you take the next step toward your goal.

"6. Include recreation and fun in your goals. Plan some healthful recreational activity at least once each week.

"7. Make sure that your goals are consistent with your self-esteem. If you have to kick someone else to achieve your goal you won't be happy reaching it.

"8. Make sure that your goal represents something you want to do not just what you think you ought to do. Regardless of what your parents or friends think you ought to do examine your own heart and mind."[3]

That is excellent advice. Listen to it. Follow the example of others and you too can be amazingly successful.

Five Per Cent Excel

In America today only one person out of every 1,220 taxpayers is a millionaire; one out of every 144 taxpayers earns from $25,000 to $50,000 a year; one family out of nineteen earns $10,000 a year—that's about 5 per cent. That means that 95 per cent of the people earn less than $10,000 a year. Now if you are negative you will say that the reason you aren't in that select one-of-nineteen group is because you lack education or because you were not at the right place at the right time, or you didn't have the right pull, or you didn't marry a woman with wealth, or some other excuse. Don't forget the words of Andrew Carnegie, "No man becomes rich unless he enriches others." That's how he made his $500,000,000. He did it by lowering the price of steel from $160 a ton to $20 a ton. He benefited all Americans.

Yes, the reason you are in the 95 per cent category if you are, is because you planned it that way. You did not set a goal. Let me question very seriously if you should set a goal for money alone. The goal should be to render a greater service than someone else. If you do this the money will come rolling in.

---

[3]Albert, *Ibid.,* pages 195-198.

Emerson said, "If a man has good corn, or wood, or boards, or pigs to sell, or can make better chairs or knives, crucibles or church organs than anybody else you will find a broad, hard-beaten road to his house though it be in the woods."

Have you heard Charles M. Simmons' record, *The Magic Key?*[4] Simmons gives us some marvelous advice:

I. Ask yourself the question, "What do I want to accomplish today?" Most people never ask it. People who fail never plan. Remember nothing becomes dynamic until it first becomes specific.

II. Ask yourself, "How strong is my desire?"
A. Do you get up early in the morning?
B. Will you contact ten people today by phone or letter?
C. Will you make an advance plan to be enthusiastic even if you don't feel like it?
D. Why not carry a hundred dollar bill? It gives you money consciousness and a sense of success.
E. Do you buy and wear good clothes? It pays. You see clothes cover 96 per cent to 98 per cent of the man. Clothes do make the man.
F. Do you read good inspirational books? And of course the best inspirational book is the Bible.
G. Go to church on Sunday with your family. Make it a family affair.
H. Ask for that order. Go out expecting to give better service to your client than anybody else in this world.

---

[4]You can secure it by writing 630 North San Mateo Drive, San Mateo, California. Another outstanding record is Earl Nightingale's *The Strangest Secret in the World.*

III. Now ask yourself, "What is my deadline?" Set a timetable for reaching your long-range goals. Write out a check to yourself for a certain amount at a certain time. Then expect to cash it.

IV. Ask yourself, "What is my exact plan of action?" And then, "How do I start?" "How do I go about it?"

Such advice will make you a dynamic man. I challenge you to try it.

Five Success Suggestions

Five suggestions for success are:

1. Pay the price. Results are directly proportionate to the effort we put forth. We must understand emotionally that as we sow so do we reap.
2. Can you practice imagination? Can you see yourself achieving every bit of the goal you've attempted?
3. Practice courage. Talk positively on your goal. Refuse to believe that there is any circumstance sufficient to its defeat.
4. Save 10 per cent of what you earn. Make your dollars your slaves to work for you.
5. Action. The achievement of this program of success demands immediate dynamic action. This then is the example of goals.

CHAPTER 9

Benefits of Goals

Your key for personal success for today is found in the benefits of goals. There are abilities in goals. You can be successful.

French moralist, Jean de la Bruyère said, "In this world there are only two ways of getting on—either by one's own industry or by the imbecility of others." You may "get on" the latter way, but you haven't been successful, for success is the persistent achievement of a challenging and worthy goal. The greatest benefit of a dynamic goal is that you yourself measure up to the fullest possibility of the total capacity of all of your talents, mind power and potential.

Goal Happiness

One of the outstanding benefits of goals is personal happiness. Life is too short to be unhappy. But you will never be happy until you are achieving a worthy challenging goal. And remember it cannot be selfish nor can it be evil. A worthy goal will benefit you. It will benefit your family. It will benefit your community. It will benefit your church. It will benefit your society, yea, even the nation. You see, your abilities are very closely related to your desires. If you desire little you will exercise little of your capacity. I will tell you who the outstanding athletes are. They are the ones who paid the greatest price, such as Leroy Jordan of Alabama football fame who in the fall of 1962 made All-American. Although smaller than many other college linemen, Leroy Jordan made up in determination, dedication, and desire what he lacked in weight and natural ability. He wanted to play college football and dedicated himself to this purpose rather than dissipating his abilities in a hundred inconsistent activities. I saw Leroy in the Orange Bowl January 1, 1963. There was an example of outstanding dedication to a goal. Remember that high school athlete you knew who had such natural ability? Where is he now? Lost in the swamp of mediocrity. He didn't have a goal. All of that ability was wasted. No purpose, no goal.

Remember when you were young you used to hear people say that rich people aren't happy. Only poor people are really happy. Do you believe this? Is this true? Marcus Antoninus remarked, "No man is happy who does not think himself so." A man may have riches and be miserable. That man is not a successful man. But the man who has set a dynamic goal is happy because he is persistently achieving that worthy, challenging goal. And this in itself brings about peace and happiness of mind. Augustine said, "Happiness comes in the attainment of our desires and in our having only right desires."

Failure Sours

"Men, on the average, will be kindly or hostile in their feelings toward each other in the proportion that they feel their lives unsuccessful or successful."

—Bertrand Russell

"The common idea that success spoils people by making them vain, egotistic and self complacent is erroneous; on the contrary it makes them for the most part humble, tolerant and kind. Failure makes people bitter and cruel."

—W. Somerset Maugham

A person may have a hundred million dollars and be a failure. And the widow who sets her goal to provide the best possible education for her child and to give him the best possible character training may die a pauper but leave an immortal influence. This truly is success—the persistent achievement of a worthy, challenging goal.

Goal Enthusiasm

As Dale Carnegie has so well put it, "If you want to be happy set yourself a goal that demands your thoughts, liberates your energy and inspires your hopes. Happiness is within you. It comes from doing some certain thing to which you can put all of your thought and energy. If you want to be happy get enthusiastic about something outside yourself."

The only way to lick an evil idea is with a greater idea. There are those who have set themselves to destroy us. Khrushchev said, "We will bury you." Their timetable calls for 1973 and many believe they are ahead of schedule. J. Frederic Dewhurst said in his book *America's Needs and Resources*: "Of all the great nations the one that clings most tenaciously to private capitalism has come closest to the socialistic goal of providing abundance for all in a classless society."

An interesting thing about our world is that in America today we have the purest example of what the fanatic false philosophies of communism seek to offer. Here about 7 per cent of the population live on farms and produce food for the other 93 per cent while in the Soviet Union it takes some 46 per cent of the people on farms to inadequately produce food for the rest. Furthermore the fantastic productive power of industry gives the average working man benefits that make him wealthy in comparison with what 90 per cent of the people of this world have. Of the total income in our nation less than 5 per cent is earned by those making $50,000 a year or more. Here under capitalism we have the two most precious possessions of all men—individual liberty and free enterprise, the pursuit of his goals to the benefit of others and to the satisfaction of his own needs.

Earl Nightingale tells the interesting story about a king in a European country who, as an experiment, took an aimless individual and put him in a cage, provided a warm bed and three good meals every day. For some time the man kept screaming, "Let me out. Why am I here? I've done nothing wrong." Then the king would come to see him each day and say to him, "Why you have nothing to worry about. You are warm in winter. You have no problems. All of your needs are met. You have adequate food. What else do you want?" Day after day he satisfied the sensate desires of this individual.

Finally one day a stranger passing by said, "Oh, that poor man, locked up in a cage. It must be terrible." The answer of the individual amazed him. He said, "I have everything—three good meals every day; no longer have to worry about working; I'm safe and protected; absolute security; everything I want I have right here." Was he successful? Tragically, terribly wasteful. No concern for his family. No interest in leaving an example of influence and inspiration to succeeding generations. No contribution to the social and spiritual needs of others. A slave. That's all he was.

How many people do you know like that who've never learned, much less enjoyed, the benefits of a dynamic goal?

Act now on setting a long-range goal. You can be successful, but there is no easy way to dynamic success.

Henry Ward Beecher has said, "Victories that are cheap are cheap. Those only are worth having which come as the result of hard fighting." Never forget those words, "What the mind can conceive and believe the mind can achieve."

61

Goethe, the German philosopher, said, "Before you can do something you must first be something." In other words you must act the part.

1. Set one goal at a time—the goal that is most meaningful for you at this particular time.
2. Think about it all the time. Build mind pictures of your achieving it. Use the five senses to bring your total personality to bear upon it.
3. Drive it into your subconscious mind. Remember your subconscious mind takes orders. It is fantastically creative. It never rests. Make your subconscious mind your willing servant by bringing to fruition the goal that you have set for it.
4. Write out this goal in simple clear language.

By all means you will want to get and read and re-read the book by Napoleon Hill, *Think and Grow Rich*. Mr. Hill says that you should write out a goal. It should be simply stated. Something like this: From January 1, 1966, through December 31, 1970, I will receive $250,000. In return for this sum of money I will give undying loyalty to my firm, unquestioned faithfulness to my family, dedicated service to God through my church and the best program of personal improvement for myself possible. Such a goal as this will make you a dynamic individual. You can be successful.

You may wish to write a ten-year goal, then break it down into five-year segments. Certainly divide it into one-year periods and have monthly check-ups and weekly planning and a program of daily improvement. You see, you can be better than you think. It's all up to you. You usually use less than 10 per cent of your total mental power. You waste so many hours every day. You fret away in worry so much energy fruitlessly all because you didn't plan by setting a dynamic goal to achieve.

Yes, you *can* be successful. You *can* accomplish great things through the persistent achievement of a challenging worthy goal. Your key for personal success is through goals, but you must act now.

Goals Can Change Your Life

Goals, the check points on your journey of success:

1. What date do you expect to achieve the purpose you set for yourself earlier?

2. List changes in attitude, conduct, habits and associations necessary to reach this goal.

    A.

    B.

    C.

    D.

3. Set up your goals in yearly segments from now until its realization.

4. Review these goals with your team, whether business or family to encourage their whole-hearted cooperation.

5. Commit yourself unswervingly to the accomplishment of these goals by printing them to post on the wall of your office, on calling cards or other places of daily contact. These are symbols that stimulate you to excel.

PART THREE
IMAGINATION

CHAPTER 10

Vivid Imagination

John Masefield said, "Man's body is faulty, his mind is untrustworthy, but his imagination has made him remarkable." Your key for personal success for today is imagination, the power and motivation of a magnificent mind, reaching beyond itself to scale heights never before imagined. Vivid imagination hunts for the ideal solution to life's problems and goals and then a dynamic imagination has the power to change what is found, to sift the information and bring the best results.

Two college presidents, Dr. Donald Cowling and Dr. Carter Davidson, say that the functions of the imaginative, creative mind are these: (1) Ability to concentrate. (2) Accuracy in observation. (3) Retentiveness of memory. (4) Logical reasoning. (5) Judgment. (6) Sensitivity of association. (7) Creative imagination.[1]

Seven Steps to Imagination

In the book *Applied Imagination,* Osborn[2] outlines the steps in the creative and productive imagination. (1) Orientation; pointing up the problem. (2) Preparation; gathering pertinent data. (3) Analysis; breaking down the relevant material. (4) Ideation; piling up alternatives by way of ideas. (5) Incubation; letting up, to invite illumination.

---

[1] *Our Changing World,* No. 891.
[2] Alex Osborn, *Applied Imagination* (New York: Charles Scribner's Sons, 1953), page 115.

(6) Synthesis; putting the pieces together. (7) Evaluation; judging the resultant ideas.

Dr. Maxwell Maltz in the book *Psycho-cybernetics* says: "Creative Imagination is not something reserved for the poets, the philosophers, the inventors, it enters into our every act, for imagination sets the goal, the picture which our automatic mechanism works on. We act, or fail to act not because of will as is so commonly believed but because of imagination.

"A human being always acts and feels and performs in accordance with what he imagines to be true about himself and his environment."[3]

"Were it not for slow, painful and constantly discouraged creative effort," said James Harvey Robinson, "man would be no more than a species of primate living on seeds, fruits, roots and uncooked flesh."

Inventive Imagination

"It was imagination," said Victor Wagner, "that enabled man to extend his thumb by inventing the vise, to strengthen his fist and arm by inventing the hammer. Step by step man's imagination lured, led and often pushed him into the astonishing heights of power he now so apprehensively occupies."

An Imaginative Man

One of the truly imaginative men in business in America is Joseph Treadwell who in 1956, at thirty-two, became owner and manager of Treadwell Ford Agency, the downtown Ford dealer in Mobile, Alabama. Let me tell you about just a few of the things that Joe Treadwell does to stimulate business with his imaginative mind. Each November and December he has a Christmas tree on the sales

---

[3] Maltz, *Ibid.*, page 28.

floor. Everyone who buys a new Ford car during that two-month period receives a Christmas gift and he publicly advertises that this bag on the tree will have at least $101, maybe $1,000 or somewhere in between. You can imagine how people who are short of cash for Christmas would prefer buying a new Ford that will guarantee them at least a $101 for Christmas spending.

On other occasions he has given every purchaser of a new car a three-days-and-two-nights trip in the Smoky Mountains of East Tennessee at Gatlinburg, or he may give them a three-days-and-two-nights trip with all expenses paid to Miami Beach. Again he has given a barrel of gas with every car, that is fifty-five gallons of free gasoline. On occasions he has loaded up all of his salesmen in the black hearse that he bought and has taken them out to shopping centers where they will go around and place, "Will you take (a certain amount)?" on the windshield of the automobiles.

He has advertised, "Buy a Ford from the man in the red coat" and every salesman wore a bright red coat, a bright red hat and carried a red walking cane. On other occasions he has had fifty common carriers with four, five or six Fords on each one all together with big signs saying, "Trade at Treadwell Ford. I'm going to Treadwell Ford." Imagine fifty truck loads of Fords all led by police motorcycle escort going criss-crossing through the downtown streets of the city of Mobile before they wind up at Treadwell. He has gigantic fish fries and invites the public to join him.

On a billboard in a prominent location in the city he has raised a brand new Ford automobile and has hired a model at $100 a week, three hours in the morning and three hours in the afternoon. She sat in the car or stood by the car up on the billboard waving to the people as they drove by.

He put a tall acid jug on the sales floor and every time he caught a salesman not smiling he made him put at least ten cents in the acid jar.

To stimulate his associates he does many things. On one occasion he sent a box filled with crumpled bills and with a note saying that all the taxes were paid on it. Inside this box were one thousand three wadded up $1.00 bills and one five dollar bill. He gave it as a gift to his general manager. People in the automobile industry all over America know how imaginative Joe Treadwell is. It pays off. At least 2,000 new Fords are sold every year.

Meditative Moments

Many ask, "Well, how good is imagination? Isn't it all daydreams?" Samuel Johnson has said, "Many have no happier moments than those that they pass in solitude, abandoned to their own imagination, which sometimes puts sceptres in their hands or miters on their heads, shifts the scene of pleasure with endless variety, bids all the forms of beauty sparkle before them, and gluts them with every change of visionary luxury." But is this what imagination really is? I think not. Certainly, creative imagination dreams, but productive imagination furnishes the dreams to the wheels of reality.

"Imagination rules the world." —Napoleon

"Imagination is more important than knowledge." —Albert Einstein

"Imagination makes man the master of animals." —Shakespeare

"Imagination governs the world." —Disraeli

Let's study this important dynamic of life's fullness further.

CHAPTER 11

Imagination Defined

Your key for personal success is imagination. What is imagination? We are studying how you can be an imaginative, dynamic, outstanding individual.

I think the best definition of what imagination does is from Dugald Stewart, "The faculty of imagination is the great spring of human activity, and the principal source of human improvement. As it delights in presenting to the mind scenes and characters more perfect than those which we are acquainted with, it prevents us from ever being completely satisfied with our present condition and with our past attainments and engages us continually in the pursuit of some untried enjoyment or of some ideal excellence. Destroy this faculty and the condition of man will become as stationary as that of the brutes." And the Bard of Stratford on Avon, William Shakespeare, said, "The poet's eye, in a fine frenzy rolling, Doth glance from heaven to earth, from earth to heaven; And as imagination bodies forth The forms of things unknown, the poet's pen Turns them to shapes, and gives to airy nothing A local habitation and a name. Such tricks hath strong imagination . . ."

Three Laws of Association

The key to creative imagination is association. Dr. Alex Osborn in his book *Applied Imagination* said that association is developed by the three laws of the Greeks discov-

71

ered for us[1]: First, contiguity. This means nearness, as when a baby's shoe reminds you of an infant. Contiguous means touching, in contact with, or in close proximity without actually touching, or near. For example, a dictaphone says to me "executive" and a successful executive because the successful executive is one who's conservative of his time and knows that with the use of the dictaphone he can produce more.

The second law of association is similarity in that the picture of a lion will remind you of a cat. The metaphor implies similarity. Allegories, fables and parables are likewise founded on similarities. For example, a happy child will remind you of home or of parents but it also may suggest a new opportunity, such as the new year brings.

Third, association is accomplished by contrast. For example, a midget might remind you of a giant or a hobo might remind you of a millionaire.

Audio Association

Association also works through sound. The song, "A Pretty Girl Is Like a Melody" reminds me of a beautiful recording of that song with a soprano obligato that I played on numerous occasions while a disc jockey with an armed forces radio station in Tsingtao, China, immediately after World War II. It was the most popular song the marines and sailors called for.

Of course combination is the essence of creativity. Dr. Easton has said, "A creative thinker evolves no new ideas. He actually evolves new combinations of ideas that are already in his mind."

Our actions through our life are the result of associations with earlier convictions, ideas and beliefs. For example Cecil B. DeMille, who produced so many of the great

---

[1]Osborn, *Ibid.*, pages 110-112.

Bible motion pictures, said: "I have no doubt that my father's vivid reading of Biblical stories planted in my impressionable mind a reverence and respect for the Bible, perhaps even a sense of its dramatic value, which in subsequent years was to turn me to the Great Book for themes to thrill motion picture audiences." How many times have you been discussing something with someone when they suddenly said, "Hey, that gives me an idea."

I've often found that my most creative times have been while hearing someone else speak. I make it a rigid rule never to go to hear someone else speak, whether at a convention, church, civic club, or whatever without taking my note pad with me, for many times, in fact on most occasions, I get ideas from things that were said. "Ideas are flighty things. That which now seems perfectly clear may later get away from you. Make a habit of jotting down ideas as they occur to you. Although many of them will not work out they may suggest other thoughts." —Daymon Aiken

Your imagination is vividly activated through creative association with other ideas. You can be successful.

CHAPTER 12

Brainstorming

Your key to personal success is imagination, and you develop your imagination by brainstorming. Brainstorming is simply using the brain power of a compatible group to storm a problem. There are two-way values of brainstorming. (1) It automatically excites the individual's own imagination. (2) It stimulates the associate power of all others present. It brings out their best. It challenges them to think creatively.

"When you really get going in a brainstorming session a spark from one's mind will light up a lot of bang-up ideas in the others just like a string of fire crackers."

—Fred Sharpe

The results of brainstorming are truly amazing. The United States Treasury has found that it secured 103 good ideas in 40 minutes on the subject, "How can we get more Federal employees to sell more United States Savings Bonds?" They received eighty-nine ideas in thirty minutes on the subject, "How to reduce absenteeism." My experience has been that you often get the best results in a shorter period of time. Sometimes it bogs down after fifteen or twenty minutes. Then stop and rest for awhile and come back with a fresh approach or a new problem.

What are the principles of brainstorming? Alex Osborn discusses them[1]: Ideation can be more productive if criti-

[1] Osborn, *Ibid.*, pages 156-158.

cism is concurrently excluded. Don't undermine any creative idea. If you pause to criticize someone else's idea you lose the initiative and creativity of your own. Furthermore it breaks the positive thought of the entire group. It also creates hostility and divides the group. No adverse judgment of ideas should be allowed.

"If you try to get hot and cold water out of the same faucet at the same time you will get only tepid water. And if you try to criticize and create at the same time you can't turn on either cold enough criticism or hot enough ideas. So let's stick solely to ideas. Let's cut out all criticism during the session of brainstorming."   —Alex Osborn

Free Wheeling

The second basic rule in brainstorming is that free wheeling is welcomed—the wilder the ideas the better. Your wild idea may bring forth a ready response, a constructive gem from someone else. Remember it is easier to tone down than to think up. Let the crazy ideas come and speak the first thought that comes to your mind. It may be a jewel.

The More the Better

Quantity is important. The more ideas the better. The greater the number, the more likely a winner. It has been found that the last fifty ideas produced at a brainstorming session have averaged higher in quality than the first fifty. Quantity breeds quality.

Creative Power

The fourth principle is a combination: improvement comes as a result of brainstorming. Other participants may improve upon your idea, creating a much better suggestion. Remember group ideation is far more productive than individual ideation.

Remember also that brainstorming is fun. The two guides to the success of a brainstorming group are: (1) How many good ideas did you find later? (2) Did the group enjoy it? Good brainstorming really is an enjoyable event. If it's done at work you will find the people may feel a bit guilty being paid for having a wonderful time. What's wrong with that?

In dozens of experiences of brainstorming in church groups, economic groups and social groups I have found that the leader is the key. If the leader will state a positive idea, be firm about the rules of brainstorming, set a definite time limit, stop at the end of the time limit, make it a game—a joyful experience—don't let them tire, rest or take up other subjects, you will find it to be a great and tremendous experience.

Judge Ideas Later

Once you have received the ideas do not grade them or judge them. Let a committee or individual do it at a later time. You may want to use a dictating machine or a tape recorder or have a secretary take the ideas down in shorthand. Be sure that you get *all* of the ideas. What seems unimportant at the time may later prove to be valuable.

Imagination is a gold mine. How much better if you have a number of gold mines going for you! Brainstorm your way to success.

CHAPTER 13

Creative Leisure

Your key for personal success today is imagination, and your imagination is at its best in leisure ideation. It has been found that in testing 702 individuals, women are 25 per cent more creative than men. Why do you suppose this is true? Isn't it for the very same reason that women live longer? Women are more creative and live longer because they break the strains of the day in leisure activity. They do not work at the same frenzy as the man who is at the office or laying bricks or selling, therefore their physical body rests more and their minds are more productive and more creative.

Creativity in Leisure

How many times have you been on the golf course when the idea came that solved the problem at the office? How many times have you been driving down the highway and suddenly, out of the blue, the solution came? Your conscious mind had been telling your subconscious mind for a long while that you had a problem and your subconscious mind was at work on it. In leisure, when the intensity of the conscious effort is relaxed, the subconscious mind takes over. Then when you are ready to listen to the subconscious mind suddenly the idea is consciously placed before you.

Your Idea Hot House

The word incubation indicates intentional relaxation. In medicine it refers to the phase in the development of an infectious disease between infection and the first symptom. In imagination it means the relaxed atmosphere by which we let our subconscious mind bring to consciousness the solution to our problems.

Dr. Hornall Hart, professor emeritus at Duke University says, "Pay attention to your hunches. I even pay attention to my wife's, they are better than mine." When we are relaxed these flashes come seemingly out of nowhere but literally they are the response of a creative mind. They are not mere freak phenomena to be examined as curiosities. When our bodies are as relaxed as a sack of flour these flashes are more readily before us.

Harry Hepner, professor of psychology at Syracuse University, said, "The appearance of a good idea seemingly comes from nowhere . . . Failure to record the flash or to follow it through may entail a tragic inability to do so later." Ralph Waldo Emerson encouraged us to "Look sharply after your thoughts. They come unlooked for like a new bird seen in your trees and if you turn to your usual task they disappear."

My personal experience reveals that many times a thought, an idea or a message, address, or a sermon, comes suddenly out of the blue. I always keep a notebook in hand and I write down these thoughts and I keep the notebook with me at all times. In a moment of leisure again a further development of the thought comes, an illustration here, a humorous anecdote there, and the body of the message springs into view. This is incubation.

Let It Simmer

Edna Ferber wrote, "A story must simmer in its own juice for months or even years before it is ready to serve." Remarked Constance Robertson, "I have found that it pays to hold a plot in suspension and not to worry it or force it. At the right point I go into a long lull. Then I tackle my typewriter and write whatever comes. My story then seems to reel itself off in a most extraordinary way." This was the key to Edison. Most of us know that he would go for days and not go home to sleep, but few people knew that he had a sofa in his office and he would catnap there from time to time. Here some of his most outstanding ideas came into being. Here his creative mind brought forth the so-called flashes of ingenuity.

Lowell Thomas recommends a prescription from Yoga which calls for a deliberate, sustained period of silence— just an hour of silence, sitting still, neither reading nor looking upon anything in particular.

Furthermore do not be a rigid slave driver. Flit from one idea to another. You will find that the truly outstanding ideas will keep coming back to you from time to time. Play these hunches as an organist plays all of the console to bring forth the tremendous tunes from all the pipes.

One time of challenging ideation for me is in worship. When hearing the minister bring forth the message, whether in convention or in church. I have found some amazing and seemingly miraculous solutions to problems that have been confronting me before.

Dr. Norman Vincent Peale holds that for creative medi-tation "there is nothing like peace-drenched mountains with their deep, sun-bathed pensive valleys. Here our minds clear and our ability to think creatively returns."

Of course, the best leisure ideation comes during peri-ods of rest following conscious work.

Add Years to Your Life

Furthermore a definite value of leisure ideation is in lengthening your life. A recent study at the University of Chicago reveals that men who think creatively actually are young at fifty and appear to be aging slowly but men who work with their hands seem to be old at fifty and are aging rapidly.

So let me urge you through conscious effort to plant the seeds of knowledge, of suggestion, of information, of fact and trust the fabulous power of your creative mind to bring you the solution during leisure ideation. Leave your desk. Go to the golf course. Go out on the ocean fishing or in your lake nearby. Work in your garden. Spend time at your stamp collection or whatever it is that you enjoy doing. Get away from the tedious and leisurely enjoy life. In doing so you are not wasting time; you are using it to the best of your ability.

CHAPTER 14

Hindrances of Imagination

Your key to personal success is imagination. You can become an imaginative, creative person. But these are hindrances to creative imagination. Italian Zoologist Battista Grassi has divided mankind into three classes: (1) Those who work with their minds. (2) Those who pretend to do so. (3) Those who do neither. "Unless you are in the first class," said Grassi, "you will probably fail to summon up the energy to make yourself do the things you have to do to get the most out of your imagination."

Daydreams Are Deadly

The first hindrance is daydreaming. I'm speaking here of idle and purposeless fantasy. Dreams with no roots, dreams with no reality—these are hindrances. Truly creative dreams are the solution to, as well as the desire of, our aspirations and goals in life.

Psychiatrist Freud said, "Every neurosis has the result and therefore probably the purpose of forcing the patient out of real life, of alienating him from actuality." This then is the weakness of daydreams that have no root nor purpose, no plan nor goal in life. They destroy rather than build up.

James Russell Lowell has said, "Solitude is as needful to the imagination as society is wholesome for the character." We are not talking about the leisure ideation that solitude brings. This is wonderfully creative. We are talking about the unreal, impractical, irrational daydreaming that leads an individual to escape from the reality of purpose and actually is a division of the mind.

The Morbid Movie of Worry

The second hindrance to imagination is worry. This is Public Enemy No 1. More people have been destroyed and are being destroyed every year by worry than any other single cause. The Bible says, "Ye cannot serve God and mammon." You cannot serve two masters at once. Neither can you be an enthusiastic, vibrant, alert, creative individual and be saturated with the viciousness of worry. Worry is corrosive, corruptive and destructive. Dr. Harry Fosdick has labeled it "anxious fear." He says, "Worry is like running reels of morbid movies through our minds." Therefore we must change reels. We must run the reel of vibrant purpose, of joyful living, of enthusiastic endeavor, of dynamic purpose, then we will destroy the hindrance of worry.

How to Battle the Blues

The blues are the third hindrance to imagination. At breakfast one morning a lady is supposed to have said to her husband, "I'm down in the dumps. I believe I'll go buy a new hat." Her husband replied, "So that's where you've been getting them."

Recent scientific studies reveal that everyone has both a high peak of emotional intensity and a low level of emotional discouragement each thirty-day period. If you let the blues master you there will come a time when you will be in a constant thirty-day period of deep and decided depression. There are some positive things that we can do to overcome the blues. Let me suggest some that I have practiced. I keep in my office a stereo record player with some of the finest music. When I am discouraged I play the music, turn it up high so that the whole vibrancy of the exhilarating strains will drive my moods of despair into the ground and lift me up to heights of joy. I have a record player in my car that is connected to the radio, and when I can't get good radio music I turn on *Music Man, South Pacific, Oklahoma,* semi-classical and classical numbers that lift me to emotional heights. Another way to whip worry is to enjoy the presence in spirited conversation of exhilarating people. We become what the crowd we run with is. Be with enthusiastic people and you will be enthusiastic.

Another way to whip worry is to spend some creative hours with your favorite hobby. You will find that this will bring new spirit, new vision, new outlook and help you to lift the dread disease of worry. Remember to make the blues your slave not your master.

Total Mind Control

Evil thoughts are the fourth hindrance to imagination. Charles Haddon Spurgeon said, "A vile imagination, once indulged, gets the key of our minds, and can get in again very easily, whether we will or no, and can so return as to bring seven other spirits with it even more wicked than itself; and what may follow no one knows." F. W. Robertson, another great English cleric, has said, "Imagination enobles appetites which in themselves are low, and spiritualizes acts which, else, are only animal. . . . But the pleasures which begin in the senses only sensualize."

Remember there is only one principle that all philosophers of all ages have agreed upon, and that is this, "We become what we think about." "As a man thinketh in his heart so is he." Show me what a man is thinking and I will tell you where he will be a few years from now. Our senses should be the servants and slaves that lead us to outstanding success. Remember the greatest success is he who performs the greatest service for the most of mankind. Don't

83

make the senses your god. Make the service of God and mankind your purpose and then you've really begun to live.

Overcome the hindrances to imagination. Be your own master. Don't let daydreams, worry, the blues and evil thoughts drive you to despair. You can be successful. Become so today.

CHAPTER 15

Developing Imagination

Your key for personal success is imagination. How can you develop an imaginative mind? You can be successful. One of the best ways to develop your imagination is to simply force yourself to work at it. George Meyer, when asked how he turned out the song *For Me and My Gal,* snapped back, "I just sat down and went to work." Clarence Budington Kelland, a prolific fiction writer, confesses that he would hardly turn out anything if he didn't force himself to work each morning immediately after breakfast whether he feels in the mood or not.

Here are two ways to get started:

1. Concentrate. Focalize your psychic energy upon one goal. Write out your purpose. Intensify your efforts upon it. Stay with it. Bring all the power, the experience, the background, the facts and the knowledge you can accumulate upon that one purpose. Spend time meditating on it.
2. Then team up with a compatible group, collaborate with others who will help you accomplish it. A great man delights in helping others. I have found that the more successful a man is the more helpful he will be to others. He wants to share his knowledge with others, particularly younger people. Therefore go to outstanding people round about you. Call upon them, their knowledge, their background and their experi-

ence. Ask them to help you in achieving this purpose. You will be amazed how readily they will reply.

In his book *How To Win Success Before Forty* Damroth tells how to make ideas pay off.[1] (1) We must apply idea ability to the job. (2) Let your ideas flow freely, be a wildcatter. (3) Concentrate on the big idea. (4) Don't quit until your idea is a reality. Stay with it.

Make Your Moods Your Servants

Alex Osborn says we need to establish a working mood. He suggests this is similar to pulling ourselves up by a boot strap. Even self-confidence can be self-induced to some extent. As a baseball player swings two bats before stepping up to the plate we need to flex our imagination when approaching a creative task. Osborn tells of ad writer Allen Ward, who accomplishes amazing results in ideation. Listen to Ward's formula: "I have no sure way of uninhibiting myself for creative thinking, but I've found that one good way to get into a working mood is to close my door and try to forget everything but the job before me. Then I pull my typewriter to me, wrap my legs around it and start to write. I write down every line that comes into my head—crazy, dull or however it sounds. I find that if I don't it may linger there and block others. I write as fast as I can. Then after a long while some cogs that haven't worked start to whir and something striking begins to type itself out on the yellow sheet before me like a telegraph message. That's the hard way and about the only way I know."

Some of the world's most outstanding writers have been those who have known firsthand the experiences they relate. Certainly Hemingway lived his experiences. He wrote of his experiences. Therefore, the more varied our experi-

---

[1]William G. Damroth, *How To Win Success Before Forty* (Englewood Cliffs, N.J.: Prentice-Hall, Inc., 1956), page 91.

ence the more definite our imagination. Of course we can increase this imagination and make it firsthand experience by reading. Become a prolific reader. Develop your reading rate. I have had for many years a reading rate machine that has more than doubled my reading rate. The late President John F. Kennedy was able to digest an amazing amount of reports because he could read at 1200 words a minute. He literally had developed his reading rate to a phenomenal amount. Read biographies. Read constructive fantasies. Read books of faith and inspiration. And by all means read the Bible.

Act Out Your Success Role

You can develop imagination by role playing. Imagine yourself in the shoes of a particular person. Imagine yourself as President of the United States. Begin at the first hour in the morning and imagine yourself through every conference, through every meeting, through every council activity, through every telephone call, through every responsibility during the day. Play the role of that person. You will be able to imagine yourself in his very shoes.

This is especially helpful if you are selling. Imagine yourself in the shoes of the purchasing agent that you are calling upon. Find out about the problems that he is facing. Set out to serve him and his company by proving that you have the solution. Then you are his ally, you're his friend, you're his associate; you aren't someone competing for his time, you're one who is there to help him. Imagination places yourself in his shoes through role playing.

Then finally let me urge you to practice mental pictures in achieving imaginative goals. Harry Emerson Fosdick said, "Hold a picture of yourself long and steadily enough in your mind's eye and you will be drawn toward it. Picture yourself vividly as defeated and that alone will make victory impossible. Picture yourself vividly as winning and that alone will contribute immeasurably to success. Great living starts with a picture, held in your imagination, of what you would like to do or to be.''

I have a life-insurance salesman friend in Missouri who will someday become a $75,000 a year vice-president with his nationally-known insurance company. He is playing the role. He has pictured himself there. He is taking every possible means of personal improvement. He is paying the price of long hours, of diligent work. He is a cooperative team member. It is inevitable that he will be the vice-president of that firm, or maybe the president.

Produce and Star in our Own Movie

Imagine yourself sitting before a large motion picture screen. You are on the screen. The important thing you see in these pictures is a vivid and detailed projection of the person you want to become. See yourself moving about that screen, achieving the very things that you are dreaming of. Earl Nightingale says this is one of the best ways to lose weight. Picture your slim self walking across that motion picture screen with all the vitality of life that can truly be yours. Spend a little time each day, an increasing amount of time as each day goes by, picturing yourself on that motion picture screen, the truly successful, dynamic individual you wish to become. Napoleon practiced soldiering in his imagination for many years before he actually went on the battlefield. Webb and Morgan in their book *Making the Most of Your Life* tell us, ''The notes Napoleon made from his readings during these years of study filled, when printed, 400 pages. He imagined himself as a commander and drew maps of the islands of Corsica showing where he would place various defenses, making all of his calculations with mathematical precision.''[2]

---

[2] *Our Changing World,* No. 747.

Conrad Hilton imagined himself operating a hotel long before he ever bought one. As a boy he used to play that he was a hotel operator. Henry Kaiser has said that each of his business accomplishments was realized in his imagination before it appeared in actuality. Dr. Albert Edward Wiggam called mental picturing of yourself "the strongest force within you."

Dr. Leslie Weatherhead has said, "If we have in our minds a picture of ourselves as fear haunted and defeated nobodies we must get rid of that picture at once and hold up our heads. That is a false picture and the false must go. God sees us as men and women in whom and through whom He can do a great work. He sees us as already serene, confident and cheerful. He sees us not as pathetic victims of life, but masters of the art of living; not wanting sympathy, but imparting help to others and therefore thinking less and less of ourselves and full, not of self-concern, but of love and laughter and a desire to serve."[3]

Imagination

You are successful the moment you imagine your purpose.

1. Imagine yourself in the act of accomplishing your purpose. Use the five senses to place yourself at the moment of achievement.

For instance, say that your purpose is to build a $500,000 building at your alma mater named for your parents.

    A. Can you see yourself projected across the screen of your mind through imagination in the very act of handing the keys to the President of the College?

---

[3]Osborn, *Ibid.*, page 149.

Visualize the building—red brick, white columns. two stories, etc.

B. Can you smell the flowers on the speaker's stand, the corsages worn by the ladies present and the special bouquet handed to your mother?

C. Can you taste the joy of achievement, realizing that thousands of students will respond to life's highest challenges as a result of your gift?

D. Can you hear the band playing in the background, the burst of applause, the deep and sincere words of appreciation from a faculty, alumni and students?

E. Can you feel the key in your left hand, the President's warm handclasp in your right in the very act of presentation?

2. Now make your purpose come alive by writing out below your crowning event of a lifetime using the five senses.

3. Schedule brainstorming sessions with each compatible group that can help you achieve your purpose. Remember big men delight in accomplishing glorious things.

PART FOUR
BUILD CONFIDENCE AND SUCCEED

CHAPTER 16

Whip Worry

One woman's way of dealing with worry was, "I've joined the new Don't Worry Club and now I hold my breath. I'm so afraid I'll worry that I'm worried half to death." Your key for personal success is building personal, individual self-confidence by whipping worry.

John Edmund Haggai in his book *How to Win Over Worry*[1] says that worry is Public Enemy No. 1. He says that mental illness is costing this nation two-and-a-half billion dollars a year; that many more Americans commit suicide (the result of stress, duress, anxiety and worry) than die from the five most common communicable diseases. For instance, in 1957, 220 people died of polio, 15,980 committed suicide. Seventy-five hundred more people committed suicide than were victims of homicide. A total of 10,170 people died as a result of ulcers. At least 17,000,000 Americans are suffering from some form of mental illness. During World War II more than 300,000 of America's finest young men were killed in combat. During the same period of time over a million civilians died from heart disease, primarily the result of worry. One doctor states that worry causes heart trouble, high blood pressure, some forms of asthma, rheumatism, ulcers, colds, thyroid malfunction, arthritis, migraine headaches, blindness and a host of stomach disorders in addition to ulcers.

You cannot have confidence until you whip worry.

---

[1]John Edmund Haggai, *How To Win Over Worry* (Grand Rapids, Mich.: Zondervan Publishing House, 1959), pages 15, 16

What People Worry About

Notice these statistics about things people worry about: Things that never happen, 40 per cent; things they can't change, 30 per cent; needless worry about health, 12 per cent; petty and miscellaneous worrying, 10 per cent; real problems, 8 per cent. Therefore 92 per cent of the things people worry about are ruinous and uncontrollable. Furthermore worrying is sin, for it not only destroys man's health but even can cause him to commit suicide. Phillips translates Philippians 4:6-8 thusly, "Don't worry over anything whatever; tell God every detail of your needs in earnest and thankful prayer, and the peace of God, which transcends human understanding, will keep constant guard over your hearts and minds as they rest in Christ Jesus. Here is a last piece of advice. If you believe in goodness and if you value the approval of God, fix your minds on whatever is true and honorable and just and pure and lovely and praiseworthy."[2]

Davidson, in his book, *How I Discovered the Secret of Success in the Bible*,[3] tells how to build confidence: "(1) You must know your product. Know what you are doing. Master your job. (2) You must avoid all exaggerations. You must practice the art of understatement rigorously and conscientiously. (3) You must be willing and able to prove your case with facts developed from several different angles. (4) You must present your case in a tone of quiet authority without apology or uncertainty." Then, there is nothing to worry about. You have all the facts. You have people's confidence and friendship. You are then whipping worry.

---

[2]J. B. Phillips, *The New Testament in Modern English* (New York: The Macmillan Company, 1958).
[3]Clinton Davidson, *How I Discovered the Secret of Success From the Bible* (Westwood, N.J.: Revell, 1964), page 50.

Worry Produces Nervous Breakdowns

Dan Custer[4] says that worry is the interest we pay on trouble before it is due. It never solved any problem. It is completely destructive and disintegrating. Still, many of us continue to indulge in it. Worry is a malfunction of the mind. The wrong use of the mind results in disease. Therefore, worrying is against the law. The Buddhists say, "The two devils of the emotional kingdom are anger and fear. Anger, the brain passion, and fear the freezing passion." The Apostle Paul said, "God has not given us the spirit of fear; but of power, and of love, and of a sound mind."[5] We are not born with fear. It is a cultivated mental disease that destroys. Therefore, a sound mind is an integrated mind— a mind in one piece; a mind working harmoniously together. When worry controls the mind it leads to abulia, or loss of the power of the will, because the mind is divided and cannot act in one channel. Abulia is often a nervous breakdown. This literally means divided mindness. The victim has quit struggling and yields to a depressed and passive manner. Worrying is injurious to the human body. Furthermore, it is injurious to social fellowship, and to business relations and family affairs. Worry is suicidal.

In the Thirty-Seventh Psalm David wrote, "Trust in the Lord, and do good; so shalt thou dwell in the land, and verily thou shalt be fed." The way to whip worry is to crowd worry out of your mind with positive spiritual thoughts.

Forgive Yourself

Over more than a dozen years of counseling with people who had many problems, I have found that a guilt com-

---

[4]Dan Custer, *The Miracle of Mind Power* (Englewood Cliffs, N.J.: Prentice-Hall, Inc., 1960), pages 220-221.
[5]II Timothy 1:7.

plex has brought more worry and emotional destruction than most any other thing. The person with a guilt complex has never learned to forgive himself. Therefore he is punishing himself. When you punish yourself you are violating life's most important and most dynamic motivating principle—self-preservation. Such action comes from a puritanical, religious atmosphere on the part of some and a fear of punishment on the part of God by others. The nature of God is forgiveness. In I John 1:9 we have the passage, "If we confess our sins, he is faithful and just to forgive us our sins, and to cleanse us from all unrighteousness." Learn to forgive yourself so you then can whip worry.

Dr. John A. Schindler[6] writes about the dangers and destructive powers of E.I.I., emotionally induced illness. He says that over 50 per cent of those seeking medical aid have it. In a thousand different cases emotionally induced illness is as common as all of the other 999 diseases put together. Dr. Schindler reports that at the Oschsner Clinic in New Orleans they found that 74 per cent of 500 consecutive patients admitted to the department handling gastro-intestinal diseases were found to be suffering from E.I.I. In 1951, a paper from the Yale University Out-Patient Medical Department indicated that 76 per cent of patients coming to that clinic were suffering from E.I.I.

These people literally were worrying themselves to death.

---

[6]John A. Schindler, *How to Live 365 Days a Year* (Englewood Cliffs, N.J.: Prentice-Hall, Inc., 1954), pages 3-4.

An Emotion Greater Than Worry

There is one other emotion that is just as dynamic as worry. Worry is dangerous to every crowd, for the one who worries contaminates all the others round about. But here is another contagious solution. It is enthusiasm—the vital quality that arouses you to action. Self-control is the balance wheel that directs your action and will lead you to be positive and powerful and overcome the destructiveness of worry.

To be a well-rounded, well-adjusted, well-balanced individual you must have self-control and enthusiasm. Remember, there is only one thing in all this world that you hold total control over and that is your mind. You can master worry. You can whip worry by the positive power of enthusiasm. You see, you are the sum total of your dominating and most prominent thoughts.

For example, if your family is having a discussion—let's say you are involved in an argument. You have raised your voices in disagreement. The doorbell rings. Immediately the entire family stops talking. You do not want to be embarrassed in front of visitors. So you crowd out the emotion of disunity and you put on a front for the visitors. In the same way you can crowd out the emotion of worry and instill in its place enthusiasm, positive thinking and personal self-confidence.

Harold Sherman tells an interesting story of the positive power of P. T. Barnum, the great showman.[7] Once awakened from a sound sleep in the middle of the night he was told, "Mr. Barnum, one quarter of the circus has been completely destroyed by fire." Barnum sat up, blinking his eyes. "What are you going to do?" asked the messenger,

---

[7]Harold Sherman, *How to Turn Failure Into Success* (Englewood Cliffs, N.J.: Prentice-Hall, Inc., 1958), pages 22-23.

expecting Barnum to leap from the bed and start issuing orders. "I can do nothing tonight," Mr. Barnum replied, "so I'm going back to sleep." There you have it. With confidence, he had learned to whip worry.

Crowd worry out with enthusiastic action. Forgive yourself, for guilt feelings deny creativity and strength. Face the fact that worry always destroys. It never helps.

CHAPTER 17

Fight Fear

Your key for success today is to fight fear with faith and with facts. You can be a self-confident, triumphant, successful individual.

Napoleon Hill says that there are seven basic fears: "(1) The fear of poverty. (2) The fear of criticism. (3) The fear of ill health. (4) The fear of loss of love. (5) The fear of old age. (6) The fear of loss of liberty. (7) The fear of death."[1] Let's build self-confidence in fighting these fears.

We must fight fear with facts. Emerson has said, "Trust thyself, every breast vibrates to that iron string of trust." When your mind and message is filled with facts you become a radiant dynamic individual.

In Carl Sandburg's book, *Abraham Lincoln: The Prairie Years,* we have this illustration: "A listener to one of Abraham Lincoln's speeches gives the picture. 'As his body loosened and swayed to the cadence of his address and as his thoughts unfolded drops of sweat stood out on his forehead; he was speaking not only with his tongue but with every blood drop of his body.' A scholarly man said, 'His manner was impassioned and he seemed transfigured; his listeners felt that he believed every word he said and that like Martin Luther he would go to the stake rather than abate one jot or tittle of it.' "[2]

---

[1] Hill, *Think and Grow Rich,* page 82.
[2] Carl Sandburg, *Abraham Lincoln: The Prairie Years* (New York: Harcourt-Brace and Company, 1926), page 72.

Now let's look at the facts. What is the worst possible thing that could happen to you? Put your mind in reverse for a moment and let's just anticipate—loss of health or job, whatever it is. What would you do if that were to occur? Sit down and write out a course of action, step by step. Next, plan to make the best of that worst possible thing, perhaps even use it for improvement (such as getting a better job). When you face the fact that the worst that could happen to you can be dealt with, and that it is unlikely to occur in the first place, you can revel in the joy of life's pleasures and achievements.

Take Your Own Inventory

Play up your good points. Just sit down and make an inventory. In the left-hand column list all of your faults and failures. In the right-hand column positively, carefully and honestly list all of your good features—pleasing personality, good education, fine family background, etc. Unless you are neurotic, you will find yourself way ahead of the game.

In one of his radio addresses Earl Nightingale refers to a quote by Balzac: "By resorting to self-resignation the unfortunate consummate their misfortunes." As long as the followers of Mohammed have predominately in their teaching, "Allah wills it" and this fatalistic philosophy, the people of that state will never dominate the world by thoughts, their philosophy, or their leadership. But we have followers of fatalism here. Such statements: "Well, that's the way things go." "That's the way the cookie crumbles." "That's the way the ball bounces." Now if this statement is a dismissal of a mistake or misfortune, then all right, but too often it is the destruction of initiative. Frank Pierce says that by facing the facts you control your destiny to a great extent.

Fight Fear with Faith. Fear is amazingly contagious. One person can infect and ruin otherwise amiable relationships. Fear hampers our ability to think and to reason effectively. Extreme fear can paralyze our capacity to act. Fear even increases pain. It is known that 75 per cent of pain that is felt while a person is tense and jittery will disappear when a person is totally relaxed. Don't try to flee from your fears; face them with a positive faith. Admit them, but crowd them out with faith. Open the closet of your mind. Grab the fears in the dark recesses. Hold them out into the sunlight of God's love and truth and trample them into the dust. Levy has said, "A person under the firm persuasion that he can command resources virtually has them."

Napoleon Hill commented on this subject, "Is it not strange that we fear most that which never happens; that we destroy our initiative by the fear of defeat when in reality defeat is the most useful tonic and it should be accepted as such."

You fight fear with faith and with facts by acting the part of confidence, by getting all of the information. Right at this moment determine that you will not be the victim of fear, but you will be the victor with faith. You will not let fear frustrate and ruin your present and your future. You will not fail to fight. And, furthermore, don't contaminate other healthy positive minds by the contagion of fear. If you will not be victor, then go like a hermit to a cave in isolation of your own defeat. But you do not have to do that. You can be victor.

CHAPTER 18

Dominate Doubts

Your key to confidence is to dominate your doubts. Shakespeare has said, "Our doubts are traitors and make us lose the good we oft might win by fearing to attempt." Doubts are good when they can be controlled. Doubts are good when they lead us to a keen evaluation. Gathering the facts, and seriously studying the situation, help bring caution and wisdom. Only fools never have doubts.

But a great majority of people let their doubts rule them. You must admit your inadequacies to overcome doubt. Face the fact that you do not excel in everything. Acknowledge that you have weaknesses. In the very process of admitting your inadequacies you dominate your doubts. See, a problem well stated is half solved. When a person can face the fact that he is inadequate in a certain area, that person will go and find help somewhere. This is the way to dominate your doubts. You are more important than the emotion of doubt. Samuel Johnson has said that "Nothing will ever be attempted if all possible objections must first be overcome."

Let the doubt give you wisdom; let the doubt be satisfied; let the doubt raise its head and then when maturity, wisdom, experience, and knowledge have led you to realize that the doubt is satisfied, move on. According to Shakespeare, "Modest doubt is called the beacon of the wise—the tent that searches to the bottom of the worst."

The trouble is that many people do not have modest doubts. They have magnificent, mountainous doubts that crush them.

Don't Let Doubts Destroy You

Remember that doubts are destructive. They destroy action. They tear up the peace and serenity and happiness of a man's life. Listen to Robert South, English clergyman and author: "There is no weariness like that which rises from doubting—from the perpetual jogging of unfixed reason. The torment of suspense is very great; but as soon as the wavering, perplexed mind begins to determine, be the determination which way soever it may be, it will find itself at ease."

Eliminate your doubts by speaking your convictions. Don't be a Mr. Milquetoast. "The man who speaks his positive convictions is worth a regiment of men who are always proclaiming their doubts and suspicions," said Pliney the Elder. Daniels, a mountain philosopher from Tennessee, used to say, "Don't figger how you can't; figger how you can." So gather the facts and act. Don't wait. Dominate, dictate, control your doubts. P. T. Munger so well said, "Knowledge and personality make doubt possible. But knowledge is also the cure of doubt; and when we get a full and adequate sense of personality we are lifted into a region where doubt is almost impossible, for no man can know himself as he is, in all the fulness of his nature, without also knowing God."

Your Pause That Refreshes

Doubt should be the "pause that refreshes" on the pathway to personal success. But don't let the "Coke break" last all day. Don't let the five-minute period stretch into four hours. This truth is expressed by English clergyman Caleb Colton when he said, "Doubt is the vestibule

103

which all must pass before they can enter the temple of wisdom.—When we are in doubt and puzzle out the truth by our own exertions we have gained something that will stay by us and will serve us again.—But if to avoid the trouble of the search we avail ourselves of the superior information of a friend, such knowledge will not remain with us; we have not bought, but borrowed it.''

And Goethe sums it up with his statement, "Give me the benefit of your convictions, if you have any, but keep your doubts to yourself, for I have enough of my own." Don't spread your doubts; dominate them.

Crab grass grew in my yard when I first moved to South Florida. At that time I wanted any kind of grass to grow there—anything but sand. Later I killed the crab grass in order to grow beautiful St. Augustine grass. Similarly the doubts we have are temporary expediencies that help us move into the full palace room of power and achievement.

Gain self-confidence by dominating your doubts. Only a fool never has doubts, but a wise man never yields to them. He brings them rigidly under control. Be a dictator—over doubts, that is. Dominate them and you will be successful.

CHAPTER 19

Act Aggressively

Your key for today is to act aggressively. Seize the day. Grapple with the hour. Assault the minute. To gain courage you must act aggressively. Remember our actions are our moods. Positive assertive action will drive away despondency.

In order to act you must first have confidence in yourself. You are better than you think you are. You can accomplish; but you must act—act now and act aggressively.

Why do you fail to act aggressively? Is it that you do not know your job? We are down on that with which we are unfamiliar.

Each year in America our economy loses billions of dollars because of insufficient, untrained, uninformed employees. An aggressive company will train its people. Now if you are not adequately trained for your task and there is no plan on the immediate horizon for training you, what should you do? The answer is train yourself. Read books on your field. Every field in America has some kind of training procedure and books that you can secure. Also read books on personality development.[1]

There is no excuse for becoming a failure. Act aggressively by learning and mastering your job. Then it becomes a joyous privilege and not a tedious task.

---

[1]For instance, Dale Carnegie's *How To Win Friends and Influence People*, Gabriel's *Twenty Steps to Power and Influence and Control Over People*, and Battista's *The Power to Influence People*.

Go Upstream and Succeed

Let me urge you to do the opposite of the majority of people. A man without purpose is applying only about 30 per cent of his ability. If you do not have purpose, multiply your present salary by three and the figure you get is the one that you will be making if you apply your total ability, experience, knowledge and capacity by dynamic purpose. But you must violate the norm. Earl Nightingale says that only 5 per cent of American men are outstandingly successful. Dare to be different, and I believe you will find that you can be outstandingly successful.

In May, 1962, the stock market had a sudden drop. It was the most sustained paper loss since 1929. Frenzy and frustration swept the market. People called their brokers and yelled, "Sell." J. Paul Getty, one of the world's richest men, watched the situation very carefully and then ordered his brokers to buy. He bought at a low price. Within fifteen months the market was back ahead of where it was in May, 1962. Getty and others who bought at the low level became amazingly wealthy because they dared to be different. They went against the stream.

Paul J. Meyer, the million dollar personal success man, has the following dynamic points of success.[2]

"1. Crystallize your thinking. Determine what specific goal you want to achieve and then dedicate yourself to its attainment with unswerving singleness of purpose.

"2. Develop a plan for achieving your goal and a deadline for its attainment. Plan your progress carefully, hour by hour, day by day, month by month. Organize activity and maintain the enthusiasm of the well springs of your power.

---

[2]From a conversation with Paul Meyer.

"3. Develop a sincere desire for the things you want in life. A burning desire is the greatest motivator of every human action. The desire for success implants success consciousness which in turn creates a vigorous and ever-increasing habit of success.

"4. Develop supreme confidence in yourself and your own abilities. Enter every activity without giving mental recognition to the possibility of defeat. Concentrate on your strength instead of your weaknesses; on your powers instead of your problems.

"5. Develop a dogged determination to follow through on your plan regardless of obstacles, criticisms or circumstances. Opportunities never come to those who wait, they are captured by those who dare to attack." Act aggressively.

Dress the Part

A practical way to overcome discouragement and to develop your action is the way that you dress. For example, wearing hard heels gives you a sense of purpose and achievement as you walk forcefully down the street. The clicking of the heels is an act of aggression and certainty.

Recently a friend of mine bought me a suit. When I have an important engagement or a speaking opportunity I wear that $175 suit. It does something to my mood. Self-confidence is destroyed in the presence of a person who is much more attractively dressed than yourself. Don't let this happen. You will find that a $100 or $125 suit will last twice as long as a $40 suit. And in all of the time you are wearing it, it will increase your effectiveness and efficiency by giving you self-confidence.

Ninety per cent of a man's body is covered by clothing. That leaves only his hands and face to be the "real person." Therefore clothing creates an important impression. Consult your tailor. Get a professional opinion. Don't wear the clothes that you like; wear the clothes that are best for you—that bring out your best. Wear the clothes that help you act aggressively. I love the story of the dynamic young man just out of college who applied for a position at a bank. The personnel officer asked him what he was capable of doing, and the young man replied that he wanted to be a vice-president. The personnel manager, quite shocked, said, "Why we already have twelve vice-presidents." The aggressive young man replied, "That's all right. I'm not superstitious."

Seize the day! Grab hold of life! Wrestle some opportunity! Get your share of success! Don't bog down in the quagmire of distrust, fear and frustration. By acting aggressively you can climb the mountaintop of glorious achievement. You can be successful.

CHAPTER 20

Possess Your Mind

Your key to personal success is to control your mind and master your emotions. How many people do you know who really do *not* control their own minds? Some have yielded to others. Many have given their minds to habits of destruction—the alcoholics, dope addicts and pleasure-mad individuals who exist only for self-satisfaction.

True greatness is attained in service to others. So possess your mind. Do not be a victim going over the falls; be a victor climbing the rapids to achievement. "You have not only the power to think but, what is a thousand times more important still, you have the power to control your thoughts and to direct them to do your bidding . . . You are the sum total of your dominating and most prominent thoughts," observed Napoleon Hill.

You change your manner and tone of voice to hide your true feelings from those you do not want to share them with. You control yourself because you want to. Now do the same with your mind. Master it. Control it. Make it serve you.

The Bible says, "As a man thinketh in his heart so is he." Our dominant thoughts make us what we are. In I Peter 1:13 we have these words: "Gird up the loins of your mind." Use your thoughts and control them.

Happiness Is a State of Mind

Everyone wants to be happy. But happiness is not a goal; it is a state of mind. "A merry heart doeth good like a medicine: but a broken spirit drieth the bones" (Proverbs 17:22).

An old Dutch proverb says, "Happy people are never wicked." You can do something about being happy. Abraham Lincoln said, "Most people are about as happy as they make up their minds to be."

Drive away the dregs and disease of despair. Determine you are going to be happy.

Napoleon Hill lists the following twelve great riches of life: "(1) A positive mental attitude. (2) Sound physical health. (3) Harmony in human relationships. (4) Freedom from fear. (5) Hope of achievement. (6) The capacity for faith. (7) Willingness to share one's blessings. (8) A labor of love. (9) An open mind on all subjects. (10) Self-discipline. (11) The capacity to understand people. (12) Financial security."[1]

These are certainly worthy goals for all men to attain but, remember, there is nothing in all this world that you influence more than your own mind. In Romans 6:16 we have these words: "Know ye not, that to whom ye yield yourselves servants to obey, his servants ye are to whom ye obey; whether of sin unto death, or of obedience unto righteousness?" Look again. Either our minds are mastered by our wills and become servants to our goals of success or our minds can be enslaved to destructive habits, to corrosive conduct and to ruinous deeds.

Life is for living. Life is for attainment. "Possess your mind and you will have confidence."

---

[1]Napoleon Hill, *The Master Key to Riches* (Los Angeles: Willing Publishing Company, 1945), pages 29-34.

Build Confidence and Succeed

A confident, continuous, positive attitude assures you of a habit of succeeding:

1. State your purpose with bolder confidence than you have previously.

2. You can whip worry with enthusiastic action. Outline your action.

    A.
    B.
    C.
    D.

3. You can fight fear with facts:

    Fact 1. You're a free man in a free society.
    Fact 2. You have increasing desire to excel.
    Fact 3. You can find the solution to any problem.
    Fact 4. You now have a purpose greater than yourself.
    Fact 5. You are among the top 5 per cent in the nation.
(Fill in the others yourself.)
    Fact 6.
    Fact 7.
    Fact 8.

4. You can dominate and dictate your doubts:

A. Who's greater, the unlimited you or that negative emotion Doubt?

B. Aggressive action will destroy doubt. Describe your immediate action.

C. Improve your wardrobe and lift your moods. What clothes do you need now?

5. You can possess and empower your mind. List the constructive ways you will reconstruct your positive mind.

A.
B.
C.

PART FIVE
THE POWER OF
PERSISTENCE

CHAPTER 21

Persistence Produces Power

Your key for personal success is persistence, for persistence produces power. Let me tell you the story about one of America's most outstanding failures. In 1831 he failed in business. In 1832 he was defeated for the Legislature. In 1833 he again failed in business. In 1834 he was elected to the Legislature. In 1838 he was defeated for Speaker; in 1840 defeated for Elector; in 1843 defeated for Congress; in 1846 elected to Congress; in 1848 defeated for Congress; in 1855 defeated for Senate; in 1856 defeated for Vice-President; in 1858 defeated for Senate; in 1860 elected to President of the United States.

His name? Abraham Lincoln. Who else could have been able to bear the adversity that Lincoln bore during those tragic days of the Civil War? Nearly half of his cabinet was opposed to him. When asked why he didn't fire them he said, "Don't I rid myself of my enemies by making them my friends?" At his death they all stood and honored him with total loyalty. He was able to hold the Northern states together by the power of his dedication and conviction, and he saved the Union by the force of that conviction. Yet in the process he destroyed one of America's greatest blights—slavery.

Lincoln learned persistence by being victor over many adversities in the formative years of his life. The proving ground of greatness is how we bounce back from life's troubles and tribulations. Persistence is the power that produces amazing achievement. Bacon has said, "Great efforts come of industry and perseverance; for audacity doth almost bind and mate the weaker sort of minds."

Learn from Every Disappointment

After one particularly happy vocational experience of several years a friend said, "You know, you've had it so good. Things have gone so easy and so well with so little opposition that one of these days you may find yourself in hot water because you haven't, by necessity, had to learn how to deal with problems, opposition and difficulties." Since there is no substitute for personal experience, my friend had a point. My answer that many people cause their own problems by failing to count the cost, failing to consider all of the facts and then starting off half cocked before they gain the fellowship of the people involved, was a halfhearted reply. The truth of his statement had driven home. The man who has had to pick himself up from the disappointments and difficulties of life has learned a valuable lesson. Nothing deters him. Nothing frustrates him. Nothing upsets him. He has traveled that course before and he knows the answer. And he is persistent.

Never forget the words of Marshall Foch, the French Commander in World War I, when the battlefield situation was as tragic as could be: "My center is giving way, my right is pushed back, situation excellent, I am attacking."

"Perseverance gives power to weakness, and opens to poverty the world's wealth. It spreads fertility over the barren landscape, and bids the choicest fruits and flowers spring up and flourish in the desert abode of thorns and briers." —S. G. Goodrich

How to Be a Genius

How prone we are to write off the outstanding achievement of another person by saying, "Well, he's a genius," "Look at his opportunities," "Look at his education," or some such trite statement. Never forget Thomas A. Edison's remark, "Achievement is 2 per cent inspiration and 98 per cent perspiration." What is a genius? Genius is the power of making continuous effort. You don't even know when you've approached or you've crossed the line of failure and success, it is so fine. But I'll tell you when you've crossed it—when you continue to persistently pursue your goal—when you let nothing deter you nor detour you— when your purpose pulsates and your goal guides and your motivation challenges and inspires—then that's genius.

On March 15, 1915, the British Navy attacked the Turks at the Dardanelles. There was a terrific Naval barrage from the guns on the shore. Three ships had been sunk and finally, just at noon, the British Navy withdrew never to take that point during that engagement. What they didn't know was that the Turks had only sixty seconds of ammunition left and at that very moment were preparing to surrender. Had the British Navy been persistent and continued to press the battle they would have taken the Dardanelles, split the enemy forces, closed the war years earlier and saved millions of lives. Oh, the tragedy of failing to persevere.

The Turtle Won the Prize

Remember that childhood story of the hare and the turtle? The most promising boy in my high school class is today, at forty, a hopeless alcoholic. He was the hare—a big spurt and then a good time. Hang the goal. But there was another boy, picked on, poked fun at, limited in athletic ability (never did letter, just went out for the basketball team) but continuously at it. Where is he at forty? An amazingly successful insurance executive—a millionaire. He was persistent.

Pathway in Your Brain

The subconscious mind never argues. It takes orders and never rests. Therefore the conscious mind must consistently and persistently command the subconscious mind to bring forth the results of its ceaseless labor. Thus we are building a conditioned consciousness, a habitual feeling or a habitual condition by which we achieve. Remember, "As a man thinketh in his heart so is he." We become what we think about. The persistent command drives a pathway, a channel, a canal, a ditch, a roadway through the impressions of our mind and brings forth the desired result.

One study in business found that 80 per cent of the sales were made after the fifth call. Forty-eight per cent of the salesmen quit after the first call, 25 per cent quit after the second call, 12 per cent quit after the third call, 10 per cent of the salesmen keep calling and make 80 per cent of the sales. Persistence pays off. Persistence provides power. Do you want it? It's up to you. Do you realize how bored some people are the second and third time they hear anything? How do we learn? By repetition. What's the principle of advertising? Repeating the same story over and over and over. For example: How many settlers were killed by the Indians west of the Mississippi River? Only thirty-six. But from reading all of the stories and seeing all the movies and TV extravaganzas of the Indian uprisings in the West you would think that millions of Americans had been slaughtered by the Indians. You see the story has been told so long and so often, with so much impact and color, that we believe the Red River actually was named that because its banks flowed with the blood of the settlers. Repetition makes impact. So be persistent and you will accomplish.

Repeat and Reap Results

In his book, *How I Discovered the Secret of Success in the Bible,* Davidson says, "What makes repetition so powerful a factor in effective suggestion? What purpose does it serve? (1) The human mind cannot act on what it does not understand. Repetition, especially when it presents a proposition in many ways, serves to make the idea clearer. (2) Repetition wears down the resisting power of those contrary ideas which entangle your idea or suggestion and prevent its ready acceptance by your prospect's mind."[1]

Let me quote you that tremendous statement by Irving Black on this principle: "No doubt a good many of us have seen a pile driving machine at its work. Poised in mid-air is the weight of the driving part of the machine. Suddenly this weight of several tons is let loose . . . We would think that the log would be driven down its whole length with this terrific impact but it is hardly moved a fraction of an inch. Again that same terrific impact and again there is that slight embedment in the ground. And so on this process continues for weeks until the proper foundation is made. It is this cumulative process, this constant hammering, this continuous driving force, that finally erects a foundation upon which to build a permanent structure. It is this same law, this cumulative law, that causes men of obscurity to become famous. It is this steadiness of purpose that lifts men out of the chaos of poverty into the heights of prosperity. It is this sincerity of accomplishment that differentiates between the doer and the wisher."[2]

---

[1] Davidson, *Ibid.*, pages 79-80.
[2] *Ibid.*, page 81.

Pile Drive Your Way to Success

Pick out your foundation, drive your stake in it and start pile driving, hour after hour, day after day, impact upon impact. You can achieve through persistence. There is no other emotion, no other thing that is as powerful as persistence. You can have anything you want if you will pay the price of persistence, staying after the effort. Let your goal be, "Day by day I'm on my way." Say it over and over again and you will succeed.

Great Men Work

"Though you may have known clever men who were indolent, you never knew a great man who was so; and when I hear a young man spoken of as giving promise of great genius, the first question I ask about him always is, does he work?"   —John Ruskin

Dr. David Seabury, the psychologist said, "One could not overstate what attention refocused could do for a person if consistently, insistently, incessantly and persistently carried out. No aberration could remain in control of anyone if this process was earnestly fulfilled. Nor would the supposed external barriers to success, health and happiness, long remain as obstacles. Every negative has its positive, every loss a potential gain, every evil a hidden good. Such a statement is not mere optimism but the simple provable truth. To turn attention to finding and using the good with which to overcome the evil is one of the greatest secrets of true living. From doing so we will give our human attention a natural basis for fulness and power."

Engineers have proven that troops in cadence cannot cross a bridge. It will break if they try. Well do I remember in the military how, when we approached a bridge, we would fall out of step and walk across careful not to be in cadence. Yes, repetition is one of the most powerful forces in the world. You can be successful through persistence. I challenge you to do so today.

CHAPTER 22

Persistence Empowers Purpose

Your key for personal success today is persistence, and persistence empowers dynamic purpose. You can be successful.

What is the first response that comes to your heart when you are faced with a problem? That's right—to quit, to give up. A boy was burned so horribly that his legs were expected to be amputated, but he didn't give up. They said that he wouldn't walk again but he did. He made a pathway, holding onto the picket fence. He disciplined himself in steel will. He paid the price in fantastic persistence. As a result he became one of the world's greatest distance runners. His name—Glenn Cunningham. He discovered that persistence empowers purpose.

If you are persistent long enough, you too will determine and develop amazing purpose.

Your Job and Long Life

John E. Gibson, in a news article entitled *Science Looks at Your Job,* reports that your profession actually affects the length of your life. For example, educators and lawyers, two groups that have to pay the most persistent price in achieving their service in life, live longest. Next came scientific and engineering pursuits, third were philosophical and theological callings. Doctors ranked next. Then painters and musicians, followed by writers and actors. Explorers and poets averaged the shortest life span. Furthermore this study showed that the individuals who achieved the greatest distinction in their professions averaged much longer life spans than the less eminent.

These same professions rate the highest in prestige as well. For instance, doctors have the highest prestige rating in the minds of most people, with college professors, scientists and bankers running a very close second. An army psychologist found that professions averaging the highest intelligence scores were accounting, engineering, medicine and chemistry. Occupations ranking next highest in the I.Q. department included writers, educators, lawyers and dentists. "In a wide scale study conducted by the University of Minnesota Investigators it was found that the persons whose occupations made continuous demands on their intelligence, mental ability, tended to increase more definitely with age. Furthermore, many people of high achievement do not have above average I.Q.s but the quality most successful men *do have* in common is persistence and the capacity to make fullest use of their abilities."[1]

The reason these professions rank so high in achievement, in long life and in prestige is that these men were persistently after their purpose in life. And as their persistence empowered their purpose, their purpose was a motivating factor to develop persistence. You cannot have one without the other.

Recently there has been talk about men with super-bodies, that is men who work long and strenuous hours under tremendous pressure. Some of these men have found that health problems developed—a heart condition—and they were forced to take a rest period. One study showed that while these men were recuperating from a heart condition, even when they were supposed to be resting, they actually had established another business. Do

---

[1] *Our Changing World*, No. 641.

they really have super-bodies? No. Actually they have super-purpose and powerful persistence.

Control Your Length of Life

You may ask, "Are you suggesting that people can actually control the length of their life?" Yes, I most emphatically am. Medical science agrees that the most important factor in any illness is the will to live. On a number of occasions I've seen people get well by the sheer persistence and determination to do so. And I've seen other people die simply because they felt they didn't have anything to live for. The man who is persistently serving a worthy purpose will care for himself. He will take care of his body. He will see that the necessities and needs are met—that adequate recreation is a part of the routine of his life. Furthermore the man who persistently is empowered to achieve a worthy purpose (for we've said that the science of success is the persistent achievement of a challenging worthy goal) is not as prone to be fraught with worry and frustration and hyper-tension. You see, he's beyond himself. He is not constantly looking inward at his own personal problems.

Be Failure-Proof

To be failure-proof you must have an unconquerable faith, totally consistent and goal-directed emotions, a will surrendered to a cause greater than yourself, and an idea for achievement or service that has incubated its time and is now ready to hatch into acceptability.

Be the Master of Your Moods

One of the great powers of developing persistent purpose is to control our moods. Thanks to the recently developed field of Business Men's Records there is available for you today a planned program to develop persistent purpose. Paul J. Meyer, president of Success Motivation Institute of Waco, Texas, and other firms, have a number of outstanding recordings that you can use to cultivate your purpose. I purchased a transistorized record player that I can take in my brief case along with several records. Then in a hotel room, or in an office waiting for a conference, or whatever the circumstance, I can cultivate and develop my persistence. Never let those moments be wasted.

Change Possibilities to Probabilities

First, you must be upset with discontent. Inventor Charles Kettering said, "A problem well stated is half solved." Then, second, you must vividly imagine the long-range goal. Third, you should build excitement by listing all the benefits to yourself, your family, and to everyone involved. Fourth, you must dedicate yourself, commit yourself, surrender yourself, to the attainment of this goal.

The achievement of your goal is assured the moment you commit yourself to it. The realization will require time.

Imagination dreams, goals direct, enthusiasm propels, and persistence produces.

God Give Us Men

The decision is yours. Will you pay the price of persistent effort—never giving up, never wavering, never swerving from your purpose—always staying at it? You will succeed. Martin Luther changed the whole course of theological history. Remember his words, "It is neither safe nor prudent to do aught against conscience. Here I stand—I can do not otherwise. God help me. Amen."

> God give us men! A time like this demands
> Strong minds, great hearts, true faith and ready hands;
> Men whom the lust of office does not kill;

Men whom the spoils of office cannot buy;
Men who possess opinions and a will;
Men who have honor; men who will not lie;
Men who can stand before a demagogue
And damn his treacherous flatteries without winking!
Tall men, sun-crowned, who live above the fog
In public duty and in private thinking;
For while the rabble, with their thumb-worn creeds,
Their large professions and their little deeds,
Mingle in selfish strife, lo! Freedom weeps,
Wrong rules the land and waiting Justice sleeps.

—J. G. Holland

No Man Is an Island

We become what the people we associate with are. Therefore your persistence in achieving a worthy purpose will be a part of the total triumph of good, the total triumph of democracy, the total triumph of all that's wholesome in your society. At the same time laziness is cancerous; it is catching. One person who has found that he can get by on the unemployed rolls is a challenge to others to do the same. All you have to do to fail is to do nothing. That's it. Simply drift downstream with the tide. But there is no power, no muscles, no strength, no character involved in that fatal activity. There is strength and character and power energized when we fight the stream, particularly when it is mountainous, turbulent, hard to go upstream.

Bogardus's book *Leaders and Leadership*[2] has meant more to my life than possibly any other book except the Bible. In it Borgardus quotes Admiral Dewey, "Perhaps some boy may have since excelled me in the length of time that he

---

[2]Emory S. Bogardus, *Leaders and Leadership* (New York: Appleton-Century-Crofts, Inc., 1934), page 298.

could hold his head under water but my record was unbeaten in my day."

John Wesley, who traveled on horseback over land and by slow sail ship at sea, traveled a total of 250,000 miles in his lifetime, preaching as often as fifteen times a day throughout fifty years. "He had read books while making his horseback journeys and yet, when past eighty he complains that he cannot read and work more than fifteen hours a day." The doctors told him that he would have to slow down. He did—by only preaching eight times a day. Of Charlemagne, Bogardus said, "He was so hardy, they tell us, that he would hunt the wild bull singlehanded, so strong that he felled a horse and rider with one blow. Add to these external traits a tireless energy, an iron will, a keen love of order and of justice, deep-seated religious instincts and under all an exuberant animal nature; such is the man as he appeared to his contemporaries."

When Thomas A. Edison was working on the phonograph he had difficulty reproducing the letter S. He would work eighteen and twenty hours a day for weeks and weeks at a time before he came up with the solution. He would not quit.

Booker T. Washington said, "I have begun everything with the idea that I could succeed."

The Priest Who Persevered

Francisco Palou, in his book *The Life of Junipero Serra,* tells of the persistence of this Catholic priest to reach his work in the west: "When the Governor saw what a plight he was in he said; 'Your reverend well knows that you cannot accompany the expedition. We are only six leagues from the place from which we set out. If your reverend will permit they will carry you back to the first mission in order that you there become well again and we will go on with our journey.' But our venerable father, who will never give up, replied in this manner: 'Please do not speak to me further about the matter because I trust in God who will give me strength to arrive at San Diego, if He's given me strength to come this far, and in case this is not His good pleasure for me, I shall resign myself to His holy will. Even if I die on the road I will not go back, but you can bury me here, and I shall very gladly remain among these pagan people if such be the will of God for me.'"[3]

Persistence and purpose provide tremendous courage. Lyman Abbott in his book *Henry Ward Beecher* tells the following incident: "In Elizabeth City, New Jersey, Beecher was to address a crowd of ruffians who declared that they would kill him if he attempted to speak there. Surrounded by a loyal band he was ushered into the hall and to the platform. As he began to speak he said: 'Gentlemen, I have been informed that if I attempted to speak tonight I am to be killed. Well I am going to speak and therefore I must die. But before you kill me there is one request that I am going to make. All you who are to stain your hands with my blood just come up here and shake hands with me before you commit the crime for when I die I shall go to heaven and therefore I shall not see any of you again.'"[4] They heard him out. Who could stand against such courage and persistence?

Courage Overcomes the Coward

When Samuel Gompers was presiding over a heated meeting of the American Federation of Labor held in Albany, New York, he was rushed upon and attacked. "John Brophy rushed from the rear of the room, scaled the bar and jumped upon the platform where I was standing. He

[3]Francisco Palou, *The Life of Junipero Serra* (Pasadena, Calif.: George W. James, 1913), page 71.
[4]Lyman Abbott, *Henry Ward Beecher* (Boston: Houghton-Mifflin Company, 1903), page 316.

pointed a revolver in my breast. It was certainly a startling scene. I did not touch the revolver or make any attempt to touch his hand but with my left hand I caught the lapel of his coat and extended my right palm forward and in as emphatic a tone as I could command, said: 'Give me that pistol.' He did not give it to me and still louder and with all the emphasis I could command I repeated my demand. At the third repetition he dropped the pistol into my hand and then bedlam broke loose. I then protected him from them.''[5]

Gompers was dedicated to his beliefs of labor. Persistence had developed purpose and courage. He would not be deterred.

You can build a tower of fantastic success but you must first draw in your mind's eye the architectural sketches. Then you must lay a brick every day. If you lay a brick a day or several a day and everlastingly stay at it, your castle will be built, your tower will be achieved and you will stand there for all to see and respect as long as you live and, yea, much longer even than that.

The decision is yours. You can be successful but you must pay the price of persistence, for persistence empowers purpose. You cannot continue to do any one thing with persistence without developing amazing purpose in the process.

The Power of Persistence

Persistent action produces the power and the habit of succeeding:

1. Restate your major purpose. Now add the persistent action necessary for its achievement.

---

[5]Samuel Gompers, *Seventy Years of Life and Labor* (New York: E. P. Dutton and Company, Inc., 1925), page 277.

2. How will you cultivate the habit of this persistent action?

3. Genius is the power of making continuous effort. What are the five benefits you will enjoy once you have attained your purpose?

    A.
    B.
    C.
    D.
    E.

4. To the 95 per cent who fail you will be a genius. State the reasons you have failed to be persistent in the past.

    A.
    B.
    C.

State how you will overcome each.

    A.
    B.
    C.

CHAPTER 23

Persistence Pays High Profits

Your key for personal success for today is persistence. You can be successful by paying the price of persistence. Persistence produces peace. Let's take two men. One is aimless, no purpose, no direction, no goal. He is a hobo if he is broke; he is a playboy if he has inherited a fortune. Is he happy? You tell me.

Now let's take the second man. He is persistently achieving a worthy, challenging goal, whether it's the milkman who delivers this important item to your front door or the corporation lawyer. He knows where he is going. He has the joy of achievement. He brings his pay check home weekly or monthly with a sense of accomplishment. He returns a certain portion of it to the religious and benevolent needs of his community. He invests at least 10 per cent of it as a safeguard against rainy days and old age. He is meeting the obligations of his family. Now tell me which man is at peace?

Yes, persistence produces peace and contentment in a man's heart. Real peace comes when we are using our abilities, our powers, our God-given talents for the achievement of a worthy goal. The more purposeful, the busier an individual, the happier he is. Dean Briggs[1] emphasized this: "Do your work. Not just your work and no more, but a little more for the lavishing sake, that little more which is worth all the rest. And if you doubt as you must; and if you

---

[1] Dean LeBaron Russell Briggs of Harvard and later President of Radcliffe.

suffer as you must—do your work. Put your heart into it and the sky will clear. Then out of your very doubt and suffering will be born the supreme joy of life.

The mother whose primary goal in life is to send her children forth in maturity as outstanding citizens of the land, who is joyfully contented with the efforts of giving these children the best that she can in character training and in personal guidance will not be neurotic. Her purpose demands persistence, and her persistent efforts day by day produce joy and peace in her heart.

A Motto to Make Your Work Joyful

How do you like your job? Do you get up in the morning eager to go to work? Do you have difficulty leaving your work in the afternoon to go home to your family and civic and church responsibilities? Do you enjoy taking your work home with you, not out of necessity but out of the vibrant joy of achievement? Do you find yourself having difficulty crowding in a vacation and the day off? I'm not suggesting that you become a work addict as some have become because they are neurotically involved. But do you work for the sheer joy of it? Do you like your job?

Recent studies have revealed that a lot of people, in fact the majority of people, do not like their jobs but when asked the question, "What would you like to do?" they have no answer. Notice the negativism of it: not happy where they are but not knowing where they want to go— no joy, no peace, because no persistence. They are living for a dollar rather than for a purpose.

Let one of your mottoes be, "The greatest use of life is to so use your life that the use of your life will outlive your life." Find a purpose beyond yourself and persistently bring all of your talents, ability, mind power, personality to bear upon achieving that goal. You will have peace in your heart and you will be able to sleep comfortably at night.

Louis Kossuth has said, "The palm-tree grows best beneath a ponderous weight, and even so the character of man . . . The petty pangs of small daily cares have often bent the character of men, but great misfortunes seldom."

The Harder the Training the Better the Product

The burden of a great and glorious responsibility involving a dynamic purpose that you are persistently pursuing doesn't break your back, nor does the load of it bring abulia or a nervous breakdown. I have observed Coach Frank Broyles, now at the University of Arkansas, in training his team, bringing them to the peak of physical perfection and timing and team play as they exact to a science the laws of football achievement. His record in the Southwest Conference, year after year being champion or co-champion, is proof that the finer the training the better the product. Persistence brings peace in the achievement and satisfaction of arriving at the goal. Coach Bud Wilkinson, then at the University of Oklahoma, had his players climb, in tennis shoes, the stadium steps from the playing field all the way to the top, bringing their physical facilities to the height of perfection. His teams through the years have proven the importance of persistence, and there is peace in being a member of a championship organization.

Those of us in the ranks didn't understand what was being done during those agonizing months of strenuous training in 1944 and 1945 as our division was being honed to a peak of military perfection, through the jungles and on the beaches, fording the rivers and climbing the mountainous ranges on Guadalcanal in preparation for the invasion of Okinawa. However our Divisional Commander, Major General Lenuel C. Shephard, Jr., knew what he was doing and the Sixth Marine Division received the Presidential Unit Citation because he led us in persistently paying the price of purpose. Peace was the result. We are talking about the personal peace of individual achievement that comes in a man's heart when he knows he has done his best, and that best is a part of all the good that's round about him everywhere.

Persistence Provides a Bride

Did you hear about the young man who was in love with a young lady but his company transferred him out of town for a year? He knew that persistence paid off so he decided he would hold her attention by mailing her a postcard every day for a year, and he did. At the end of the year she married—the postman. Now the persistence of that daily visit by the postman brought him to the attention of the young lady. She couldn't resist such persistence.

Hugh Blair has said, "Industry is not only the instrument of improvement but the foundation of pleasure . . . He who is a stranger to it may possess, but cannot enjoy, for it is labor only which gives relish to pleasure . . . It is the indispensable condition of possessing a sound mind in a sound body, and is the appointed vehicle of every good to man." You see, joy hovers about the head of the man who loves his own occupation.

In the Bible, Job 11:15-19 (ASV) says, "Yea, thou shalt be steadfast, and shalt not fear: For thou shalt forget thy misery; Thou shalt remember it as waters that are passed away. And thy life shall be clearer than the noonday; Though there be darkness, it shall be as the morning. And thou shalt be secure, because there is hope; Yea, thou shalt search about thee, and shalt take thy rest in safety. Also thou shalt lie down, and none shall make thee afraid."

Remember those times when you started a task and then stopped in the middle of it? You let something else divert your attention or you simply did not pay the self-discipline of completion. Not only were you embarrassed when associates called for the information and you didn't have it;

not only were you hurt when you passed the deadline and your work and others suffered; but you lost self-respect—you didn't complete your job. Never forget that what you think about yourself is merely an opinion of what others think about you, for others' attitudes reflect themselves in our outlook, our moods constantly. If others are appreciative of our efforts, our work, and our presence, this reflects itself in our personal outlook. Certainly if they are negative toward us we will be negative in turn. So gain this peace of self-achievement by persisting and you will be successful.

Your Eight-Point Pathway to Success

In his book *How To Turn Failure Into Success* Harold Sherman has given the code of persistence. Let me quote it for you: "(1) I will never give up so long as I know I am right. (2) I will believe that all things will work out for me if I hang on to the end. (3) I will be courageous and undismayed in the face of odds. (4) I will not permit anyone to intimidate me or deter me from my goal. (5) I will fight to overcome all physical handicaps and setbacks. (6) I will try again and again and yet again to accomplish what I desire. (7) I will take new faith and resolution from the knowledge that all successful men and women have had to fight defeat and adversity. (8) I will never surrender to discouragement or despair no matter what seeming obstacles may confront me."[2]

John Ruskin has said, "God intends no man to live in this world without working; but it seems to me no less evident that he intends every man to be happy in his work." Calvin Coolidge said, "Nothing in the world can take the place of persistence. Talent will not; nothing is more common than unsuccessful men with talent. Genius will not; unrewarded genius is almost a proverb. Education

---

[2]Sherman, *Ibid.*, page 138.

will not; the world is full of educated derelicts. Persistence and determination alone are omnipotent. The slogan 'Press on' has solved and always will solve the problems of the human race.''

It is all up to you. You can be successful. You can have peace in your heart and look at every day with joy and purpose. You can come to the end of life's journey with fulfillment and achievement and hosts of friends who pay you the praise for a life wonderfully and richly invested and productive. I challenge you to find a purpose; pursue that purpose with persistence and you will have peace in your own heart.

CHAPTER 24

Persistence is Education

Your key for personal success is to accomplish endurance through persistence. The word persistent means to persevere, tenacious. Tenacious means adhesive, determined.

Clarence Day in his book *Life With Father* suggests the power of persistence with the following statement: "Father declared he was going to buy a new plot in the cemetery, a plot all for himself. 'And I will buy one on a corner,' he added triumphantly, 'where I can get out.' Mother looked at him, startled but admiringly, and whispered to me, 'I almost believe he could do it.' "[1] Here's a statement of a man so persistent in his daily pursuits that his loved ones actually expected him to be effective in eternity.

Have you ever gotten to that place in your life when you wondered if it were worth it all? When you've been striving so hard and the answers have not yet come? You were just about ready to quit. But do you remember the occasion when you pressed on just a little bit more and suddenly everything fit into place? You were amazed to find the answer so close, the light of morning so near. Remember the darkest is just before the dawn.

Max Otto has written a statement that pertains here: "Along the upper reaches of the Ohio where the foothills of the Allegheny mountains hem in one of America's beautiful streams you sometimes awake at daybreak to find

---

[1]Clarence Day, *Life With Father* (New York: Knopf, 1935).

that a heavy mist has obliterated the landscape leaving only a narrow circle of it dimly visible about you. When this happens you resign yourself to the weather and wait for a change or you may do what you have on hand with the best cheer you can muster, calling to the neighbor whose shadowy form you can see though you cannot be sure what he is doing. If you keep busy the mist rises. You see the river rolling on toward the Mississippi. Then you see the opposite shore, the houses of the city, the taller buildings, the towers of the schools, the steeples of the churches highest of all. Slowly the mist climbs the hills, hangs for a little like a torn veil on the summit, then vanishes, disclosing a blue sky. And the work you began in the fog you continue in the sunlight."[2]

Court Three Ladies at Once

Enduring a little bit longer may bring fabulous inroads of achievement pouring out upon you far beyond your fondest imagination. The world belongs to him who patiently perseveres. It is yours. It is waiting for you to attain it. But, remember, fortune and fame and success—all of these are fickle ladies that have to be pursued. Like the proverbial old maid—they want to be wed but they want to be sure they are wanted. They have some question marks about the sincerity of your purpose. They have seen other friends hurt down through the years, so these three are waiting for you to prove yourself. If you endure, persevere, persist, you soon will have their hand. It's up to you.

Opportunity always comes disguised as hard work but God never shuts one door but He opens another. Life's great opportunities often open on the road of daily duties. You must keep enduring, day after day, never turning back, and you will be successful.

[2] *Our Changing World*, No. 574.

Work Is Love Made Visible

In *The Prophet* Kahlil Gibran wrote, "Work is love made visible. And if you cannot work with love but only with distaste, it is better that you should leave your work and sit at the gate of the temple and take alms of those who work with joy."

"Work is love made visible." Remember mother's love expressed in so many wondrous ways? Remember the days of the depression—how limiting they were? My father was pastor of a church in a small town. He had been there three years and they were one year behind in his salary and they only paid him $100 a month. How the love of my parents showed itself in so many wondrous ways. Work is love in action.

The home is a haven and a heaven on earth, a refuge from man's most difficult hours at work. A man can take anything at work if there is joy and happiness and peace at home. A man can accomplish much more at work if he feels his work is love made visible, that he is doing it because it is an expression of his love to his children and to his wife, and perhaps to his aged parents. You can endure and in endurance there is success.

Education Sets Income

Persistence pays off in so many wondrous ways. Do you realize that a high school graduate will earn $50,000 more in his lifetime than a man who quits before graduation? This means that every day a youngster stays in high school is worth $70 to him. And, of course, a college education is worth approximately $150,000 more in a man's lifetime than a person with an eighth grade education. The persistence of those formative years pays off tremendously in all of life's effectiveness.

Endurance is success. Goethe said, "He who moves not forward goes backward." Nothing stands still. Time isn't waiting for you to decide what you are going to do. Therefore, endure, persist, persevere, stay with it, pursue it.

Is there anything worse than self-doubt, self-pity, self-condemnation? This destroys endurance and persistence. Hillyer has written, "Self-doubt is caused by the fact that every human activity involves some other person whose praise or blame seems unduly important. We set a goal of perfection before ourselves and groaningly conclude that it cannot be achieved. But perfectionism is a dangerous state of mind in an imperfect world. The best way is to forget doubts and set about the task at hand. While the battle is being fought or the cake is baking in the oven, leave the outcome to the future where it belongs. If you are doing your best you will not have time to worry about failure."[3]

Who is calling the signals of your life? Remember what I said earlier—that your mind is the only thing in this world that you hold total control over. Now master it. Don't submit your mind, God-given and fantastic in its possibilities, to any other human. Keep your mind as the power of your own achievement. Therefore don't let others' criticisms, or doubts, or questions, or cynical rantings affect you. Determine what you are going to do. Let nothing in this world keep you from accomplishing it. Persist every day; endure, and you will achieve.

---

[3] *Our Changing World,* No. 788.

CHAPTER 25

Persistence Produces Results

Your key for personal success is persistence because persistence produces results. You can be successful.

Recently in the Montgomery, Alabama, airport I met a successful businessman, a Mr. Smith from Atlanta. The friend who introduced us told me about Mr. Smith's tremendous success in his wholesale auto parts business. Upon congratulating him he answered, "Oh, I've been lucky." But success is not luck. Success can be predicted: it can be assured. I asked further about Mr. Smith and here's the story:

Auto parts dealers found they were having difficulty getting parts. Supplies were arriving too slow so Mr. Smith suggested to his associates that he open up a clearing house in Atlanta. He assured them that for 2 per cent of the volume above cost he would set up a clearing house that would guarantee them their parts much more readily, quicker—far greater service than they were then having. They all agreed to enter into the covenant. In 1962 that warehouse did $10,000,000 of business. Now you figure what 2 per cent of that is. In 1963 they are expecting to do $13,000,000 of business. Luck? No, it is not luck. Mr. Smith had an idea and he persistently pursued that idea. Today the results are there as a reward, as a crowning achievement of persistently pursuing a worthy idea.

In Matthew 7:7 we read: "Keep on asking and the gift will be given you; keep on seeking, and you will find; keep on knocking and the door will open to you. For everyone who keeps on asking, receives, and everyone who keeps on seeking, finds, and to the one who keeps on knocking, the door will open."[1] That's it. If you keep on working, keep on asking, keep on seeking you inevitably will reach your goal.

There's No Such Thing As Luck

Some people destroy initiative by their attitude toward luck which can be as futilely fatalistic as *"Allah wills it."* Abe Lincoln had terribly bad luck in elections but persistence produced the Presidency. We should learn more from our defeats, by examining them more carefully, than we do from our victories. I've found in reading about hundreds of individuals, in personally observing dozens of friends, and in my personal experience that the harder one works the luckier one becomes.

Persistence Produced the Pontiac

At the outbreak of World War II, Doug Lewis, now Dean of Men at Hannibal-LaGrange College at Hannibal, Missouri, had a new Oldsmobile convertible. A personal friend of his, a Pontiac dealer in a small town in Missouri, wanted to buy the car. He entered into this covenant: if Doug would turn the car over to him then this Pontiac dealer assured Doug that the first car he received at the end of the war Doug Lewis would have. Remember how difficult it was to get cars those days, how few came off the assembly lines? Doug waited weeks and then found out that one car had been delivered to his friend, some hundred or more miles away from where he was living. He called him long distance and said, "I'm ready for my car."

[1]Charles B. Williams, *The New Testament in the Language of the People* (Chicago: Moody Press, 1937).

The man began to stumble and said, "Now wait. I promised you the first car after my wife got one, my salesmanager, my service manager, a demonstrator. You will have the first one I have for sale. I've got to supply my stock first." Doug didn't argue with him. He simply took a bus, arrived in the small town on Thursday afternoon, went down to the Pontiac dealer's office, greeted him, sat around and talked to him. It came time to close up. The dealer said, "Come on up to the house and have supper." And Doug did. He brought his bag along. After the supper they sat around talking. Then the dealer said, "Spend the night." Doug said, "I'll be happy to."

The next morning they had breakfast. Doug followed him down to the shop. All day he hung around. Went home with him that night. Spent the night. The next day, followed him around all day. Didn't say a word about the automobile. Saturday night Doug spent the night. Sunday he went to church. He stayed with the dealer all Sunday afternoon and Sunday night. On Monday he went to the office with him. Finally on Tuesday morning the dealer took the keys out of his pocket, threw them in Doug's lap and said, "Take it. You've worn me out." That's persistence. Results come to him who will persevere. It's up to you.

Think Big

In his book *The Magic of Thinking Big,* Schwartz has said, "(1) Believe it can be done. Believing a solution paves the way to solution. (2) Don't let tradition paralyze your mind. Be receptive to new ideas. Try new approaches. Be progressive in everything you do. (3) Ask yourself daily, 'How can I do better? How can I be better?' (4) Ask yourself, 'How can I do more?' Capacity is a state of mind. (5) Practice asking and listening. Ask and listen and you will obtain raw material for reaching sound decisions. Remember big people monopolize the listening; small people monopolize the talking. (6) Stretch your mind. Get stimulated. Associate with people who can help you to think of new ideas, new ways of doing things and forever persevere."[2]

After a beautiful concert a lady rushed up to the pianist and gushed, "I'd give *anything* to play as you do." When the pianist replied, "Oh, no, you wouldn't," a hush fell over the group. Trying again the lady said, "I would too give anything to play the piano as you do." "No you wouldn't, if you would you could play as well, possibly a little better, than I do. You would give anything to play as I do except time, except the one thing it takes to accomplish the task. You wouldn't sit and practice hour after hour, day after day, year after year." Then she flashed a warm smile. "Understand," she said, "I'm not criticizing you. I'm just telling you that when you say you would give anything to play as I do you really don't mean it."

You can have most anything in this life if you will pay the price for it. It's up to you. The question is, "Will you persevere? Will you stick to it? Do you have the bull dog determination? Results are waiting. Achievement is just around the corner. But you must not waver; you must not chase rabbits when you are hunting quail."

The Most Critical Time in Your Life

According to Napoleon there is a fifteen-minute period in every battle when the decision will go either way. The General who knows that period and throws everything he has into the battle will win. But the General who does not know it or who is so cautious he will not commit his reserves, will lose not only the battle but inevitably the campaign.

***

[2]Schwartz, *Ibid.,* pages 80-81.

This is the problem in so many lives. People do not know when that critical time is and even if they knew they would not commit everything they have. There comes a time in the shadow of success when you must burn your bridges behind you.

The Romans came to the cliffs of Dover. They first were repulsed and sent back home. When they came again the Saxons were on the cliffs looking down, far outnumbering the Romans. But the Romans landed and taking all their supplies ashore, turned with one dramatic and decisive event that carried the day. They set fire to their wooden ships and pushed them back out into the English Channel to burn to the waterline and to sink. Then with great resolve they unsheathed their swords and turned to march with forceful resolution into the face of the battle. The Saxons fled. Such persistence, such total commitment was unimaginable. The day was won for the Romans by default.

Do you know when the time is to commit yourself, and are you willing to do it? The results of persistence are yours. There is no way for you to fail. You have learned the law of success and you are challenging that law and demanding that it work for you, not against you. I challenge you to be successful. You can be. The decision is yours.

Persistence Pays High Profits

Persistence is the pile driver that produces the expressway to success:

1. Your major purpose is yours the minute you begin persistent action for its achievement.

A. List the time needed daily for such action.

B. State how you will make this the habit of your life.

145

2. List below Harold Sherman's eight-point pathway to success:

A.

B.

C.

D.

E.

F.

G.

H.

3. What changes in your life, business, family, schedule, etc., will you make in order to persistently pursue your purpose?

A.

B.

C.

D.

E.

PART SIX
MOTIVATION

CHAPTER 26

What Motivates Men?

Your key for success today is that you are motivated by what you believe.

George Elliot[1] said, "We must not inquire too curiously into motives. They are apt to become feeble in the utterance: the aroma is mixed with a grosser air. We must keep the germinating grain away from the light." But experience proves she was wrong. For motives are as vital as our heartbeat. H. W. Beecher hit the truth when he said, "God made man to go by motives and he will not go without them, anymore than a boat without steam, or a balloon without gas." Find what motivates men and we can touch the button, we can turn the key that makes men achieve miracles.

Six Basic Needs

In *How To Live 365 Days a Year, Schindler* lists these six basic needs[2]:

1. The need for love. There is but one indispensable human emotion and that is tenderness. A person is affected all of his life by the amount of love he received as a child, or the amount he failed to receive. Of course, his romantic love affects him in youth years and in the married years. Certainly, old people must be loved as well.

---

[1]Pseud. of Mary Ann (or Marian) Evans.
[2]Schindler, *Ibid.*, page 198.

2. The second basic need is security. Some psychiatrists believe the child's entire personality is affected if he is weaned too early in life.

3. The third basic need is for creative expression. Achievement is the tremendously satisfying factor in life. Determine the area you have most talent in and achieve there. You will find great satisfaction.

4. The fourth need is for recognition. Who wants to be a mere number? Who wants to be only a statistic? This organized world tragically submerges the individual into the mob. Recognition, in my opinion, is the most dynamic of all motivating factors.

5. The fifth is the need for new experiences. One of the satisfying factors of my life has been planning for that next new experience. As soon as I reach one event I immediately set my goal on the next. I like to have engagements months—even years—in advance, and day-dream about those coming events.

6. The sixth basic need is self-esteem. When we lose our self-esteem we die within. The greatest danger in America today is not the man with the super-ego. The greatest menace is the man with an inadequate ego structure. Recently a survey revealed that 75 per cent of young people entering colleges and 75 per cent of business people applying for work with personnel offices sold their ability short.

Four Principles of Motivation

In the book, *The Magic Power of Emotional Appeal,* the author[3] says that there are four principles of motivation:

1. Self-preservation. This, of course, is the strongest of all. When a man has his back to the wall and his very

---

[3]Roy Garn, *The Magic Power of Emotional Appeal* (Englewood Cliffs, N.J.: Prentice-Hall, Inc., 1960), page 20.

life is at stake, he will fight with supernatural
strength.
2. Recognition. This, is the second most important. No
man wants to be a zombie, yet so many are. They've
lost their identity—their self-respect.
3. The third principle of motivation is romance. Certainly, when there is romance in a man's work and a
romance in his home, his life is dynamic.
4. The motivation of money. And this, in my opinion, is
the poorest of all four.

Every man is individualistic. Every man is different. We
must learn our man. We must understand him. When we
determine which of these motivating principles is most
meaningful for him and we turn that key, we can make his
life a magnificent obsession rather than a meaningless odyssey.

Goethe said, "If you treat an individual as he is, he will
stay as he is. But if you treat him as if he were what he
ought to be and could be, he will become what he ought
to be and could be." The words of the song, "Wishes are
the dreams we dream when we are awake," must help each
individual to dream at night and wish at day. Men are
motivated by dreams, desires, and wishes. Archibald Alexander has said, "Men are more accountable for their motives, than for anything else; and primarily, morality consists in the motives, that is, in the affections."

Motivate Yourself

The emotionally mature man is so much better able to
motivate himself than the man of mixed, confused and
immature emotions. Some of the things that are important
in helping motivation are: the capacity to trust others; the
ability to be self-critical; the power of sex ability; a deep
sense of self-assurance; and the ability to manage and ad-

minister without becoming personally involved in the details of work.

When a man is motivated he achieves. He is successful. His wishes bring forth dedication in his work for he cannot remain on the plain of mediocrity; he must scale the mountains.

Remember the tragic sinking of the atomic submarine, the *U.S.S. Thresher.* How shocked we all were when the reports came out of the shoddy workmanship in building that tremendous submarine—substandard welding, faulty assembly, and poorly soldered electrical connections. As a result of this lack of motivation a hundred men died.

Recently I purchased a sports model automobile. Hardly having driven out of the agency, I discovered the radio would not work properly. The reason—dozens of poorly soldered connections. You see, some mechanic was not properly motivated.

This is carrying over into the tragic drop out of school children. No motivation. Instead of preparing themselves by both high school and college and then technical preparation for a career, many young people are looking just for a job. They learned it from their parents. They got it honestly.

Motivate and Excel

Dr. John W. Gardner, President of the Carnegie Foundation, has said, "An excellent plumber is infinitely more admirable than an incompetent philosopher. The society which scorns excellence in plumbing because plumbing is a humble activity, and tolerates shoddiness in philosophy because it is an exalted activity, will have neither good plumbing nor good philosophy. Neither its pipes nor its theories will hold water."

Properly motivated men are men of purpose and dynamics and dedication.

One of the really outstanding contributions to this study of motivation is by Bob Conklan on his record, *The Key to Motivation*. He says, "It is beliefs, not benefits that truly motivate." To this I agree. Here are some of the questions he suggests that you ask yourself:

1. Are you working for beliefs or benefits?
2. How do you react to criticism?
3. What effect does your belief have on your talents?
4. Does your belief truly motivate?

Bob is right. The man who believes that his work is contributing to the good of others, to the strengthening of society, to the benefit of many other individuals, to the advancement of his own family, and to the strengthening of the principle of Americanism, that man is truly motivated.

"It is beliefs not benefits that motivate." Men are motivated by what they believe. What do you believe? Is the work that you do of blessing to all men your employment touches? If so, you will be a motivated man.

CHAPTER 27

How to Develop Energy

This is your key for today—develop dynamic energy and you will be successful.

Energy is the ability to act. It is invisible determination, and all healthy people have energy for that which excites them.

Buxton has said, "The longer I live, the more deeply am I convinced that what makes the difference between one man and another, between the weak and the powerful, the great and insignificant, is energy, invisible determination, a purpose once formed, and then death or victory. This quality will do anything that is to be done in the world; and no talents, no circumstances, no opportunities will make one a man without it."

A number of incentives that you might use to energize yourself and your employees are: advancements, awards, challenges, competition, compliments, contests, family award, goals, honor plaques and pins, management development recognition by having employees' names on office doors, superior office furnishings, prestige, prizes, special schooling, special assignments, trips, and happier working conditions.[1] Try these and see how they work with you, for in the final analysis you will have to determine for yourself what works best for each given situation. Remember, every man is different and the factors that energize one man may not move another man at all.

---

[1] Edward J. Hegarty, *How To Build Job Enthusiasm* (New York: McGraw-Hill).

154

Be an Outgoing Person

Have you ever noticed that truly-energized individuals are emotionally well adjusted? Remember this when you are thinking of the importance of building emotional security in your children. They will be able then to face the trials and tribulations of life. Well-adjusted, outgoing individuals can be hit by the hardest tragedies and yet get up and kick despair in the face as they climb to their feet. You see, they are too interested in others and the world in general to worry about themselves. I've seen such individuals carry their load of burdens for years and yet no one actually knows it's there. They had hidden it in their capacity for energetic action. They have happy, outgoing, enthusiastic expressions. Yes, the energetic person is capable of facing life's storms and calmly sailing through those troubled seas because his eye is on the stars and not on the seas.

In one of his programs of *Our Changing World* Earl Nightingale listed fifteen ways to keep miserable[2]: (1) Think about yourself. (2) Talk about yourself. (3) Use the personal pronoun "I" as often as possible. (4) Mirror yourself continually in the opinion of others. (5) Listen greedily to what people say about you. (6) Insist on consideration and respect. (7) Demand agreement with your own views on everything. (8) Sulk if people are not grateful to you for favors shown them. (9) Never forget a service you may have rendered. (10) Expect to be appreciated. (11) Be suspicious. (12) Be sensitive to slight. (13) Be jealous and envious. (14) Never forget a criticism. (15) Trust nobody but yourself.

Now, in order to be energetic and emotionally mature do the very opposite. Think about others. Talk about oth-

---

[2] *Our Changing World,* No. 676.

ers. Don't even use the word "I." Do what you know is right regardless of whether anyone agrees with you or not. Don't worry about what others think. Don't care whether they respect you or not. Don't look for such action. If you do, you will never serve others, for you will selfishly want to be served.

When you have completed a service, move on to another. Earn the joy out of the action itself and then forget it has been done. Don't expect to be appreciated. Never let jealousy or envy enter your mind, and acknowledge that a criticism is from a person who needs help and is sick within himself. Pray for such an individual. Exercise kindness. Turn the other cheek toward him and learn to trust everybody, for in so doing you will truly trust yourself. Someone has said, "He that does good for good's sake, seeks neither praise nor award, but he is sure of both in the end."

Here's How to Build Energy

"You have two types of energy. One is physical, the other is mental and spiritual. The latter is by far the more important, for from your subconscious mind you can draw vast power and strength in time of need."[3] Here is the formula for building dynamic energy:

1. Set the goal. Nothing becomes dynamic until it first becomes specific.
2. Keep your body in rigid physical condition. Dr. Thomas Kirk Cureton, Director of the Physical Fitness Laboratory at the University of Illinois, says that a man can be as fit at fifty as he was at twenty if he wants to. Dr. Cureton says that a man must first train his whole body and, second, he must push himself to

---

[3]Napoleon Hill and Clement Stone, *Success Through a Positive Mental Attitude* (Englewood Cliffs, N.J.: Prentice-Hall, Inc., 1960), pages 181-182.

the limit of endurance and exceed the limit with each workout. This then is the art of record breaking—doing more each time than the time before. Therefore enter into a program of physical fitness. Keep your physical body healthy.

3. Eat the right food. By all means take vitamins regularly. At thirty-four I was tired, lacking physical energy. Then I started taking vitamins. At forty I had a lot more energy than I had at thirty-four.

4. Make opportunities to be of service to somebody every day. Practice the Golden Rule. Remember that most people you meet have far greater problems than you have. And never forget that some people can lick their problems if they have a little bit of encouragement, a little bit of kindness.

5. Express your appreciation and kindness to others. Thank the waitress for bringing you the menu. Thank the elevator operator for holding the door or letting you off at your floor. You will be amazed at how this kindness lifts and radiates your day. In 1958 I was on a speaking mission to Yugoslavia. When you enter that country you take your passport to each police station in the village or city that you are in. The police hold your passport until you move on to the next place. In the larger cities it is held at the hotel desk. You leave it when you arrive, you pick it up when you leave. The police check every day, several times a day. In that communistic state they know immediately where you are at all times. I simply treated the communist police as I would anyone, thanking them for their service, smiling in their presence, engaging in conversation through my interpreter, Aaron Jelowich. On each occasion they reflected this kindness. They were gracious to me. I asked my interpreter, "Why?" He said, "Because

these people sometimes go for a solid year and never have one kind word said to them. They are so appreciative of your kindness they are kind to you in return." If an atheistic communist wants love, how much more does the person you come in contact with every day!

6. There comes renewed energy in every point of achievement. Remember you are not working for others' praises, you are working because you believe in what you are doing. And when it's accomplished there is that sweet peace that floods your heart and mind and being.

Energy Unlimited

The greatest discussion of energy that I have found anywhere is in the chapter on energy in Bogardus's *Leaders and Leadership*.[4] An outline of that chapter follows:

1. Application. Work is the steppingstone to leadership. "John Wanamaker shocked Washington when as Postmaster General he came to work at 7:30 A.M. two and one-half hours ahead of official Washington. In 1928, at the age of eighty-two, he was in his office in Philadelphia from 8:00 A.M. to 6:00 P.M."
2. Endurance. "Great strength and physique lead to undertaking and accomplishing great tasks."
3. Persistence. "Tenacity of purpose is a quality of leadership. It brooks no discouragement. The harder the game is made, the greater the heights to which the player rises."
4. Courage. "Energy finds expression in an elemental courage that implies leadership. Religious motivation may transform energy into indomitable courage."

---

[4]Bogardus, *Ibid.*, page 106.

5. Assuming Personal Responsibility. "If there is one thing that inspires followship more than another, it is to have someone step out ahead, shoulder a double load, and set the pace. Everyone is also stimulated to assume responsibility."
6. Versatility. "Versatility may keep work and recreation in balanced proportion—versatility keeps a person from getting in a rut. Many positions in themselves require marked versatility."

Develop dynamic energy and you will be a successful person.

CHAPTER 28

Motivation's Source

Your key for success today is to develop a projected plan and you will be motivated.

Many people shotgun their motives in all directions, but motivation must be rifled. This is accomplished through a projected plan that scales the heights of achievement.

It's Out of Your Paycheck

The man who is not able to motivate himself must pay his supervisor for doing it for him. Lloyd Conant is quoted by Earl Nightingale as saying, "As long as a person must be supervised, a part of his income must go to his supervisor." That's why the presidents of large corporations make so much money. They are self-motivated. That's why the pay falls off directly proportionate down the line. A part of all the shop foreman's incomes must go to pay the manager and a part of each employee's wages must go to pay the foreman over him.

Frank E. Pfeiffer, President of the Reynolds and Reynolds Company, says, "Management is the means of making things happen and administration is a routine of following certain set procedures whether they produce results or not." Are you a manager or an administrator? True motivation comes when the man has a real dynamic plan of what he is going to accomplish and motivates himself day by day toward the achievement of that purpose.

160

W. L. Burton, vice-president of sales of the Maritz Sales Builders in St. Louis, Missouri, says, "These following are the standard job inducements: (1) A challenging compensation plan. (2) Sales territories with adequate potential for future growth. (3) Opportunities for advancement. (4) Good products adequately advertised. (5) Prices in line competitively with quality offered. (6) Good service. (7) Sound credit policies. (8) Competent job training and field training. (9) Fair marketing policies."

These job inducements, however, are not the right motivational plans for the best development. Notice the emotions involved in what Mr. Burton calls the eight basic motives that stimulate salesmen to greater effort: "(1) Personal gain. Money, power or prestige. (2) Desire for praise and recognition. (3) Avoidance of monotony and boredom. (4) Pride—job satisfaction. (5) Fear and worry. (6) Desire to be needed. ((7) (Love of family. (8) Conscience—obligation to others."[1]

Your Plan for Achievement

True motivation comes from a projected plan. Would you try this one on for size:

1. Plot your goal written out in one sentence. Build excitement and satisfaction of the five senses in reaching that goal. It must be primarily of benefit to others. If you set it just for yourself you will never bring the excitement to bear upon it. Remember, greatness is service.
2. Set a year by year checkup with your family and with your business. Plan an exciting, extended vacation with the entire family each year. Get away from the routine. Go to distant places. See interesting things.

[1] *Our Changing World*, No. 673.

You will have the joy of anticipating it. You will have the joy of the trip itself. You will have the joy of talking about it and showing the films of it later. Primarily, you will have the joy of doing a wholesome activity with your family.

Check up on the spiritual enrichment of your family. Are you deepening them in the principles of your church? Are you taking them to worship each Sunday?

And now for your business. Are all of the employees enjoying their work? Are they deriving a real sense of achievement in their daily activities? And are you practicing the principles that Lincoln used at the Lincoln Electric Company in Cleveland?

3. Are you building a month by month program of personal achievement? Have you attended Dale Carnegie's course or Napoleon Hill's *Science of Personal Achievement*? Have you gone to a specialized study at a University or some other academic center? Have you given yourself the best possible training for your vocation? Each month check up to see if you are better prepared to do your work than the month before.

4. Plan a week by week program of happiness, success and achievement. Plan your week so thoroughly that you will arrive to work on Monday morning eagerly anticipating the next five days. Schedule your activity on Friday afternoon for the following week as Frank Bettger so successfully did to become one of America's outstanding insurance salesmen, a thousand-dollar-a-night speaker and author of so many best-sellers in selling. Schedule your golf game or games so that you are truly recreated. Plan and perform some meaningful hobby, whether it's chess, tennis, bridge, or whatever. Make your week meaningful. And, of course, the most meaningful experience of all is to

worship God. Vitally relate yourself to the church of your choice. Become active in it. Join in the character building program for youth. Become a regular and faithful contributor to the cause of your church in its program.

5. Live in day-tight compartments. "Sufficient unto the day is the evil thereof," says the Bible. Let yesterday's problems die with the dusk. If you don't, tomorrow's achievements and opportunities will not rise with the sun. Through playing of outstanding business records, through reading of inspirational books, through your personal devotional life, through your family fellowship, and through your associates at work, you can motivate yourself.

Develop a projected program and you will be motivated.

CHAPTER 29

Excitement

Your key for success today is dynamic excitement. You can be motivated and successful.

Charles Buxton said, "Experience shows that success is due less to ability than to zeal. The winner is he who gives himself to his work, body and soul." True motivation is fantastically exciting. The motivated man bounces out of bed in the morning, eagerly arrives at work, enthusiastically greets his associates, purposely faces every day's events whether they are problems or successes, finds challenges in every human relationship, and finds personal power to greet every emergency. He is truly a joyful, vibrant, dynamic individual who lives life to the fullest.

One of the interesting facets of communism has been the tremendous exodus of motivated men to the free world. About three million of the best educated leaders, teachers, physicians, scientists, engineers, architects, and other highly skilled specialists have fled to the west. Street signs in Miami today are also in Spanish. Hospital corridors give instruction in Spanish because so many of Cuba's outstanding leaders have fled to the west. The reason— communism does not have the power to motivate men. When men lose liberty they lose motivation. Can the Red world long survive without the dynamics of motivated men?

Get a Glory

Archibald Rutledge tells the story of an engineer on a tiny tugboat crossing a southern river who kept his engine room meticulously clean and went about his work with amazing vibrancy. Asked why he did things so enthusiastically he replied, "Cap'n, it's just this way—I got a glory." If you look on your job of pumping gas in the corner service station as the lower rung toward the presidency of your oil company and the providing of everything you desire for your family and heritage, then you've got a glory. But if you look upon that job simply as making money, then you've lost the glory or you never had it to start with.

Watch Who You Run With

Let me state again: the tremendous importance of developing excitement comes from the people we associate with. We draw emotional strength from the people we are around. If you have a pessimistic friend and you are associating regularly you yourself will be pessimistic. We become what the crowd we run with is. Pick your crowd. Find an excitable, enthusiastic group and draw emotional strength from them.

Also learn to control your bitterness. Nietzsche once wrote, "Growth in wisdom may be exactly measured by a decrease in bitterness." George Washington Carver, the great Negro scientist and outstanding Christian leader, said, "No man can make me stoop so low as to make me hate him." Remember that five minutes of intensive hate burns more energy than eight hours of hard work. Excitement and achievement are directly related to the negative emotions that we've cast aside or learned to rigidly control. Your bank of energy must have regular deposits placed in it. If it does not, you will be overdrawn shortly and the bank will send you a notice. The excitable achiever is constantly filling his bank of energy with joyous, dynamic, purposeful thoughts, associations and moments of inspiration. You have just so much energy to expend. Now use it for your best achievement.

America's First Success Story

Marie B. Ray has written two interesting books that I commend to you: *How Never To Be Tired* and *The Importance of Feeling Inferior*. Let me quote Dr. Ray: "He was born to poverty and became one of the richest men in America. He started life as a printer's devil and became a great writer. He had only two years of schooling and became one of the most learned men of his day. He was of lowly birth and rose to be a first Ambassador to France. He had no training as a scientist, inventor, statesman, and became a leader in all these fields. He was without experience as a courtier and he became the idol of the court of Louis XVI. Benjamin Franklin not only wrote, he lived the first American success story. How did this boy, a nobody and a descendant of generations of nobodies, accomplish this? By a completely honest, a ruthless approach to Ben Franklin, nobody, an unalterable determination to make him a somebody. To that end he launched a direct head-on attack on every liability he possessed with the intention of turning it into an asset.

"His schooling ended at the age of ten. At night, after work, at that age, he studied arithmetic, at twelve he added formal exercises in writing, in his teens he began the study of foreign languages, eventually including French, Italian, Spanish and Latin. He was honored with degrees from Yale, Harvard, William and Mary, even the University of Oxford, in none of which he ever set foot."[1]

---

[1] Marie B. Ray, *The Importance of Feeling Inferior* (New York: Ace Publishing Company), pages 49, 55.

Abraham Lincoln and the Inferiority Complex

Another example of this power of excitement is Abraham Lincoln. No man ever started lower. No man ever had more economic, romantic and political defeats who rose to the height of Abraham Lincoln. What is this factor of dynamic excitement? Marie Ray says it is compensation. She says that there are two ways of compensation—direct and indirect. One consists of turning our liabilities into assets, the other in adopting an overall strategy that leaves the liabilities unchanged and develops other resources to rise above them.

"Without the whiplash of the inferiority complex all talent would lie dormant. It is the spark that disturbs our cloud. For a compensation to be satisfactory and thus allay our painful sense of inferiority, it must fulfill certain conditions. (1) It must be positive, not negative. (2) It must be energetic, not passive. (3) It must be an expression of our own independent thinking and acting. (4) It must be conducive to self-esteem and the esteem of others. (5) It must be socially responsible and valuable. (6) It must give us a normal sense of power and a feeling of goodness."[2]

Here are some of the values of compensation as psychiatrists point them out and as reported by Dr. Ray: "(1) The defective organ or faculty may be trained to function as well as, or better than, the normal one. (2) The function of a healthy organ or faculty may be substituted for the defective one. (3) A situation may be developed in which the defect becomes an advantage. (4) A psychic superstructure may be constructed so that the total personality assumes a pattern which is the compensation for all one's complexes, regardless of their genesis."[3]

---

[2]Ray, *Ibid.*, page 59.
[3]Ray, *Ibid.*, page 60.

People are moved to action by the desire of good and the fear of evil. Which is it with you? Fear or evil will not motivate for very long and the excitement is negative. But a positive, dynamic motivation is the desire for good.

Charles P. Kingsley said, "You have powers you never dreamed of. You can do things you never thought you could do. There are no limitations in what you can do except the limitations of your own mind as to what you cannot do. Don't think you cannot. Think you can."

CHAPTER 30

Motivating Yourself and Others

Your key for personal success for today is to motivate yourself and then you can motivate others.

The secret of success in motivation is satisfying wants. Therefore, you must first know what your wants are, then you can set up a plan to reach those wants. All actions are the result of motivation. Great deeds come from positive, dynamic motivating factors.

Paul J. Meyer, President of Success Motivation Institute, lists the five symptoms of executive suicide: "(1) Doubt. Doubting yourself and your ability. (2) Procrastination. (3) Devotion to false symbols. Letting symbols become your goals. (4) Complacency. Putting off. (5) Loss of purpose."

The good thing about my friend, Paul Meyer, is that he not only can state a problem but he also has the solution: "(1) Crystallize your thinking. Set a dynamic goal. (2) Develop a plan to reach that goal and give yourself a deadline on its accomplishment. (3) Develop a burning desire to reach that goal. It must become an obsession with you. (4) Develop unshakeable faith in yourself to accomplish it. (5) Create a force of iron will determination. Let nothing keep you from reaching your goal."[1]

---

[1] Paul J. Meyer, *Who Motivates the Motivator?* Record (Waco, Texas: Success Motivation Institute).

Your Mind Can Achieve

The magic ingredient of motivation is hope. Hope is that amazing desire—that dream, that expectancy of realizing what is desired and developing a belief and a plan to attain that goal. We consciously and subconsciously respond to that which is wonderful, desirable, obtainable, available and reachable. "What the mind can conceive and believe, the mind can achieve."   —Stone and Hill

These hopes come from spiritual, social and personal values. The social worker, the religious worker, the missionary, are motivated to work long and financially unrewarding hours because there is spiritual motivation toward bringing peace and happiness and hope to those they serve. These desires and aspirations are self-generating. They come from within and with each hope achieved, each plateau scaled, others come.

One of the social factors in motivation is status seeking. Now when status can be used for worthy motives to achieve benefit to others, personal satisfaction, good to the family, and be uplifting to the downtrodden masses, then status is wonderful. But, too often status becomes just a symbol—living like the Joneses, owning the company car, the job title, the upper echelon bonus. Then status is corroding and corruptive and ruinous. It is selfish and is no longer social.

Personal values become meaningful when they bring security for our family, assurance of a college education for our children, the necessities of life for aged parents and ourselves, and enough financial security to share our economic achievement with others through the church, social agencies, community fund, etc.

Be a Self Starter

In Nelson Doubleday's personal success program Samm Sinclair Baker has a very fine little booklet on *How To Be a Self-Starter*. Baker's plan of action (page 12) is as follows:

"1. Study the situation, the need, and the opportunities. Ask yourself, how can I accomplish the most good for my employer, for my family and for myself?

"2. Tabulate all of the possibilities of action. Count the cost. Evaluate the situation. Study it very carefully. Get all the facts. Write down all the possibilities. Evaluate them.

"3. Arrange your best possible plan of action. Plan it to minute detail. Bring trusted associates in on your plan. Consider their opinions if they are excitable individuals and can rise to the heights of the motivational appeal that you have used for yourself.

"4. Re-check the pros and cons. Evaluate before you start and while you are on your journey. Be quick to plan a program of action; be slow to make changes, but when the overpowering facts necessitate a change never hesitate to admit that you are mistaken. Don't throw good money after bad. Don't throw good hours after bad.

"5. Take the step. Remember the Chinese Proverb: 'A journey of a thousand miles begins with the first step.' Get at it. The world is watching the man of action."

Let us recall. The principles of motivation are: (1) Self-preservation. This is the most dynamic. (2) Romance. If there is a romance about your job, if there is the romance in your family, if there is the romance, the joy, the exhilaration about all that you do, then life is truly worth living. You are a motivated man. (3) Acknowledge

171

and use the matter of recognition. A motivated man will receive recognition. The successful, dynamic, excited individual is recognized when he walks into a room of strangers. His very step is charged with the vibrancy of success, and he is in a position to motivate and influence others.

Motivation

Motivate yourself and others to be a success:

1. List in order of greatest importance to you the four principles of motivation. Self-preservation, recognition, romance, money.

    A.

    B.

    C.

    D.

2. Restate your major purpose. Then add a sentence outlining the use of at least two of the above motivating principles.

3. Grade yourself on the following emotional characteristics, A—Outstanding, B—Good, C—Average, D—Poor, E—Bad:

    A. Capacity to trust others—
    B. Ability to be self-critical—
    C. Power of sex ability—

D. Deep sense of self-assurance—
E. Ability to manage without becoming personally involved—

4. You must develop greater energy to accomplish your purpose.

   A. List how you will do so; goals, develop better health, cooperate with others, etc.

   B. List your plan to achieve your purpose.

5. List the most exciting individuals you have ever known:

   A.
   B.
   C.
   D.
   E.
   F.
   G.

6. Which of their excitable traits do you need the most?

7. How will you develop those traits? Reading, special courses, etc.

PART SEVEN
BUILD BURNING DESIRE
AND SUCCEED

CHAPTER 31

Burning Desire is Power

Your key to success today is to build a purposeful burning desire.

My dear friend, Craig Jerner, professor of Metallurgy at Oklahoma University, gave me a fascinating book. It is *Incentive Management*,[1] the thrilling story of the success in motivation that James F. Lincoln has used in building the Lincoln Electric Company of Cleveland, Ohio.

For example, in 1956 Lincoln Electric employees' annual earnings were $11,209 while the average for all other manufacturers in America was $4,952. In 1957 Lincoln Electric average earnings were $10,164. The other manufacturers averaged $5,199. In 1959 Lincoln Electric employees earned $10,467 while employees of other manufacturers earned $5,648.

In 1959 the productivity per worker measured by sales dollars for Lincoln Electric was $46,152. The productivity per worker measured by sales dollars for all other manufacturers was $22,075. Why the difference?

Motivation Principles

Mr. Lincoln's first step in developing incentive is to get the desire for cooperation of those involved. A football game is not nearly as involved as is industry with its men, machinery, customers, government interference and taxa-

[1] James F. Lincoln, *Incentive Management* (Cleveland: Lincoln Electric Company, 1951), pages 80-81, 114-115.

tion, yet industry must develop the same kind of team spirit that a football team achieves in building a tremendous team effort. You have seen teams made up of outstanding stars that never jelled as a team. Consequently they had a losing season when they could have won all of their games, if they had learned to play as a team.

The individual's latent abilities are often brought out by the stress and desire inherent in the game. A specialized skill that is outstanding will often make a company, as well as a football team, dominate above all others in the field. Mr. Lincoln says, "That desire is what the leader must inspire in all of his organization. The worker must feel that he is recognized in accordance with his contribution to success. If he does not have that feeling of self-respect and the respect of others because of his skill, he will think he is being played for a sucker if he increases his output so that the owners can have more profits."

How is it that an amateur athlete often works as hard or even harder than a professional athlete who is paid for his services? Don't you think the answer is the respect and position that comes from recognition and achievement? Isn't this his reward? "The first problem an industrialist has is to make the job one in which the worker will be proud of his skill and desire to increase such skill," observed Mr. Lincoln.

Briefly, Mr. Lincoln attributes his success to a four-fold principle:

1. Challenge the worker's ability. Give him something that is beyond his present ability plus a strong desire to accomplish it. Put him into a scrimmage with his fellows to see who is best. Give him the chance to beat the top. In other words, individual challenge.
2. Make the worker know that there is no limit to his capacities except those that are self-imposed. Jesse

Owens did not break the world's record for the broad jump the first time he tried. He would never have approached his best if he had not tried and continued to try to do what he had never done before. He challenged his ability and developed it. All abilities are developed in the same way.

3. Let everyone know that advancement in the organization comes from within and this advancement depends completely on the ability of those chosen for advancement compared with all others and on nothing else.

4. Put the development pressure on yourself so that you will develop your own capabilities in making yourself a great leader. You must be the inspiration to your followers. Always expect the impossible from yourself as well as from those around you. You will frequently achieve the impossible if you will but challenge yourself.

Remember the key is to build individual participation and sense of achievement and purpose, and the team play concept that we have on an amateur athletic team. The business—industry—organization—needs to be motivated and unified with the old team spirit that we had in high school and college days.

Fred Smith, one of America's outstanding management consultants, has said, "The difference in a good organization and a bad organization is structure. The difference in a good organization and a great organization is emotional motivation." That's it! Burning desire. Do you have it? Desire is power you can change your life by building desire.

He Kept on Swinging

Babe Ruth was the world's greatest home-run hitter for 45 years. He hit a total of 714. Many people thought that record would never be broken.

On April 8, 1974 in Atlanta-Fulton Co. Stadium, Hank Aaron hit 715. I was there. He went on to hit a total of 755.

Babe Ruth also holds the record for strike outs: 1330. But he's *known* for his home runs. He kept on swinging; he never quit. HE HAD A BURNING DESIRE.

That's true in the game of baseball, in the work of Lincoln Electric, and in life as well. Remember the words of the Apostle Paul in Philippians 3:14, 15 (RSV): "I press on toward the goal for the prize of the upward call of God in Christ Jesus. Let those of us who are mature be thus minded." Did you get that? The mature person is the one who not only will seek to achieve in this life but will prepare for the next life as well.

Your Biography of Success

In that fascinating book, *The Law of Success,* Napoleon Hill in the section "A Definite Chief Aim," gives a biography of success.[2] Let me list some of these achievements: Woolworth chose as his goal the building of a chain of five- and ten-cent stores. He concentrated on it and did it. Wrigley's was the sale of a five-cent package of chewing gum. It made him millions. Edison concentrated upon the harmonizing of natural laws and he became one of the world's outstanding scientists.

Henry L. Doherty's goal was the operation of public utility plants. He became a multimillionaire. Ingersoll concentrated on a dollar watch and it made him a fortune. Statler

---

[2]Napoleon Hill, *The Law of Success* (Cleveland: Ralston Publishing Company, 1956), Vol. 2, page 50-51.

on home-like hotel service and you know of his success. Edward C. Barnes on the sale of Edison dictating machines and he retired as a young man with more money than he needs. Woodrow Wilson set his mind on the White House for twenty-five years and he became its chief occupant. Lincoln, while in New Orleans watching a slave girl being sold, said, "I'm going to hit that traffic and hit it hard." It made him President.

Henry Ford's desire was to make the automobile available to every family in America. He became one of the world's outstanding millionaires. Andrew Carnegie's goal was to lower the price of steel. He became one of the world's richest men. Gillette's desire was to give the entire world a good shave. He became a multimillionaire. George Eastman concentrated on the Kodak and you know of his success.

Russell Conwell's desire was expressed in one address, *Acres of Diamonds,* and it yielded more than six million dollars to philanthropic activities. Hearst built a chain of sensational newspapers. It made him a millionaire. Helen Keller's desire was to learn to speak and she became one of the world's outstanding citizens, a dynamic inspiration to all who know of her story. Marshall Field wanted to build the world's greatest retail store and he saw it in his lifetime. Burning desire is power.

Karl Marx's desire was to destroy capitalism. Lenin desired to bring the world under the control of communism. Beginning in 1903 with seventeen men, in less than fifty years the communists controlled one billion of the world's population. Desire is power. Rightly or wrongly, it is still power.

Take Your Annual Check-up

Did you read the article in *This Week Magazine,* by Dr. William C. Menninger of Topeka, Kansas, entitled, "What a Psychiatrist Would Like to Know About You"? Dr. Menninger tells us that we should take a little time, at least once a year, to check up on where we are going; to see what our goals, purposes, desires are. Dr. Menninger, one of the world's outstanding psychiatrists says that our lives are richer, more meaningful, more purposeful, more dynamic, if we take a regular vacation, if we have useful hobbies, if we can re-create our aims. If your temper is short; if you easily lose control of your emotions; if you find yourself fretting ceaselessly about little things that shouldn't disturb you; then you should get away and in constructive activity—whatever it is you enjoy doing that is re-creative—you can re-structure your goals and desires.

Matton said, "As physicians judge the appetite, judge you by desires." And Cicero has said, "The thirst of desire is never filled, nor fully satisfied." That's what makes desire so powerful. Upon one achievement we move on to greater achievements but desire must be controlled. Certainly, burning desire can be terribly harmful or it can be fantastically successful. You hold the key. You call the signals. It's all up to you. But you ought to make a habit of succeeding.

There's Nothing You Can't Do

"Those things that are not practical are not desirable. There is nothing in the world really beneficial that does not lie within the reach of an informed, understanding, and well protected pursuit. There is nothing that God has judged good for us that He has not given us the means to accomplish, both in the natural and moral world. If we cry, like children, for the moon, like children we must cry on."
—Edmund Burke

Desire is the inward motivating power that propels. Like a fan jet it gives tremendous thrust as the jet shoots forward. Recently I carefully examined a small executive two-engine jet, carrying seven or eight passengers. It has thrust of 5,000 feet per minute, almost straight up—fantastic power. This is but an illustration of burning desire. It will propel you upward to fantastic, amazing success, or the wrong, corroding, corrupting burning desire will drive you down to destruction. It is in your hands. The key is yours to turn.

Our Nation's Biggest Business

Do you realize that education is the biggest business in all of the nation today? Forty per cent of all Americans engage in some sort of educational activity. "There are two-and-a-half million kids in kindergarten; thirty million in elementary schools; eleven-and-a-half million in high school; and four million in college. There are seventeen million people in adult education and nine million in independent self-study," so says Earl Nightingale. Do you realize that this is more than seventy-five million people involved in some sort of educational endeavor? As encouraging as this is, it also means, however, that only 20 per cent of all persons of college age are going to college. What does this say about motivation? Does it suggest that a considerable per cent of these young people simply are not motivated? We are well aware that of the 80 per cent of young people of college age not in college, certainly a group of them are not qualified for college work—either from lack of preparation or by natural endowment. However, it is reasonable to assume that at least 30 per cent of college age young people who are not in college are capable of doing college work. But, you see, they lack burning desire.

In case you are one of these let me build a little desire with these statistics: A man with less than eight years in school earns an average of less than $3,000 a year. The high school graduate, about $6,000 a year. The average income for the college graduate is more than $9,000 a year. This means that the college graduate in his lifetime will earn approximately $150,000 more than the high school graduate. There is another important factor and that is, that the college graduate is prepared in a much larger area of vocational achievement than the high school graduate. He is better prepared to find and to enjoy a place of outstanding service.

The world was shocked some time ago to learn of the terrible effects at birth of a certain drug given to mothers during pregnancy. In London, England, alone 1200 cases of malformation at birth were attributed to this drug. Don't you imagine that the physicians who saw these babies being born, some without arms and legs, some evidently mentally deformed, wondered if they should even start the breath, be true to their oath? But the physicians had no choice, they had given themselves to prolonging life.

They Should Have Failed

History tells us of some outstanding examples of people with physical defects, who achieved truly wonderful things. Charles Steinmetz, the electrical inventor who died in 1923, was deformed at birth. He lived to make outstanding contributions to all mankind. There are others who had physical defects—Beethoven, Edison, Julius Caesar, both President Roosevelts, James Ferber, Helen Keller, to name a few. The physical defect was simply another challenge to be successful.

Washington Irving said, "Great minds have purposes, others have wishes. Little minds attain and are subdued by misfortunes; but great minds rise above them." And John Foster said, "When a firm, decisive, spirit is recognized it is curious to see how the space clears around a man and leaves him room and freedom."

Napoleon Hill suggests that burning desire is made up of the following six ingredients: "(1) Self-reliance, (2) Personal initiative, (3) Imagination, (4) Enthusiasm, (5) Self-discipline, (6) Concentration of effort." "Any dominating idea, plan or purpose held in the mind through repetition of thought and emotionalized with a burning desire for its realization, is taken over by the subconscious mind and acted upon through whatever natural and logical means may be available."[3]

"No one has ever been known to succeed without applying the principle of definiteness of purpose . . . The first step from poverty to riches is the most difficult. It may simplify my statement if I tell you that all riches and all material things that anyone acquires through self effort begin in the form of a clear, concise mental picture of the thing one seeks."
—Andrew Carnegie

> My wants are many, and if told,
>   Would muster many a score;
> And were each wish a mint of gold,
>   I still should long for more.

—John Quincy Adams

Desire builds desire. This is the fantastic power of it.

Your Formula for Burning Desire

The amazing book, *Success Through a Positive Mental Attitude,* gives an explanation of burning desire and how it works.

"1. . . . your subconscious mind begins to work under a universal law: what the mind can conceive and believe the mind can achieve. Because you realize

---

[3]Napoleon Hill, *Think and Grow Rich* (Greenwich, Conn.: Crest, 1960), page 36.

185

your intended destination, your subconscious mind is affected by this self-suggestion. It goes to work to help you get there.

"2. Because you know what you want, there is a tendency for you to try to get on the right track and head in the right direction. You get into action.

"3. Work now becomes fun. You are motivated to pay the price. You budget your time and money. You study, think and plan. The more you think about your goal the more enthusiastic you become. And with enthusiasm your desire turns into a burning desire.

"4. You become alerted to opportunities that will help you achieve your objective as they present themselves in your everyday experiences. Because you know what you want, you are more likely to recognize these opportunities."[4]

When Charles M. Schwab asked Andrew Carnegie for his first promotion Mr. Carnegie grinned broadly and replied, "If you have your heart fixed on what you want there is nothing I can do to stop you from getting it." That's burning desire.

Five Steps to Success

In his book, *How To Sell Your Way Through Life,* Napoleon Hill lists the five fundamental steps to success: "(1) Choice of a definite goal to be attained. (2) Development of sufficient power to attain one's goal. (3) Perfection of a practical plan for attaining one's goal. (4) Accumulation of specialized knowledge necessary for the attainment of one's goal. (5) Persistence in carrying out the plan."

---

[4]Hill and Stone, *Ibid.,* page 25.

He also lists some of the advantages of a definite aim: "(1) Singleness of purpose forces one to specialize and specialization tends towards perfection. (2) A definite goal permits one to develop the capacity to reach decisions quickly and firmly. (3) Definiteness of purpose enables one to master the habit of procrastination. (4) Definiteness of purpose saves the time and energy one would otherwise waste while wavering between two or more possible courses of action. (5) A definite purpose serves as a road map which charts the direct route to the end of one's journey. (6) Definiteness of purpose fixes one's habits so that they are taken over by the subconscious mind and used as a motivating force in driving toward one's goal. (7) Definiteness of purpose develops self-confidence and attracts the confidence of other people."[5]

Abe Lincoln Had Purpose

There is no finer example of desire than the life of Abraham Lincoln. Carl Sandburg in his book *Abraham Lincoln: The Prairie Years* quotes the following: "As he walked back to New Salem he saw ahead of him a tough piece of work to do; he had to transform his blank ignorance of surveying into a thorough working knowledge and skill . . . Many nights (school master) Graham's daughter woke at midnight, and saw Lincoln and her father by the fire, figuring and explaining. Lincoln was fagged, with sunken cheeks and bleary red eyes; 'You're killing yourself,' good people told Lincoln, and among themselves they whispered that it was too bad. In six week's time, however, Lincoln had mastered his books, the chain, the circumferentor, the Three Horizons, and

---

[5]Napoleon Hill, *How to Sell Your Way Through Life* (Cleveland: Ralston Publishing Company, 1958), page 161.

Calhoun put him to work on the north end of Sangamon County . . .

"Lincoln was challenged to vote for the moving of the capital to Springfield in return for his vote for a measure that he considered against his principles. The debate continued for two days. Then Lincoln spoke: 'You may burn my body to ashes and scatter them to the winds of heaven; you may drag my soul down to the regions of darkness and despair to be tormented forever; but you will never get me to support a measure which I believe to be wrong, although by so doing I may accomplish that which I believe to be right.'[6]

Beethoven also had great drive and ambition. Listen to what H. A. Rudall says about him in his biography, *Beethoven*, "Winter and summer, Beethoven rose at day-break, when he immediately seated himself at his writing table, and continued writing until his usual dinner time at two or three o'clock. His labors were unbroken except for excursions into the open air, but never without a notebook in which to jot down whatever fresh ideas might occur during his rambles."[7]

Houdini, the magician, is another example. Here is a statement from Harold Kellock's, *Biography of Houdini*, "His training for his various immersions, stunts, and feats such as remaining encased in a steel casket under water for an hour and a half were peculiarly arduous. For months on end, several times a day, he would practice going under water in his own bath tub, holding a stop watch to test his own endurance, lengthening the period of immersion each day until he could stay under for more than four minutes without grave discomfort—accustoming himself to get along with a minimum of oxygen, so that he

---

[6]Sandburg, *Ibid.*, page 170.
[7]Quoted in *Our Changing World*.

could feed his lungs sparingly with a few cubic feet of air in a little casket and endure for an almost unbelievable time."[8]

Burning desire is a habit and can be cultivated. Success is the progressive achievement of a worthy, challenging goal. You can make the habit of success by developing purposeful burning desire.

---

[8]Harold Kellock, *Houdini* (New York: Harcourt-Brace and Company, 1928), page 1.

CHAPTER 32

Burning Desire for Recognition

Your key to success today is to build recognition and your burning desire.

Your happiness in life is directly proportionate to your ability to achieve. Achievement brings recognition. Some of the world's greatest people have achieved because of the power of an inferiority complex that thrust them forth to attempt fantastic things to be recognized as individuals.

What do you expect out of life? Do you know where you are going? Are you telling yourself that others will soon sit up and listen to you? That you are fed up with their ignoring you? That you've had enough of no one paying any attention to you and they are going to watch you? Then you are on your way. You are developing a burning desire for recognition.

Depression comes from being ignored. It is tragic to be just a face in the crowd. So stand out from the crowd. Set a big goal in whatever area you can best achieve in, a goal that will acknowledge you as an outstanding successful, dynamic individual. You are on your way to personal success when you do so.

Remember, as a child, reading the first circular about the circus coming to town? Remember how you anticipated going to a baseball game? Remember how you looked forward to the first swimming experience of the summer? Yes, you lived for weeks on that one dream. Now you must do the same thing as an adult. You must set a tremendous goal out there and develop your desire to reach it, because that goal will lead you to personal happiness. In the achieving of it you bring about the recognition your conscious mind desires and must have.

One of the human relations rules that has made the Dale Carnegie Course so powerful is, *Throw down a challenge.* The "well done" of the boss, your name in the company newspaper, a human interest story in the daily paper about you, the spoken admiration of friends and associates, as well as the anticipated, "Well done thou good and faithful servant" of the Lord—all are means of thrusting people forward.

A Sense of Confidence

Many times we need external aids to buoy up our spirits, our moods. Clothes and external conditions can be controlled to a great extent by our own attitudes and conduct. One amazingly successful automobile salesman who specializes in selling luxury cars to wealthy individuals tells of his formula for success in Bristol's *The Magic of Believing.* "Not only do I take a shower," he said, "and change all my clothes, but I go to a barber shop and get everything from a shave to a shampoo and a manicure. Obviously, it has something to do with my appearance, but further than that it does something to me inside. It makes me feel like a new man who could lick his weight in wildcats."[1]

In one of his challenging radio programs entitled *Consciousness of Competence,* Earl Nightingale discusses the secret of success of the outstanding star, whether he be in athletics, show business or in the business world. Earl says that there are three facts: "(1) Each of these stars is in the work which comes the closest to perfectly matching his

---

[1] C. M. Bristol, *The Magic of Believing* (Englewood Cliffs, N.J.: Prentice-Hall, Inc., 1948), page 167.

191

natural talents. He's where his abilities lie. (2) These people are dedicated totally to what they are doing. Everything else takes second place in their life. (3) They have supreme confidence. They can assault their work with boldness, with assurance, with confidence because they know they can succeed."

I have seen men in combat with that same sense of assurance. In fact, toward the latter part of the Okinawa campaign I had a little bit of it myself. The vast majority of my friends were either killed or wounded in combat; yet I wasn't touched. It was almost a fatalistic sense of assurance that whatever happened I would come through it all right. My name simply wasn't written on one of those bullets.

Novalis said, "Happy those who here on earth have dreamed of a higher vision. They will the sooner be able to endure the glories of the world to come." And Thomas Carlyle said, "There is no man, no woman, so small but that they cannot make their life great by high endeavor."

> I held a truth, with him who sings
> To one clear harp in divers tones,
> That men may rise on stepping-stones
> Of their dead selves to higher things.
> —Alfred Tennyson

Thought on Fire

Burning desire will reflect itself in fiery words. William Jennings Bryan defined eloquence as, "The speech of one who knows what he is talking about and means what he says—it is thought on fire . . . Eloquence is when a speaker is tremendously enthused about worthwhile things concerning which he is thoroughly informed."

Furthermore it is impossible to achieve true recognition without service to others. The greatest recognition is in the individual heart when we know what we have done—what we've given our life to—that has lifted up the downtrodden, given hope to the distressed, and encouragement to the downcast.

Dr. Kenneth McFarland, possibly America's greatest after dinner speaker, in his book *Eloquence in Public Speaking* quotes the following, "Dr. Edward Rosenow, formerly with the Mayo Clinic in Rochester, Minnesota, told of the experience that caused him to become associated with the field of medicine. When he was a small boy living in Minnesota, his brother became acutely ill. The family sweated it out until the doctor arrived. As the physician examined his sick brother, Edward Rosenow kept his eyes riveted on the anxious and anguished faces of his parents. Finally, the doctor turned to his parents with a smile and said, 'You can relax, folks, your boy is going to be alright.' Young Edward Rosenow was profoundly impressed with the change that announcement brought over his parents. In relating the incident in later years he said, 'I resolved then and there that I was going to be a doctor so I could put light in people's faces.' "[2] That's it. That is true recognition. And let me say that the burning desire is there when you wish to be recognized for the service you have rendered to others, not necessarily external recognition but internal recognition of a job well done—of putting light in people's faces, of easing the pain of a troubled heart, of giving purpose to a wasted rascal, of bringing harmony to a broken home, of giving joy to a troubled boy.

Is Anything Really Impossible?

"We all have possibilities we don't know about. We can do things we don't even dream we can do. It's only when

---

[2]Kenneth McFarland, *Eloquence in Public Speaking* (Englewood Cliffs, N.J.: Prentice-Hall, Inc., 1961), page 31.

necessity faces us that we rise to the occasion and actually do the things that hitherto have seemed impossible."

—Dale Carnegie

"Life does not consist mainly—or even largely—of facts and happenings. It consists mainly of the storm of thoughts that is forever blowing through one's head."

—Mark Twain

We must corral those thoughts, direct those thoughts, harness those thoughts toward our recognition.

"I desire so to conduct the affairs of this administration," said Abraham Lincoln, "that if at the end, when I come to lay down the reins of power, I have lost every other friend on earth, I shall at least have one friend left, and that friend shall be down inside of me." This is the internal recognition that desire brings to reality. Winston Churchill said the same thing when he said, "So long as I am acting from duty and conviction, I am indifferent to taunts and jeers. I think they will probably do me more good than harm."

Henry Ford said, "All Fords are exactly alike, but no two men are just alike. Every new life is a new thing under the sun; there has never been anything just like it before, and never will be again. A young man ought to get that idea about himself; he should look for the single spark of individuality that makes him different from other folks, and develop that for all he's worth. Society and schools may try to iron it out of him; their tendency is to put us all in the same mold, but I say, 'Don't let that spark be lost; it's your only real claim to importance.' "

"There is a time in the lives of most of us when, despondent of all joy in an earthly future, and tortured by conflicts between inclination and duty, we transfer all the passion and fervor of our troubled souls to enthusiastic yearnings for the divine love, looking to its mercy, and taking thence the only hopes that can cheer—the only strength that can sustain us."

—Edward George Bulwer-Lytton

Build Burning Desire and Succeed

Burning desire is the jet propulsion to success:

1. You will need others to help you achieve your major purpose. List the individuals and groups who will help you build burning desire.

2. Make a list of the most exciting, enthusiastic individuals you have ever known, or heard about. Try to name at least 20.

3. List below the books you must get to help you establish a consistent program of improving your burning desire. (Start with the Bibliography at the back of this book.)

4. Through victory over worry, association with vibrant people, an ever improving program of creative study, and the regular statement of your burning desire, you will make a habit of succeeding. List your next immediate action to achieve burning desire.

CHAPTER 33

How to Achieve Burning Desire

Your key for success today is to make the habit of succeeding and achieving. You must develop burning desire to achieve an outstanding purpose that will motivate and unify the total powers of your being.

In one of his programs from *Our Changing World* Earl Nightingale gives a formula for making a million dollars:

"1. Get into a line that you will find to be a deep personal interest, something you really enjoy spending twelve to fifteen hours a day working at, and the rest of the time thinking about.

"2. Learn all you can about this line, and what everybody else in the same line is doing, especially the more successful ones.

"3. Submit yourself completely. That is, surrender yourself to this, one line then make up your mind to succeed at it.

"4. Develop patience. Realize that one of the most important ingredients of success is realizing how long it takes to succeed. In fact, you must be in your line a minimum of five years, and be solidly in the black by that time, to even be considered successful. Most real success will come back to the first five years.

"5. Learn to ignore the unimportant and distraction. You've only got so much time, make sure you use it to its best advantage.

"6. Create, don't compete. Think ahead and move with intelligent boldness into new and perhaps unexplored areas of development. Lead, but don't follow."[1]

Excellent advice by a master of success. This then is your formula for succeeding. You can be successful. It's all up to you. You call the signals of your life.

There is no short cut to achievement. There are many who would think that the only way to excell is by pull or by fraud or by someone in a high place recommending you. Even if you get the position you can't hold it unless you have mastered the principles of success; unless you know the field thoroughly; unless you can match any and every other man of equal position not only in your firm, but among all competitors as well. Actually, pull may be the worst thing that could happen to a young man trying to succeed. It can destroy.

Kate Smith didn't have pull. Here was a young woman with everything going against her. She didn't know anyone to recommend her, she was large but she had a great voice. It took her many years to get started, but she had the nation applauding her. You see, you can't stop burning desire. If your desire is strong enough you will achieve.

A word of caution from Matthew Henry: "Inordinate desires commonly produce irregular endeavors. If our wishes be not kept in submission to God's providence our pursuits will scarcely be kept under the restraints of His precepts." Be sure that your burning desire is the right one—that your goals are God's goals.

How to Change the Business Pattern of a City

Years ago I shopped at a store whose motto was, "The store that will never know competition." The owner-man-

---

[1] *Our Changing World,* No. 892.

ager, who had been trained at Marshall Field in Chicago, had a burning desire to change the mercantile habits of a metropolitan area, and he did exactly that by the magic of competition and the motivation of advertising. He not only lowered prices, produced jobs, developed a competitive spirit among merchants, but directly and indirectly, his influence brought dynamic new life to an entire city. He had a burning desire to achieve.

Climb on the Bumps

Nothing can stop the man who has this desire to achieve. Eric Butterworth, in *Good Business Magazine,* tells the following story: "A little boy was leading his sister up a mountain path. She complained, 'It's not a path at all. It's all rocky and bumpy.' 'Sure, the bumps are what you climb on.'" Nothing stops the man who desires to achieve. Every obstacle is simply a course to develop his achievement muscle. It's a strengthening of his powers of accomplishment.

Did you hear about the boy in Decatur, Illinois, who answered an ad in the magazine about a book on photography, but received a book on ventriloquism instead? He kept the book, studied it, made a wooden dummy to practice with and became internationally known. That's right, Edgar Bergen and Charlie McCarthy. He took the bump of disappointment and stepped on it to a highway of success.

Don't be like the boy during World War II who said, "I wouldn't mind going to war and being a hero if I knew I wouldn't get hurt." The hurts of life's journey are but the exercise bar of achievement. They are the push-ups to outstanding success.

When General Dwight Eisenhower addressed the troops before Normandy, he said, "There is no victory at bargain basement prices."

Is there a more thrilling story of desire and purpose in achievement than that of Florence Nightingale? It was impossible for her to find a hospital in Britain that would train her to be a nurse so she might go to the battlefield and meet the needs of wounded soldiers. She went to Germany and there served an apprenticeship in want and embarrassment. Early in the Crimean War she literally changed the whole world's concept and attitude toward caring for the wounded in military battles. Upon her deathbed when more than ninety years of age, Florence Nightingale in a semiconscious condition was heard to say, "I am watching the altar of murdered men, and I shall be eternally fighting their cause."

How to Stay Young

Bristol quotes one outstanding man who, though beyond seventy, gives the following secrets of success: "I make it a plan, and have for years, to start something new—that is, new for me—at least, once a week. It may be only the making of some simple gadget for use in the kitchen or it may be an entirely new sales plan or reading an unfamiliar book. I find in following this plan not only that I keep my body and mind active, but also put to use a lot of imaginative qualities that otherwise might fall asleep and atrophy. This idea of man's retiring when he is sixty is to me a great mistake. As soon as a man retires and quits being active mentally and physically he is on his way to his grave in short order. You've seen what has happened to fire horses when they are retired. You know what happens to an automobile when you leave it outside unused and neglected; it starts to rust and it's soon headed for the junk shop. Humans are the same; they rust out or wither and die when they go on the shelf."[2]

---

[2]Bristol, *Ibid.*, page 153.

Your Driving Force of Destiny

The reason burning desire is so necessary in success is that we put forth the effort directly proportionate to the power of emotionally exciting ourselves to achieve. Desire is the driving force of destiny. Desire can accomplish amazing feats.

What are you striving for? Where are you going? Do you know? You cannot begin to build burning desire until you plan the program, until you establish the purpose, until you outline the goals—the road signs along the fabulous journey of dynamic purpose—and in this you must expect to achieve.

You realize there are two types of energy, one is physical and the other is mental and spiritual. Now the mental and spiritual energy is far more important, for a subconscious mind can bring forth great power and strength whenever needed.

How He Broke the Four Minute Mile

Dr. Roger Bannister broke the four-minute mile for the first time on May 6, 1954.[3] Dr. Bannister believed, along with his trainer, that it was necessary first to mentally assent that he would break the four-minute mile. Then his body could be developed to the point of physical perfection to accomplish this outstanding feat. Not only did he do it, but just four years later on August 6, 1958, five runners ran the mile in less than four minutes in one race in Dublin, Ireland. In those same four years the four-minute mile was performed forty-six times by Bannister and other runners.

The man who taught Roger Bannister this secret was Dr. Thomas Kirk Cureton, Director of the Physical Fitness Lab-

---

[3] Hill and Stone, *Ibid.*, page 182.

oratory of the University of Illinois. Dr. Cureton says that any man can be as fit at fifty as he was in his twenties if he knows how to train his body. He says that a few principles are involved: (1) To train the whole body. (2) To push yourself to the limit of your endurance exceeding the limit with each workout. The art of record breaking is the ability to take more out of yourself than you've got. You punish yourself more and more each day you practice.

According to Your Desire

"We believe that according to our desire we are able to change the things round about us, we believe this because otherwise we can see no favorable solution. We forget the solution that soon comes to pass and is also favorable; we do not succeed in changing things according to our desire, but gradually our desire changes . . . We have not managed to surmount the obstacle, as we were absolutely determined to do, but life has taken us round it, led us past it, and then if we turn round to gaze at the remote past, we can barely catch sight of it, so imperceptible has it become." —Marcel Proust[4]

"Whatever I have tried to do in this life, I have tried with all my heart to do well; whatever I have devoted myself to, I have devoted myself to completely; in great aims and in small, I have always been thoroughly in earnest."
—Charles Dickens

"Perseverance is power to weakness, and opens to poverty the world's wealth. It spreads fertility over the barren landscape, and bids the choicest fruits and flowers spring up and flourish in the desert abode of thorns and briars."
—Samuel Goodrich

---

[4]Marcel Proust, *Remembrance of Things Past* (New York: Random House).

Take Possession of Your Mind

Andrew Carnegie said, "The man who acquires the ability to take full possession of his own mind may take possession of anything else to which he is justly entitled . . . And the man who masters himself through self-discipline never can be mastered by others."

It cannot be burning desire unless it builds fantastic determination.

"I'll not budge an inch."   —Shakespeare

"The best lightning rod for your protection is your own spine."   —Emerson

"He who is firm and resolute in will molds the world to himself."   —Goethe

"Either I will find a way, or I will make one."
                    —Sir P. Sidney

"Energy will do anything that can be done in the world; no talents, no circumstances, no opportunities will make a two-legged animal a man without it."   —Goethe

"The truest wisdom, in general, is a resolute determination."   —Napoleon

"Toil—zeal—think—hope; you will be sure to dream enough before you die, without arranging for it."
                    —Sterling

You must build in your mind's eye a fantastic desire, a burning desire to achieve, to excel. As a man thinkest in his heart so is he.

Earl Nightingale quotes Dr. Leslie J. Nason, a professor at the University of Southern California. "You can read a child's image of himself in his actions. If he thinks he's tough it shows. If he thinks he's afraid, it shows. If he thinks he's good, it shows. If he thinks he's bad, it shows. You see, he develops this image of himself in the same way we all do, by seeing how others react to what we say or do. The parent establishes the image by telling the child, that he is always misbehaving or that he is a fine little boy. The teacher in school brings out the best in the good students, or brings out the worst in the unruly students by continuing to comment on it time after time after time. But most of all we act like the person we think that we really are. It's up to us. Everyone must have some kind of a personal image to guide his behavior. It usually causes trouble only when it is wrong." These truths by Dr. Nason are so evident. But, you can change the image you've had in the past. You can make your mind do what you want it to do. You can achieve, provided you build a burning desire.

CHAPTER 34

Burning Desire Develops Competition and Pride

Your key for success today is developing competition and pride.

Earl Nightingale tells about a man who was observed running toward a large river. As he reached the dock he increased his speed and when he came to the end he threw himself as high and as far out as he could before hitting the water, landing about ten feet from the dock. As soon as he surfaced he swam back to the land and tried it again, over and over again. A friend asked him, "What are you doing?" He said, "A friend of mine has bet me a million dollars to one that I can't jump across the river and after thinking over those odds, I couldn't help at least trying." This is competition. The spirit of competition, of courage, and of personal pride is one of the outstanding emotional factors in the achievement of the American way of life.

The 25 per cent of the salesmen who make 75 per cent of all the sales succeed because they continue to stay at the job. They do not give up. They have courage and a sense of competition. Competition is to contend with another for a prize, to engage in a contest, to compete in a race or in business or in any activity, to strive to outdo, to excel as an individual or a group of individuals. It implies a sense of rivalry in striving to give one's best in outdoing others. Certainly there is the suggestion of opposition and disputing, as well as rivalry. There are obstacles to overcome. There is personal discipline involved. There is struggle and hard work and fear and frustration and friendly enemies to overcome. Charles F. Kettering has said, "I have found that if I have faith in myself and in the idea I am tinkering with, I usually win out." Now notice the sense of competition; Kettering was competing with possible scientific failure and with other businessmen. He had a goal; he had a purpose; he had a plan.

You Are Stronger Than You Think

Dale Carnegie has said, "We can all endure disaster and tragedy, and triumph over them—if we have to. We may not think we can, but we have surprisingly strong inner resources that will see us through if we will only make use of them. We are stronger than we think." William James said, "To feel brave, act as if you were brave, use all of your will to that end, and a courage fit will very likely replace the fit of fear." Ralph Waldo Emerson said, "They can conquer who believe they can. He has not learned the first lesson of life who does not every day surmount a fear."

How many times have you held off attempting a certain thing because you simply knew it couldn't be done? You had made up your mind ahead of time. Then for some reason you were forced to try and you soon realized that from a distance that which seemed impossible soon was easily accomplished, and you could have kicked yourself for not attempting it sooner.

Develop Competition

A spirit of healthy competition developed in the home with children when they are young, exercised and challenged on the athletic field and in the classrooms, then brought to fruition and richness in the business corridors

205

of adult life brings joy, accomplishment and intensive achievement.

Did you hear about the boy who was such a problem, getting into everything, that his father suggested they buy him a bicycle for Christmas, and the mother said, "Will that make him any better?" The father replied, "No, but it will spread his devilment over a wider area." The rambunctious, dynamic, devil-may-care boy is not the one you usually need to be worried about. However, I'm not suggesting that you tell such a boy to sit still while you instill. You just don't say to a ten- or twelve-year-old boy, "Don't do this or don't do that or don't move." You simply wiggle him in the right direction. He is already competitive. He has a yen for life.

The child to be concerned about is the child who is an introvert—the wall flower type, the afraid-of-his-shadow individual. He doesn't relate and he doesn't compete. Lee H. Oswald, the murderer of President Kennedy on November 22, 1963, was a loner; he did not relate.

When you get a kid out of his shell and get him to compete he begins to live. He is a part of the effort and he's beginning to bring forth his best, the totality of his ability in competition. The same thing happens to the tragic number of high school dropouts—no competition. Never forget that the man who with his college or graduate degree thinks he has the world as his own is already a failure, for he has ceased to compete. An education is to give a man a tool or to tell him where he can find the tool to make life's decisions and to meet life's emergencies and to scale life's mountainous opportunities. The man who has been educated beyond his intelligence is the one who's sitting on top of his degree and is self-satisfied.

Your Well-Integrated Personality

Have you read Dr. Alexis Carrel's book, *Man, The Unknown?* He says "that the individual who succeeds has an intensity that determines the social level of that individual and that the happiest and most useful persons are those with a well integrated whole of intellectual, moral and organic activities . . . The so-called genius, the great artist, the great scientist, the great philosopher, the great musician, the great business success, is generally a man of common ability who has overdeveloped one particular phase of his abilities and personality." So he says, "Genius can be compared to a tumor that is growing upon a normal organism."

But do you know that many of these people are unhappy? They give to the entire community the benefit of their mighty impulses, but they often are disgruntled, in disharmony and out of step with other people. Yes, Dr. Carrel says, "The happiest people and the ones making the greatest contribution to life are those with well integrated personalities." In other words, they relate to others and respond to the challenge of others in a spirit of competition that brings forth a burning desire.

You have far greater ability than you ever dare believe. Remember, the average person uses less than 10 per cent of his total mental capacity.

What a terrible excuse I used to give myself in arguing against the learning of memory techniques to improve my capacity to memorize. I would say, "You can only remember so much so if you crowd out things you've already learned then you won't have room for all you need to know." How foolish. The most fertile field in all the world and the greatest unexplored territory in all the universe—even greater than space itself—is the human mind. You learn to use every tool you can to strengthen your mental powers. Develop this sense of competition. You will find that out of it will come a greater desire to accomplish, to achieve, to stand above the crowd.

Stay Competitive and Achieve

Such a spirit of competition is what someone has well called, *designed discontent.* Remember those lines of Joel Chandler Harris: "Watch out w'en you'r gittin' all you want. Fattenin' hogs ain't in luck." The competitive man is never satisfied. He never ceases to grow; he never stops learning; he never stops achieving; he moves on from one area of achievement to another; on and on and on.

Recently there was a newspaper article telling about certain businessmen who through heavy schedules had come to times when they needed to relax and were forced by doctor's orders to take a leave of absence from their business to go away to rest. An amazing thing was discovered. These men simply weren't pleased, weren't content, weren't happy to do nothing. While they were away on a ninety-day leave it was discovered that they had started a new business, taken on the consulting for another firm, or opened up a hotel or whatever. The article went on to summarize by concluding that there are certain men who have superior bodies and superior minds and superior abilities. They actually are superior men. Were they born that way? No, they achieved through competition and pride and burning desire.

> Greatly begin! though thou have time
> But for a line, be that sublime—
> Not failure, but low aim is crime.
>
> —James Russell Lowell

> Aspire, break bonds, I say;
> Endeavor to be good

And better still, and best—
Success is nought, endeavors all.

—Robert Browning

There was a day in our world when a gentleman was a man of wealth and of leisure who owned such vast pieces of property and, in some eras, slaves, that all he had to do was count his coupons and live a life of luxury and leisure. Isn't it wonderful that that has changed? A gentleman today is a man who treats other men as if they were better than himself or at least his equal.

Burning Desire in a Single Pursuit

Remember those days at the high school track meet and running those sprints in your football uniform at practice? Remember those joyous summer games of seeing who could dive the greatest distance or swim under water the furthest; of seeing who could throw the baseball the furthest? That's what we need to continue to do—develop the spirit of competition. And when a man has done his best, has given his all, and in the process supplied the needs of his family and his society, that man is successful—that man has made a habit of succeeding.

The person who will seek to get something from someone else without paying due process for what he receives also has never learned the joy of competition. It is just as much stealing to take pay for work not done or not completed as it is to hold a pistol to a man's brow. Estimates are that four million dollars in cash and merchandise is stolen from employers every day in America. This means a billion dollars a year—a tragic indictment. What terrible proof that men have not learned the true joys of competition and burning desire.

Earl Nightingale quotes Milton Carlton, who as an eleven-year-old won a speech contest in a California

209

school. Let me repeat his words, "In speaking of men who've made outstanding success, 'They had a burning drive to succeed; they refused to accept failure as the final answer; they often turned physical handicaps into assets; they had concern for other people; and they worked hard and constant. There is very little difference in people—that little difference makes a big difference. The only difference is attitude. From the time we are in kindergarten, we've heard the story about the little engine that climbed the hill by saying, "I think I can—I think I can." ' " What a speech by an eleven-year-old boy!

Yes, competition is the key to burning desire and burning desire is the joy of achievement. Remember you can do anything in the world you want, if you can build a burning desire. Make your contest a joyful, happy, gracious one. Let your competitors be your friends; build a spirit of wholesome competition and you will find that life is truly worth living. You can make a habit of succeeding.

CHAPTER 35

Producing Burning Desire

Your key to success today is to produce burning desire and make a habit of succeeding.

What man can conceive mentally, he can bring into materialization. Regardless of how depressed you may be, you can restore burning desire immediately by returning to the goals and the purpose to which you dedicated yourself originally. Never forget that the persistent achievement of a worthy challenging goal is success.

In his marvelous book, *Eloquence in Public Speaking*, Dr. Kenneth McFarland, one of America's outstanding public speakers, says that "the indispensable quality to speaking as well as to leadership is vitality." This word is found to mean "of critical importance, of truth, imparting life and vigor, animation, living, fundamental, essential, important, significant, necessary, needful, exuberant, something having vital force." "It contains enthusiasm, along with truth and other life-giving qualities that insure the proper direction of enthusiasm."[1]

Here's How

You can produce burning desire. Let me give you a formula: First, you must have a goal; and of course, goals are purposes. Goals and purposes differ only in degree. Purpose is the long range, all encompassing dream of your life; goals are check points along the road to success. Do

[1]McFarland, *Ibid.*, page 238.

you know where you are going? Do you know what you want to do? Remember, we become what we think about. If you have a goal, you have a personal image. If you have a goal you live and breathe and walk and act with dynamics and with purpose. If you see the man on the street hurrying, head back, shoulders erect, with military bearing, forcefulness of action, there is a man with a goal. He knows what he is doing. No coward can be a crusader.

Napoleon Hill said, "Any idea that is held in the mind, emphasized, feared or reverenced, begins at once to clothe itself in the most convenient and appropriate physical form that is available."[2] And Hill also says, "The transfer of thoughts from the conscious to the subconscious section of the mind may be hastened by the simple process of stepping-up or stimulating the vibrations of thought through fear, faith, or any other highly intensified emotion, such as enthusiasm, that is, a burning desire based on definiteness of purpose.

Christopher Columbus dreamed of a new world and set out to achieve it regardless of the cost. We know what happened. Thomas A. Edison dreamed of lighting the world with incandescent lamps and he worked on his dream incessantly. Though he paid the price of 10,000 failures he gave the world light. Samuel Johnson said, "Our desires always increase with our possessions. The knowledge that something remains yet unenjoyed impairs our enjoyment of the good before us."

The second way to produce burning desire is to renew our dynamic energy. Never allow ourselves to get stale. Remember Dale Carnegie: "Is giving yourself a pep talk every day silly, superficial, and childish? No—on the contrary. It is the very essence of sound psychology." Keep excited about your work. We are excited when we are ear-

---

[2]Hill, *Master Key to Riches,* page 61.

nestly following a pathway toward a glorious, romantic, and eager achievement that is out before us. Take the ten-year-old boy who hears about a circus coming to town. He's excited.

People become stale because of several facets: too much work, or too much play, or no routine of activity, or failure to have and find balance in life. Man is a fourfold being. He is physical; he is mental; he is social; and he is spiritual. Therefore your daily and weekly activities should include creative mental stimulation. It is very important that you find this in your work. The man who dies a little bit during eight hours of work is dead at home as well.

Certainly there should be the stimulation of joyous and meaningful social intercourse, the building of new relationships with other individuals and the sustaining and strengthening of existing relationships. Of course, everyone needs a program of physical fitness and physical improvement and all of us are spiritual beings and need a daily and weekly worship relationship. Choose the church of your choice and throw yourself into it vitally. There is no such thing as communing with God in the country, at the lake fishing, or on the golf course, or in the garden. It is impossible. Through all of your life must run the joy of service.

The third way to produce burning desire is to stay competitive in your work. Cultivate and continue the joy of achievement and the spirit of competition between others involved in the same general vocation. The man who quits studying, the man who quits reading, the man who quits working, dies in his business at that time. People often say to me, "When do you find time to read?" We find time to do the things that we want to do and that are meaningful to us. I read on the plane and waiting in the doctor's office. I read at every moment, those inbetween moments that so many people waste. I read late at night after the

213

day's responsibilities while others are watching the meaningless program on television. Observe what is good; take part in that which is meaningful on television; but practice the discipline of rejecting that which has no plan or purpose in your life.

The fourth thing is to regularly congratulate yourself on your achievements. Count your blessings. Realize that you are working toward your goal, that you are achieving.

The fifth way to produce burning desire is to be creative. To do this you must push yourself. You have great and unlimited ability—ability that has never been challenged, ability that has never been extended. In some colleges and universities 75 per cent of the freshmen flunk out. Isn't this tragic? They couldn't have entered with present day examinations if they did not have the ability to finish. But they were not creative; they didn't challenge themselves; they did not set out to achieve.

I have a friend who has a doctor's degree but the minute he received it he quit learning. He is stagnated today. Tragically and corrosively he has limited his life and those round about him. He failed to be creative.

There are certain companies who have a policy only to hire college graduates. Certainly there are fields that require specialized training that only a college degree can give, but some of the most outstanding individuals this world has ever known were those who were thrust forth into dynamic action from the sense of inferiority that a lack of complete education gives. Personally, I'd rather have an enthusiastic, dynamic individual who is creative and wants to achieve, with a limited education, any day than a man with all the degrees in the world who is through learning.

Dr. John W. Gardner, President of the Carnegie Foundation, says that the American people are placing an altogether false emphasis on college education. He feels that great prestige which the college degree has achieved in our society leads people to assume—quite incorrectly—that college is the only form of continued learning after high school. Learning is for life and if you are to produce burning desire you must continue to be wonderfully creative.

You can make a habit of succeeding by producing burning desire!

How to Achieve Burning Desire

Making a habit of burning desire assures you of success:

1. Forget your inferiority complex and with bold commitment restate your major purpose.

2. Take Earl Nightingale's formula for making a million dollars and apply this six-point plan to your major purpose.

    A.
    B.
    C.
    D.
    E.
    F.

3. List the disappointments of your life that now you realize were the bumps on which you climbed to success.

4. Take the so-called impossible situation in your life and with Roger Bannister's formula outline your record breaking goal.

    A. Train your whole body. How?

    B. Push yourself to the limit each day exceeding the workout before. Now apply it to your situation.

5. Remember Bannister first decided mentally he could do it. You can too. Outline your plan to take complete possession of your mind.

6. Achieve desire by:

    A. Stating your goal.

    B. Renewing your dynamic energy. How?

    C. Staying competitive. How?

    D. Congratulating yourself on your achievements. Now you are great—say so.

    E. Being creative. How?

PART EIGHT
NOW—ACTION!

CHAPTER 36

Planning

Your key for success today is planning—planning that achieves.

An architect spends many hours with a client determining the dreams, goals, purpose, intents and uses in the heart of the client for the building. He literally picks the mind of the client. Then he puts these aspirations on paper with proper drawings and specifications so that the contractor, sub-contractor and all suppliers can perform their function properly to achieve the ideal building.

Your road to success requires planning. You must make plans, think about them, act on them.

Action is as essential to success as the motor and fuel are to the auto. But results are the only excuse for activity. We must know why we are acting and act toward the fulfillment of our goals.

Andrew Carnegie, who amassed a fortune of $500,000,000, said, " 'Knowledge is power' is only a half truth, for knowledge is only potential power. It may become a power only when it is organized and expressed in terms of definite action. Knowledge is not power, but the appropriation and use of other men's knowledge and experience for the attainment of some definite purpose is power."

A Chinese proverb says, "Journey of a thousand miles begins with first step." But in what direction? Plan your direction. When the goal is clear, the purpose is strong, the step will be decisive, assertive and forceful. Direction and determination decide destiny.

Make Big Plans Now

Daniel Hudson Burnham said, "Make big plans. Aim high and hope and work, remembering that a noble, logical diagram once recorded will never die, but long after we are gone will be a living thing, asserting itself with ever-growing insistency. Remember that our sons and grandsons are going to do things that would stagger us."[1]

Proper planning can save your life. In 1953, I started using auto safety seat belts. In March 1961, a farmer drove onto the highway, never stopping and hit me on the left side as I was driving seventy miles an hour. I turned over six times, completely demolishing the car. The car landed upside down in a drainage ditch. I walked away with only a minor wound on my forehead and spoke four hours later. I owe my life to planning.

One Thing Needed

There are many things that go to make up success: good health (not always essential), energy—a product of good health, perseverence, common sense, enthusiasm, talent. However one thing has been left out of that list—the one thing without which all of the others cannot produce success. That thing? Work. Work that is coordinated with what we want to accomplish. Another word we might use for work is action.

A circus had advertised that they had twenty-four elephants. On the day of the parade a busy executive on his way to his office was caught by the parade. He must not miss his appointment which meant hundreds of dollars in commissions. He remembered the advertisement of

---

[1] *Our Changing World*, No. 795.

twenty-four elephants. As the elephants came into view the trunk of one holding onto the tail of the one in front, he decided to count to twenty-four and gun his car across between the last elephant and the next vehicle. He counted, nineteen, twenty, twenty-one, twenty-two, twenty-three and as the trunk of the twenty-fourth came into view he gunned his car and shot across the intersection. What he did not know was that they had brought one more elephant. He hit the elephant, killed it and wrecked his car.

The circus manager and police arrived. They said, "You'll have to pay."

The businessman answered, "It's my fault, I'll pay, how much?"

"Thirty-five thousand dollars."

"What? You can get an elephant delivered from Africa for five thousand dollars. All I did was kill one elephant."

They exclaimed, "No, it isn't, you killed one elephant and pulled the tail out of twenty-four more."

The man in the story had a plan and acted on it. But he did not check his plans thoroughly and it cost him money. Failure to investigate and prepare for all emergencies can happen in our world too.

Make big plans and act on them. Check up on them regularly. You can be successful.

CHAPTER 37

Proper Attitude

Your key for success today is the proper attitude. Your success is determined by your attitude. The fruits of success—sense of achievement, peace, exhilarating keen competition, etc.—will not be yours unless your view toward your desire, achievement, success, is right. There must be an inner satisfaction that what you are doing is what you should be doing, that you are doing what you can and all you can. This then helps to motivate you. Your attitude determines your action.

> Let me be classed with the highest or lowest,
> Only with these will the senses be keen,
> You'll either find me the fastest or slowest.
> I'll never rot with the dull in between.
> —Jack Wardlow

In his book, *The Story of Man,* Carleton I. Coon says, "Hunting exercises the whole body, as few other occupations do. It places a premium on keen eyesight. Farsightedness is an asset. Hunting also places a premium on the capacity to make quick decisions, to act quickly and to work in teams. Obedience and leadership can be developed at no better school."[1]

We are hunters, on that glamorous, romantic, intriguing hunt of success. There are prices to pay, rivers to cross, mountains to climb, incurring loss of sleep and other diffi-

---

[1]Carlton, I. Coon, *Story of Man* (New York: Knopf, 1962), page 47.

222

culties, but the anticipation of the hunt, the fellowship and exhilaration of the occasion and the delightful hours of continual discussion will many times benefit the hunter.

The Golden Key—Initiative

"Initiative is that exceedingly rare quality that prompts—nay, impels—a person to do that which ought to be done, without being told to do it."

—Napoleon Hill

Elbert expressed himself on the subject of initiative in these words, "The world bestows its big prizes, both in money and hours, for one thing and that is initiative. Initiative is doing the right thing without being told."

Enthusiasm is the lubricant that oils the machinery of action. Each person has varying amounts of energy, depending on capacity for excitement, worthiness of the goal, associations around you and other factors.

Learn to store, utilize and expend your energies to your best advantage.

Five minutes of hate expends more energy than eight hours of hard work.

You can greatly improve your personality by changing your attitude. Control of temper, stern discipline of hate, jealousy, and revenge with insertion of positive thinking, love, hope, desire can make your life a magnificent obsession rather than a meaningless odyssey.

CHAPTER 38

Action Develops Courage

Action requires courage. But action also develops courage. You can be successful. Do you have the will to believe? Do you dare to walk by faith? Do you have the capacity to gather information rapidly, yet thoroughly, and then to act? An executive is one who can act.

The common attitude among so many people is: don't stick your neck out—don't get out on a limb. Many people are afraid to get out on a limb and they haven't even climbed the tree yet. Right after World War II people said, "Don't build. The cost is too high. Prices will go down." And for the next six years costs went up at approximately 1 per cent per month. They could have saved fabulous amounts of money had they built when the need was there—right after the war.

Georges Clemenceau said, "A man who likes to be convinced to act before he acts is not a man of action. Do you see the tennis player before returning the ball begin to question himself as to the physical and moral value of tennis? You must act just as you breathe." And Oliver Wendell Holmes, Jr., said, "Life is action and passion; therefore, it is required of a man that he should share the passion and action of his time at the peril of being judged not to have lived."

Make Your Own Inspiration

Great men do not wait for inspiration. The curse of action is the thought that we have to *feel* a certain matter before we act. There is nothing in this world as fickle as feeling. Our emotions are governed by our volition and follow volition. Forget emotions! Let's act.

Professional writers laugh when someone says, "I have to wait for the mood. I must court the muse and wait for inspiration." You'll never make a living writing if you do that. There are deadlines to be reached. Furthermore, the more we write, the more the inspirational material rises, for action stimulates the thought processes, brings from the subconscious the real truth and the greatest inspiration. If you act you will find that you will accomplish far more than if you wait needlessly.

Would you like to have more courage? Dale Carnegie gives five short rules, which, if you follow them, are guaranteed to increase your fortitude.

"1. Act as if you were courageous. This makes you a bit braver, as if one side of yourself had been challenged and wished to show it was not wholly afraid.

"2. Pause to reflect that others have had to face great discouragements and great obstacles and have overcome them. And what others have done, surely you can do.

"3. Remember that your life forces move in a sort of rhythm and as you feel depressed without the power to face life you may be at the bottom of your trough; if you will keep up with your courage, you will probably swing out of it by the very forces which at the moment are sucking you down.

"4. Remember you feel more discouraged and down-cast at night than during the daylight hours. Courage comes with the sun.

"5. Courage is the measure of a big soul. Try to measure up."[1]

Action Cultivates Your Own Courage

So well do I remember combat in the Pacific in the Marine Corps during World War II. If you stayed in your foxhole and worried about being shot, you would either lie there in fright and frenzy or crack up emotionally. You got out of that foxhole. You acted. And with the increased action day by day courage came. General Omar Bradley had said, "Bravery is the capacity to perform properly even when scared half to death." Bravery requires action and with action there come other responses as well.

It was Dale Carnegie who said, "I've never felt sorry for anyone, man or woman, for having to earn a living. I do look with inestimable pity, however, on anyone who has no enthusiasm for the type of work he is doing. To me, it is a great tragedy if one does not find early in life the kind of work he likes to do that he may apply in full force all the enthusiasm of youth." "If you are devastated by sorrow, by disaster or calamity, get busy doing something. Keep your mind and your hands occupied. To do this will help you as nothing else will. I know. I have tried it."[2]

In private flying I've learned that action drives away fear. It is common practice that when a person cracks up a plane, the best thing for him to do is to go up again as soon as he is physically able. This drives away fear.

---

[1]Dorothy Carnegie, ed., *Carnegie's Scrapbook* (New York: Simon and Schuster, Inc., 1959), page 6.
[2]Carnegie, *Ibid.*, page 193.

Have a Fireside Talk With Yourself

In the dark days of the depression there was fear as thick as fog clouding the minds of so many Americans. President Roosevelt called Napoleon Hill to his office in 1933 and discussed with Mr. Hill a plan to restore calm to a troubled people who had lost confidence in themselves and in their nation. Mr. Hill tells that the motto chosen was, "One for All and All for One." It was set up to cross all political party lines. All communications media, all radio, newspapers were brought in on the team. Instead of business depression they would talk about business recovery. The public schools at all levels were a part of the project. The clergy of all denominations were encouraged to preach on the positive rather than the negative. Then President Roosevelt began his series of fireside chats in a warm, friendly, folksy manner that brought tremendous confidence. We all know the answer. Almost immediately the nation began to think positively. And it began to move economically. Yes, courage follows action.

Don't you like the words of the Russian proverb, "Pray to God, but keep rowing to the shore"? Someone has said that "We ought to pray as if all depends on God, but we ought to work as if all depends on us." Courageously you can be successful.

CHAPTER 39

Action Produces Achievement

Your key for personal success for today is action, for in action there is achievement. And achievement is success. You can be successful. The man of success is the man of action. Theodore Roosevelt said, "I took the canal zone and let Congress debate, and while the debate goes on the canal does also." Teddy Roosevelt—a man of tremendous action and courage.

Action brings achievement. Earl Nightingale has come up with a formula that suggests that a person's net worth is sixteen and two-thirds times his annual salary. What is your average annual income? Multiply that times sixteen and two-thirds and you will come up with the amount you are worth. You may have earned twice that figure, of course, in your lifetime but your present cash value is sixteen and two-thirds times your annual income. If you make $10,000 a year you are worth $156,666, that is, if you are a man of action. But if you aren't a man of action you aren't a man of achievement. Phillips Brooks says, "Do not pray for tasks equal to your powers; pray for powers equal to your task. In the doing of your work shall be no miracle, but you shall be the miracle."

Prison Set Him Free

Clement Stone and Napoleon Hill tell the challenging story of action by Kenneth Erwin Harmon, a civilian employee of the Navy at Manila when the Japanese landed there in 1941. He was captured and held in a hotel for two days before he was sent to prison camp. There in the prison camp he saw a book that a cellmate had. It was entitled, *Think and Grow Rich*. He read it. He became infatuated with it and then asked the friend if he could copy it and the friend said yes.

He began feverishly, word by word, page by page, chapter by chapter, night and day, constantly knowing that soon they would be separated and he would no longer have the book. Within an hour after the last page was completed he was transferred to the notorious Santo Tomas prison camp in Manila where hundreds and thousands of prisoners of war died. All during the more than three years of imprisonment he read all and memorized much of *Think and Grow Rich*. At the end of the war when he was released, he had no fear of the present or the future. His words are, "But I was better when I left Santo Tomas than when I was interned, better prepared for life, more mentally alert. Success must be continually practiced or it will take wings and fly away."[1]

Action brings wonderful, glorious, outstanding achievement. You can be successful. The decision is yours.

Now—Action!

Action seals the habit of succeeding:

1. Since a major purpose well stated is half-achieved, re-state your major purpose in progressive tense.

  I am continuing to achieve . . .

2. Fight failure with action by taking Earl Nightingale's ten reasons why people fail[2] and stating your positive solution. (The first solution is done for you.)

[1] Stone and Hill, *Ibid.*, pages 94 and 95.
[2] *Our Changing World*, No. 567.

A. "Ignorance of the law of success."
The law of success is the persistent achievement of a worthy, challenging goal and I've got mine.

B. "Inability to concentrate on what is important."

C. "Lack of organization."

D. "Stop learning."

E. "Loss of faith in yourself."

F. "Cling to status quo."

G. "Custom is king."

H. "Do as little as you can get by with."

I. "Never evaluate yourself."

J. "Give up."

3. Since genius is the capacity for taking infinite pains, state 9 more details of your journey to success.

Begin every day stating my major purpose to myself.

4. The Golden Key is initiative: What move are you going to make—NOW?

How to
WIN
with High
Self-Esteem

To Mary, my wife, whose undying support of me is fantastic.

To Claire, Don, Laura, Elaine, their mates, and children, who affirm me constantly.

To Dr. Bob Wolgamott, whose clients in Portland, Oregon, and Tucson, Arizona, call him blessed—for his friendship and foreword.

To Wayne Nagy, an outstanding motivational speaker and the most effective high school principal I've ever known—for his foreword.

To Dr. Phyllis Beaver, whose unexcelled skills in instructional design led Florida Power and Light Company, the only non-Japanese company to receive the Deming Award for Corporate Excellence—for her dear friendship and foreword.

To Mary Kaye Bates, whose styling and final editing put the icing on this manuscript.

And to you, the reader: enjoy the new person you are destined to become.

Contents

Foreword   239

Introduction   243

Chapter 1   What Is Self-Esteem?   247

Chapter 2   How We Got This Way   259

Chapter 3   Giving Yourself Permission to Be Whole   273

Chapter 4   Taking Charge of Your Mind   283

Chapter 5   How to Raise Your Children to Have High Self-Esteem   297

Chapter 6   Build High Self-Esteem with Effective Work Production   311

Chapter 7   The Sacredness of Personhood   331

Chapter 8   Rewriting Your Tape: Why Did America's No. 1 Box Office Attraction Quit the Movies?   349

Chapter 9   Self-Esteem in Relationships: How to Enjoy Real Love   373

Chapter 10   Controlling Your Conduct   399

Chapter 11   Guidelines for a Self-Celebrating Life   419

Foreword

Mack R. Douglas has spent his entire life helping others to bring out the best in themselves. This is a gift that has brought him a life of great joy and satisfaction. Now he has cleverly crafted a book in which he passes on his gift to us if we simply follow through on each of his pages of wisdom.

In a refreshing literary approach, Mack teaches us how to improve our own self-esteem as well as of those around us. His sparkling wit and vividly described personal experiences provide the perfect background for the easy-to-follow exercises throughout the book.

Although the author has written this book simply to help each of us enhance our own self-esteem, it can be used for so many other applications. It is a wonderful treasure chest of material for any college professor to use with students who are studying in the fields of nursing, human resources, education, and psychology. Teachers for kindergarten through twelfth grade will also find it a helpful tool and, of course, parents will find it invaluable in guiding and nurturing their children.

How lucky you are to have found this book. It will change your life.

PHYLLIS BEAVER, PH.D.

As a practicing educator I am keenly aware of the need for children to develop high self-esteem. Over the past ten years I have had the privilege of being a principal of an inner-city junior high, a suburban middle school, and a culturally diverse high school. In each situation, regardless of race, ethnic background, gender, or socio-economic status, the successful students had one thing in common: *high self-esteem.*

Since education is a family affair, we are all responsible for understanding the importance of self-esteem in our own lives so that we may better prepare our children for a successful, rewarding life.

Thanks to Dr. Mack Douglas, we now have the tool to understand and put into practice the principles of life and to teach our children these important principles.

I highly recommend this book as required reading for those individuals who choose to lead a fulfilling life and to those who choose to enrich the lives of our children.

WAYNE A. NAGY
High School Principal
. Past President: Florida Association
of School Administrators

There is an old proverb that states, "As a man thinketh, so is he." Negative self-esteem or negative thinking that always focuses on one's inadequacies contributes to the image that one is less than others. This, in turn, breeds negative emotions such as sadness, anger, frustration, envy, jealousy, and fear. All of these have destructive elements that may create mental depression. Internalized anger and other emotions contribute to an over-utilization of neurohormones of the brain such as serotonin and norepinephrine. The net result of mental depression is physical depression, which in turn contributes to the development of physical illnesses such as headaches, stomach ulcers, spastic colon, and other emotionally related conditions.

During the more than twenty years that I have known Dr. Mack Douglas, I have been impressed with his ability to recognize that taking on the role of the victim is detrimental to both mental and physical health. Victimization affects one's self-esteem, one's marriage, one's standing in the community, one's ability to relate to society at large, and in one's ability to move forward in an upwardly mobile fashion to provide for his family and their needs. In this, his latest book, this dedicated author has gone to great lengths to develop a workbook that, if read, reread, and used correctly, will help turn lives around. By applying the principles outlined in this material, people no longer need to be victims, but can feel better about themselves. They find they can enjoy higher regard from their families and friends. Their role in society can be successful and satisfying.

Dr. Douglas has laid out step-by-step guidelines and principles that, if judiciously followed and put into practice, are guaranteed to make a major difference in your life. Initially, he helps you understand what self-esteem is. He then discusses how you should go about dealing with yourself, breaking the habit of being victimized by yourself and others. Next, he takes you through the steps necessary to rewrite a new vision for your life. Again, there is an old proverb that says, "Where there is no vision, the people perish." It is important that each individual break the habit of being the victim by taking control of his own life, developing a vision for the future, and in that way begin to rebuild his life. It is a reasonably well known fact that if a person is going to build a house, he must first visualize it in his mind. The plans or blueprints are next drawn, adding the distinguishing features all prior to building the house. Nearly every significant thing in the world was first someone else's vision. The San Francisco Bay Bridge was first a vision long before plans were drawn or it was finally built. In a similar manner, it is necessary for us to visualize what we wish to do with our lives. We need to begin to make the necessary short-term, intermediate, and long-term plans toward this goal. Dr. Douglas points the way to carry out this planning on a level for the physical world in which we live as well as for the relationships we enjoy or wish to enjoy.

Dr. Douglas further understands and writes well on the successful life in which the mental, physical, and spiritual realms are integrated and balanced to make man whole.

I enthusiastically recommend the steps in this book be put into practice for a successful life. I commend Dr. Douglas on his careful coordination of material for your benefit.

ROBERT C. WOLGAMOTT, M.D., FAPA
Board Certified Psychiatrist

Introduction

Thomas A. Edison said that the greatest gift parents can give to their children is enthusiasm.

The foundation of enthusiasm is high self-esteem—*that package of beliefs you carry around in your head that you have accepted to be the truth about yourself whether it is or not.*

To the person with high self-esteem this book is an inspiration to maintain that value.

To the person with low self-esteem this book can be your journey to high self-esteem. Like all journeys, it isn't always easy. There will be detours and roadblocks, and you may never totally reach your destination. But the journey will bring you the highest and most joyous experiences of your life. In order to get the most from your journey:

1. Make a commitment to yourself that you deserve high self-esteem.
2. Daily experience the conduct and activity necessary to take charge of and change your life.

Your endorphins will produce for you the most wonderful feelings you have ever known.

You are worth it!

How to
WIN
with High
Self-Esteem

CHAPTER 1

What Is Self-Esteem?

Esteem is defined as *appreciation, worth, estimate of value.*
Self-esteem is the package of beliefs that you carry around in
your head, that you have accepted to be the truth about
yourself, whether it is or not.

His mother was a forceful, domineering woman incapable
of giving love to her son. Married three times, she was di-
vorced by her second husband because she beat him up regularly. His father died before he was born, and his mother
had to work long hours to survive.

She gave him no affection, no discipline, and no training.
He was alone and rejected by his mother and other children. He was ugly, poor, untrained, and unloved. At age 13,
he was told by a school psychologist that he didn't know the
meaning of the word *love.*

Although he had a high IQ, he failed repeatedly in school
and quit during his third year of high school.

He joined the Marine Corps, but he rebelled against authority, was court-martialed, and received an undesirable
discharge.

He moved to a foreign country and married a woman
who was an illegitimate child and who bore him two children. She fought him, bullied him, and locked him in the
bathroom. After she kicked him out, he crawled back and
begged her for another chance.

She ridiculed his failure and even made fun of his sexual
impotency in front of a friend. He felt utterly rejected.

247

On November 22, 1963, he shot and killed Pres. John F. Kennedy. His name was Lee Harvey Oswald.

Born into a prominent, wealthy family with a strong mother, this person was told from birth that he was destined to be president of the United States. He had for his role model a cousin who was considered one of the greatest achievers of his day and a very popular international figure.

Handsome, cultured, well-educated, he early excelled in politics. Then, at the height of his early success, he was struck down by a devastating illness that would have left most everyone else a mental and emotional cripple.

Not him. He was destined for greater things. He went on to become president of the United States, saved his nation from its worst financial depression, and led his country victoriously through its most far-flung war. His name was Franklin Delano Roosevelt.

Two examples of self-esteem: one of low self-esteem, one of high self-esteem.

Everything you do is determined by your value judgment of yourself.

Commitment. "The quality of a person's life is determined by his commitment to excellence." (Vince Lombardi)

People with high self-esteem can and do make a commitment to a cause that's equal to or greater than themselves. Make your motto "The greatest use of life is to so live your life that the use of your life outlives your life."

People with low self-esteem cannot make a commitment to anything. They are filled with fear, doubt, and anxiety.

Relationships. We must love people and use things, not love things and use people.

All child abusers were themselves abused as children.

One hundred percent of hard-core drug abusers have low self-esteem.

"It's no exaggeration to say that a strong, positive self-image is the best possible preparation for success in life."

Dr. Joyce Brothers

The fatal attraction syndrome (developed in detail in a later chapter) is a prime example of low self-esteem. When this person fails to receive the high emotions he expected in passionate love, he starts to control and manipulate his/her partner because he fears that person will leave. When that person leaves, the victim fears the loss of not only the promised savior, but also fears a loss of himself. That's when violent action results.

One summer at church youth camp, we invited several teens from a children's home to be our guests. Gordon Minyard, sixteen years old, was two years behind in school and so filled with low self-esteem he kept his head buried between his shoulders.

My wife and I invited Gordon to move into our home as a foster child. I will never forget the day I took him to the store and helped him choose his first suit, overcoat, and dress shoes. He was thrilled. We invested several hours each night guiding him in his studies. He went out for the junior high football team and quickly became a star. Each day he raised his head a bit more until within three months he stood proud and erect. His grades were *A*'s and *B*'s. He had his first case of "puppy love." In fact, the girls called him.

What happened? Gordon needed and received a home with role models that cared for him, showed him how to achieve, and made him responsible for his actions. In the classroom, on the football field, and in social relationships, he developed high self-esteem.

Emotional Conduct of Those with Low Self-Esteem	**vs.**	**Emotional Conduct of Those with High Self-Esteem**
1. Critical of others		1. Accepts others as they are
2. Pessimistic		2. Optimistic

Be kind, compassionate, and gentle with yourself.

3. Complains about circumstances	3. Looks at circumstances with acceptance
4. Short temper	4. Seldom loses temper; slow to anger
5. Never enough money, time, etc.	5. Plans life positively around money and time
6. Rejects help from others	6. Does not ask for help, but welcomes it
7. Expects perfection in self and others	7. Expects things to go well without demands
8. Carries heavy guilt	8. Loads no guilt on self or others
9. Unloads guilt on others as control	9. Never uses guilt as control
10. Tries to manipulate others	10. Never manipulates; does persuade
11. Usually overly dependent on God	11. Believes God expects us to act responsibly
12. Has rigid rules of conduct	12. Rules of conduct are flexible within reason
13. May be devoid of character	13. Has developed reasonable character guidelines
14. Easily addicted to alcohol, drugs, job, love, or religion	14. Has control over impulses; has own inner highs that are self-generated

A Self-Esteem Evaluation Exercise

(Pick those that best apply to you.)

CONDUCT

1. My conduct is usually beyond reproach.
2. When I get in trouble with others, it's usually not my fault.

---

*If you don't prize yourself, who will? If you don't think
well of yourself, why would anyone else?*

3. I usually can influence others to do that which benefits both of us.
4. I cause trouble with my family members.
5. I am good at the things I do at work, home, etc.
6. I never measure up to what I really want to be or do.
7. I treat other people in a way so that they feel important and of value.
8. My family and some of my friends are disappointed in me.
9. I am basically a good person.
10. I can really be mean to other people.

MENTAL ACHIEVEMENTS

1. I am smart.
2. When I reach my goals, I will be known as an important person.
3. I am well-behaved in all the things I do.
4. I am an important and valued member of my family.
5. Other people at work, school, or home think I am smart and interesting.
6. I have trouble remembering things.
7. I have never used but a small fraction of my mental capabilities.
8. I am dumb about things other than the very small world I live in daily.
9. I would fear having to converse with someone with a good education.
10. I really am not very smart.

PHYSICAL APPEARANCE

1. My looks never please me.
2. I am strong.
3. I can never get my hair the way I want it.
4. I really am good-looking.

Concentrate totally on what you want to accomplish.
In time, it will be yours.

5. Nothing in my wardrobe suits me.
6. I am popular with most everybody I meet.
7. I do not feel like my figure is as acceptable as I want it to be.
8. I do have beautiful eyes.
9. No one ever compliments me about my looks.
10. I am improving in strength and looks.

FEARS

1. I am often sad and unhappy.
2. My looks bother me.
3. I really worry a lot.
4. I am often afraid.
5. Little things worry me.
6. I face my problems and overcome them.
7. I have learned that the things you worry about never happen anyway. So I don't worry.
8. Fear is a coward. When you face it with facts and action, fear flees.
9. I have learned that I can be happy by expecting to feel happy.
10. I put joy and happiness in my life by doing the things that make me feel happy.

GETTING ALONG WITH OTHER PEOPLE

1. I feel other people are making fun of me behind my back.
2. It's hard for me to make new friends.
3. I am quite popular, because I care about people.
4. If you feel good about yourself, you will treat other people the same way.
5. I feel left out of things.
6. People often pick on me.
7. I have many friends and enjoy their companionship.

"When you have a lemon, make a lemonade."
Julius Rosenwald

8. My fellow workers or classmates include me in their conversation and activities.
9. I don't know how to meet new people and it's not pleasant.
10. I am one of the most accepted and popular people I know.

HAPPINESS

1. I am a happy person.
2. I live a cheerful life.
3. I wish things were different for me.
4. Most other people I know are unhappy also.
5. I really like the life I live.
6. My family life is the greatest.
7. I am unhappy most of the time.
8. Life really is the pits.
9. I am easy to get along with.
10. Most days I'm sorry I got up.

Answers to Self-Esteem Evaluation Exercise

Positive answers receive a +1; negative answers receive a −1.

CONDUCT: 1, 3, 5, 7, and 9 are positive statements; 2, 4, 6, 8, and 10 are negative statements.

MENTAL ACHIEVEMENTS: 1, 2, 3, 4, and 5 are positive; 6, 7, 8, 9, and 10 are negative.

PHYSICAL ACHIEVEMENTS: 2, 4, 6, 8, and 10 are positive; 1, 3, 5, 7, and 9 are negative.

FEARS: 6, 7, 8, 9, and 10 are positive; 1, 2, 3, 4, and 5 are negative.

GETTING ALONG WITH PEOPLE: 3, 4, 7, 8, and 10 are positive; 1, 2, 5, 6, and 9 are negative.

The road to success is always under construction.

HAPPINESS: 1, 2, 5, 6, and 9 are positive; 3, 4, 7, 8, and 10 are negative.

Scoring for Self-Esteem Exercise

30—50 +'s	super, confident, high self-esteem
10—29 —'s	well-defined high self-esteem
1—9 +'s	a shade more high self-esteem than low self-esteem
1—9 —'s	low self-esteem greater than high self-esteem
10—29 —'s	you really don't like yourself; work to change this attitude
30—50 —'s	you have a serious condition of low self-esteem; see a counselor for growth

Some years ago, a twenty-three-year-old pianist in a dance band in Los Angeles was on his way home from a gig at 2:30 A.M. On the freeway, he noticed a black lady standing beside her Mercedes frantically waving. He pulled over and she said, "My husband is dying of cancer in St. John's Hospital in Santa Monica. He has been in a coma and I was sent home at midnight for a bit of rest. I just received word he is alert and is calling for me. My car broke down. Will you take me to the hospital?"

He agreed and went some six miles out of his way. On the way over, she found out he wanted to become a concert pianist, but didn't have a piano at home to practice. She got his address.

Upon arriving at the hospital she offered him one hundred dollars for his trouble, but he wouldn't take it. She thanked him with deep appreciation.

Ten days later, they delivered to his apartment a $10,000 baby grand piano with this message: "You gave my husband and I twenty minutes together before he died of lung cancer. He also was a musician. We both wanted you to have this

There is nothing I cannot do if I want it badly enough.

piano in appreciation of those twenty minutes, and in encouragement of your music career." Mrs. Nat "King" (Maria) Cole.

He wouldn't have gone out of his way to take her to the hospital and she and her husband wouldn't have given him the piano if they didn't have high self-esteem.

The following statements will go a long way toward building your high self-esteem. Quote and live by one each day. The life you save will be your own.

Positive Self-Action Statements to Enhance My Self-Esteem

1. I am my final authority for everything I do.
2. I accept full responsibility for all my actions.
3. I allow myself the freedom to make mistakes.
4. I make my own decisions and willingly accept the consequences.
5. I think for myself and speak and act with deliberation.
6. I stand up for my own opinions and convictions.
7. I do not vacillate—I make the best choice I can at the time.
8. I do not accept condemnation, "put-downs," or insults.
9. I do not condemn or belittle myself for my mistakes and shortcomings.
10. I do not blame others for my problems, mistakes, defeats, or handicaps.
11. I do not lean on others for unjustified financial or moral support.
12. I take deep satisfaction in doing my work conscientiously and well.
13. I face reality and resist nothing I cannot change.
14. I refuse to accept any condemnation, blame, shame, or guilt.

Purpose is the engine that drives your life.

15. I refrain from no endeavor out of fear of unsatisfactory results.
16. I do not procrastinate; I do first things first.
17. I give precedence to my own needs and desires as I see fit.
18. I accept every problem and goal as a challenge to my awareness.
19. I purge myself of any blame, shame, guilt, or remorse.
20. I do not depend on others for confirmation or approval.
21. I do not accept advice against my better judgment.
22. I am patient, kind, and gentle with myself.
23. I discipline myself in line with my life objectives.
24. I do nothing to excess—I avoid self-indulgence.
25. I fulfill all commitments, both to myself and others.
26. I follow all undertakings through to a logical conclusion.
27. I follow all undertakings through to emotional satisfaction.
28. I take the initiative in personal contacts and relationships.
29. I freely express any emotion I see fit.
30. I readily admit my mistakes and shortcomings.
31. I walk erect and look everyone in the eye with a friendly gaze.
32. I do not deny my needs, feelings, or opinions to please others.
33. I am warm and friendly toward all I contact.
34. I recognize everyone as innately "good."
35. I feel warm and loving toward myself.
36. I am authentic, true to my own needs, values, and convictions.
37. I defer to no one on account of his wealth, power, or prestige.

"Be yourself. Who else is better qualified?"
Frank S. Giblin II

38. I count my blessings and rejoice in my growing awareness.

Conclusion

Love yourself. This may be a lifelong journey. If you didn't receive permission from your parents to love yourself, then give yourself permission to do so. Nineteen times in the Bible we are commanded to love ourselves. The apostle Paul writes: "So ought men to love their wives as their own bodies. He that loveth his wife loveth himself." (Eph. 5:28) After declaring that a man should love the Lord God with his whole heart, soul, mind, and strength, Jesus says, referring to the second of the two greatest commandments: "And the second is like, namely this, 'Thou shalt love thy neighbour as thyself.' There is none other greater commandment greater than these." (Mark 12:31) You now have biblical permission to love yourself. Do it.

Free your emotions. Experience joy, peace, happiness, elation, love, etc. Learn to enjoy these positive emotions. We learn by doing.

Give love to everyone else. Look for the good in everyone you meet; ignore those things you may not admire. Do something kind, positive, and gracious to others. Train yourself to always say "thank you" for every service rendered, even if it's to the person who holds the door for you at the mall. Write letters of appreciation. Give praise for good work done to those who work with you and especially for those who report to you. You'll be thrilled at the love that is returned.

"Once your mind is stretched to a new idea it will never again return to its original size."

Oliver Wendell Holmes

CHAPTER 2

How We Got This Way

Psychologist Carl Rogers said, "God gave children to parents expecting them to be raised as princes and princesses, but parents have turned many of them into frogs."

Eleanor Roosevelt said, "I craved attention all through my childhood, because I was made to feel so conscious of the fact that nothing about me would ever attract attention or bring me admiration. I was told that I would never have the beaux that the rest of the girls in the family had had because I was a ugly duckling. . . . I was ashamed because I had to wear made-over dresses from clothes that my aunts had worn . . . ashamed because I couldn't dance and skate perfectly as others did . . . ashamed because I was different from other girls, ashamed because I was a wallflower. I still remember how thankful I was because a certain boy once asked for a dance at one of those Christmas parties. His name was Franklin D. Roosevelt.

"For over 20 years, I was devastated by self-consciousness and fear. My mother and grandmother and my aunts had been famous beauties in New York society, and I was ashamed to be the first girl in our family who was not a belle. My mother would sometimes say to visitors, 'Eleanor is such a funny child: so old-fashioned that we call her "granny."'

"The big thing that eventually gave me courage was helping people who were worse off than myself. For example, in

1910, my husband was a member of the New York State Senate, and he and 18 other assemblymen were waging a war against Tammany Hall. These assemblymen spent much of their time holding conferences in our home in Albany both day and night. So I visited the wives of these men. I was shocked to find that many of them were spending their days and nights in lonely hotel rooms. They knew no one in Albany except their husbands. . . . I found that by trying to cheer them up and by trying to give them courage, I developed my own courage and self-confidence.

"Fear is the most devastating emotion on earth. I fought it till I won."

The cause of so much low self-esteem in our country is based on three wrong principles governing so many children and teens—intelligence, beauty, and money.

Intelligence. Teachers and parents favor the smartest students. All the others feel like failures. People have different abilities. All should be judged by their application and effort. The *C* student who works just as hard as the *A* student should be given an *A*. The so-called curve grading system is wrong. That teacher has predetermined that a certain number will fail. Students having a more difficult time should be tutored, challenging the teacher to exert more effort in helping them master the course. Grades should be based on the ability to master the course, discipline applied in study habits and effort, and the development of a high level of self-esteem that will enable the student to go on to further achievement.

The problem of failing a student is that the *F* may destroy that student's self-esteem and he may not try again.

Never tell a student he is stupid or dumb. Instead, challenge him to do his best.

When faced with a mountain, we will climb over, we will
fly over, we will find a pass through, we will tunnel through,
or we will dig deep and strike gold or diamonds.

Stanley Coopersmith, professor at the University of California-Davis, in his exhaustive study of self-esteem found:

Students with low self-esteem graded 101.53 on the IQ test.

Students with high self-esteem graded 121.18 on the IQ test.

That is a twenty-point difference, resulting from how they felt about themselves.

Beauty. Everyone but the most beautiful girl and the most handsome guy is considered to be ugly. Beauty should be measured from within, not judged by external features.

Ugly means *frightful, offensive to the sight.* You can go for months and never see a truly ugly person. Yet, many children and teens call themselves ugly. Never call another person ugly. We all have differing looks. Never contrast one child with another. Pointing out the different distinctive features means all have beauty and value.

Money. In our society, the kids with the most money are considered superior. This is a false standard. Money is simply one standard of measuring values, and children and teens from homes with money did nothing to earn it. They simply happened to be born into these homes. We must do everything possible to change this social enigma.

Causes of Low Self-Esteem

1. Negative body image. Feeling inferior in contrast with someone else.
2. Criticism tapes. A pattern of acceptance from parents and others that makes the child feel unworthy because of criticism.
3. Critical blow-ups. Negative self-criticism the child gives him or herself.

It's not the amount of time you devote, but what you devote to the time that counts.

4. Chronic comparisons to others. Make each child know he is valued.
5. Demands of perfection. No one is perfect. Perfectionists are driven by feelings of insecurity, so they try to compensate by being perfect.
6. Sense of hopelessness. Negative input from others has destroyed hope.

Typical Negative Statements

I can't remember names.
It's just no use.
Nothing ever goes right for me.
I'm so clumsy.
I'm just not creative.
I can't seem to get organized.
I can never afford the things I want.
No matter what I do, I can't seem to lose weight.
I just don't have the patience for that.
It's another blue Monday.
I get sick just thinking about it.
I'm just no good.
I never know what to say.
I'd like to stop smoking, but I can't seem to quit.
I don't have the energy I used to have.
I never have any money left at the end of the month.
I'll never win anything.
My desk is always a mess.
I feel like I'm over the hill.
Nobody likes me.
It seems like I'm always broke.
Nobody wants to pay me what I'm worth.
I'm just no good at math.
I get so depressed.

*"The secret of success in life is for a man to be ready
for his opportunity when it comes."*
Prime Minister Benjamin Disraeli

Nothing seems to go right for me.
That's impossible.
I always freeze up in front of a group.
I just can't get with it today.
I just can't take it anymore.
I get a cold this time every year.
I'm really at the end of my rope.
I just can't handle this.
I've always been bad with words.
If only I were taller.
If only I had more time.
It's going to be another one of those days.
I just know it won't work.
That's just my luck.
I don't have any talent.
Everything I eat goes right to my waist.
Today just isn't my day.
I already know I won't like it.
I never have enough time.
That really makes me mad.
When will I ever learn.
Sometimes I just hate myself.
I'm too shy.
With my luck, I don't have a chance.
Things just aren't working out right for me.
I'm really out of shape.
Why should I try? It's not going to work.
I've never been any good at that.
The only kind of luck I have is bad luck.
Someone always beats me to it.
I never get a break.
Everything I touch turns to -----
Sometimes I wish I'd never been born.
I lose weight, but then I gain it back again.

---

*The more you borrow from your bank account of positive
thoughts, the more abundantly it grows.*

I just can't seem to get anything done.
I'm just not a salesman.
There's just no way.
I'm nothing without my coffee in the morning.
I'll never get it right.
I hate my job.
I'm just not cut out for that.
You can't trust anyone anymore.
I never seem to get any place on time.
If only I were smarter.
If only I had more money.
If only . . . on and on. . . .

Habits You May Want to Change

Putting things off
Working too hard or not working hard enough
Ignoring problems
Forgetting names or other important things
Making excuses
Overindulging—eating or drinking too much
Saying "yes" when you want to say "no"
Not listening
Interrupting other people when they're talking
Not telling the truth
Being a gossip
Letting your emotions control you
Giving advice that isn't asked for
Talking too much
Not taking care of details
Smoking
Arguing
Oversleeping
Being a complainer
Losing things

---

*What makes a man great is his ability to decide what
is important and to focus attention on it until it is done.*

Being sarcastic
Never being on time
Blaming others
Being disorganized
Worrying
Not setting priorities
Wasting time
Spending more money than you earn
Being overly critical of others
Starting something but not finishing it

Self-esteem has two parts: 1) a sense of personal ability, and 2) knowledge of personal value. High self-esteem is self-respect, self-confidence, self-value, self-acceptance, self-love, and self-celebration. High self-esteem assures us of confidence in coping, in facing life, in the ability to meet life's challenges and opportunities, and to feel that life works. Low self-esteem expresses a feeling that I can't cope, I can't face life's problems, and that I am not fit to function as a person. High self-esteem means living in the now. Low self-esteem means living in the pain.

Stanley Coopersmith's extensive survey on self-esteem gives us the following:

When the father had regular work and enjoyed his work—97% of his children had high self-esteem.

When the father was out of work often and away from home often—18% of his children had high self-esteem.

When the mother had regular work and enjoyed her work—66% of her children had high self-esteem.

When the mother had high self-esteem—66% of her children had high self-esteem.

When the mother showed emotional stability—85% of her children had high self-esteem.

---

*The important thing in life is to have a great aim and
to possess the aptitude and perseverance to attain it.*

When the mother was pleased with her husband's role as a parent—94% of the children had high self-esteem.

When there was no conflict between the parents—82% of the children had high self-esteem.

When the children made A's and B's—58% had high self-esteem.

When the mother created happiness in the home—91% of the children had high self-esteem.

When the children's behavior was nondestructive—88% had high self-esteem.

When the children had a lot of illness and accidents—64% had high self-esteem.

When the parents spent a lot of time with children—82% of the children had high self-esteem.

When the mother showed a lot of affection—79% of the children had high self-esteem.

When the mother and the children had good rapport—88% of the children had high self-esteem.

When the children were held to high standards—80% had high self-esteem.

When the children had constancy of rules—88% had high self-esteem.

When the children had firm and fair parental decisions—85% had high self-esteem.

When the parents dreamed of their children's achievements—88% of the children had high self-esteem.

In 1958, I had an hour-long appointment with former president Harry S. Truman, in his library in Independence, Missouri. I asked him, "Mr. President, what can parents do to raise achieving children?" He pointed to the pictures of his two grandfathers on the wall behind his desk and said, "Parents should take their children to Sunday school and church, instill within them the discipline of hard work, loyalty to family, God, and country, and set a great example."

If you have a dream, you have everything. If you have everything and no dream, then everything means nothing.

When Mrs. Truman came into his study, he introduced her and told me, "In 1952, many of my party wanted me to run again, and I would have won. But Beth said to me, 'Harry, I'm tired. Let's go home.' And we did. I owed that to her." Mrs. Truman had never liked politics but tolerated the time in Washington for Harry's sake. When she expressed her desire to go home, Truman knew it was time to honor her request.

Sources of High Self-Esteem

Every child needs
1. Parental approval
   A. For his/her own sense of personhood
   B. For his/her sense of proven ability
   C. For his/her sense of individuality
   D. To set realistic achievement goals
   E. To provide a framework of meaningful values
2. Other good examples and adult role models
3. Sibling and peer approval
4. Educational achievements
5. Skills, mastery in sports, music, hobbies, etc.
6. To learn to feed self good strokes
7. To receive God's love and acceptance
8. Affirming romantic experiences
9. Career expertise and enjoyment
10. Root-value transfer

Positive Mind Power

The only thing we control in this world is our own minds. Practice these mind power statements daily:

I believe it in my mind; I live it in my conduct; I celebrate it with great feelings. I am a unique, never-to-be-repeated miracle of God. I rejoice in the joy of God's love. I know and receive the love of my parents and family. I love myself as a

---

If you meet someone who has no smile, give him one of yours.

conduct of life. I meet my own needs, because I have a personal emotional maintenance program. I always choose to do the things that are important to me. I choose not to argue. I choose not to lose my temper. I choose to love my job. I choose to get up and go to work each day. I choose my reaction to other people.

I have a good mind and I cultivate its growth. I have a healthy body and I treat it right. I love my family and friends and I put energy, loyalty, and effort into these relationships. I have a good memory and can bring forth everything I need from my mind-computer storage bank.

I love people and am a good listener. I give attention to other people and learn from everyone I meet. I know I am becoming what the people I meet and the books/tapes I experience are. I have the courage to believe and to express my beliefs. I have the wisdom to listen and seek to learn from all the people who come into my life.

I take responsibility for my life, my career, and my relationships. I am good at my career and am constantly growing on my job. I give more than I am paid for on my job as a commitment to excellence. I love life and give my best in everything I do. I set goals for every area of my life and work toward their achievement. I invest time with my family as a vital function of life. I enjoy sharing my values, my time, and my efforts in building better family relationships.

I do not worry; I choose to program a positive course of action instead. I choose to control my thinking and my emotions, so I choose not to worry. I choose to think only those thoughts that please me, so I control my thoughts. My feelings are positive, warm, and exciting because my thoughts are clear, positive, and enlightening. I live a calm, controlled, and serene life. I choose to relax and enjoy life. I choose to pace my schedule so as to invest time in quiet solitude. I choose to enjoy great mood music to enhance my

---

You won't get what you want out of life. You get what you expect.

serenity and peace. I choose to avoid all brassy, conflicting, and chaotic sounds.

My thoughts create wholeness within me. They contribute to my peace, because I control what I think. I choose for my mind to only dwell on harmony, balance, peace, and joy. I look for the simple solution in each situation. I am dedicated to a life of unity, wholeness, harmony, peace, and joyful serenity. I am resolved to find the good in any problem.

I choose to help build a world of peace, unity, optimism, and self-celebration. I choose to do those things that are in my best interest. I determine that all my actions will benefit me and others equally. I will not violate, take advantage, or hurt any other person. I regard the personhood of every person as a sacred trust not to be abused. I am committed to the safety of other people from the brutality of evil people.

I look for and expect the best from my every activity. I look for the best and encourage the best in other people. I will not settle for less than the best in myself and in other people. I seek to create the best in me and in others. I attract the best in others because I live for the best for myself. I draw other people to myself by the power of my love and acceptance of them.

I focus the attention of my mind on those things I can change. I leave alone those things I can't change, and I seek wisdom to know the difference. If there is something I have no control nor influence over, I choose not to fret over it. If there is something I can change to the good of all, I will set about to do it.

I keep my mind so busy thinking positive thoughts that I have no time nor place for negative thoughts. I have learned to dominate my negative thoughts by replacing them with their opposite, positive thoughts. In time, the number of my positive thoughts will be greater than the number of negative

---

"If we all did the things we are capable of doing,
we would literally astound ourselves."

Thomas A. Edison

thoughts and I then will be a positive person. I keep so busy with my positive conduct, I don't have time or energy for negative thinking. Since no thought can dwell in my mind without my consent, I choose to think only positive thoughts.

I really am very special. I like who I am and approve of myself. Every day in every way, I am getting better and better. I am growing every day, because I like myself today and will like myself even more when I celebrate my improved greatness. There is no one like me in all the world; I am special. There will never be another person just like me. I've always wanted to be someone important, and I've given myself approval to do just that. I like how I feel when I achieve my best and I want to feel great all my life. I have many beautiful qualities still within me, breaking out into fulfillment. God has given me many talents and I want to develop them all. As I grow, I am sure I will discover even more talents I have not known to date.

Because I am positive, I radiate good feelings toward everyone I come into contact with. My confidence shows itself as I glow with excitement. I am full of life and I enjoy life every day. I am glad to be alive, because life is a constant growth experience. I am intelligent and I seek the solution to any problem that comes my way. I think good thoughts, do good things, and receive good feelings. I have unlimited energy and enthusiasm to put into my life. I share my excitement for life with everyone I know. I love to be around positive people, because I draw additional strength from them. I even enjoy being around negative people, for my positive energy is shared with them and I have an unlimited source.

I am a warm, sincere, loving person, whose life is unfolding daily like a rosebud. I like to see the growth in other people I share my zest for living with. I love myself as God's intent for my happiness. I love other people as God's command for my conduct. I love life for the joys I experience daily.

---

*Just remember that what you are going to be tomorrow,
you are becoming today.*

Conclusion

Now that we know how we got this way—let's do something about it.

Make a commitment to yourself to value yourself and to celebrate yourself. Never put yourself down. Don't say critical things about yourself. You don't deserve it; it's self-destructive and will hinder you from celebrating yourself. The only way you can overcome self-critical statements is to write out the self-critical statements you have been giving yourself. Opposite each of them, write out the opposite, positive statement. Remember, the only way we overcome a negative thought is to replace it with its opposite, positive affirmation. For example, replace "You dummy, you're always making mistakes," with "That's the first mistake I've made in the last fifteen minutes. That's OK, I'm human. I'll make a conscious effort not to make that mistake again. I'm learning."

Keep this list with you at all times. Each time you catch yourself putting yourself down, quote the opposite, positive affirmation. It will take time, but you're on your way.

Choose from a program of action that will dethrone the critic in your life. Here are some statements that dethrone the critic:

1. You're kicking me right now to force me to live by the rules I grew up with.
2. You're comparing me to everyone so that once in a while I'll find someone lower on the totem pole than me.
3. You're slapping me around like my parents used to do, and I believe you because I believed them.
4. You're beating me so that I'll achieve more and more and maybe feel better about myself.
5. You're insisting that I be perfect, because if I did everything exactly right, I might finally feel OK about myself.

Every man is the maker of his own fortune.

6. You're saying I can't do it so that I won't bother trying and won't have to worry about screwing up.
7. You're telling me they won't like me so that I won't be so hurt if I'm rejected.
8. You're saying she's disgusted by me so that no matter what the truth is, I'll be prepared for the worst.
9. You're telling me to be perfect so that I'll naively think that maybe I could be perfect and for a few minutes feel better about myself.
10. You're kicking me around so that I can atone for divorcing -----.

You are seeking a life of fulfillment. The inner peace, genuine self-esteem, unlimited achievement, and great human relations all can be yours. That's what we all want. Now take it.

"Problems are only opportunities in work clothes."
Henry J. Kaiser

CHAPTER 3

Giving Yourself Permission to Be Whole

Why You Deserve High Self-Esteem

1. You are a miracle of God. He didn't intend for you to be a fear-filled neurotic, compromising person. In the Bible, the apostle Timothy says in his second epistle, "For God hath not given us the spirit of fear; but of power, and of love, and of a sound mind." (2 Tim. 1:7)
2. You are of value because you exist.
3. You have abilities—many of them untapped—lying dormant, but nevertheless available.
4. With every achievement, you prove your abilities. Make an inventory of all your accomplishments and delight in them.
5. Your only limitations are in your own mind. Set your goals, work your plan, make your commitment, and you will prove your worth.

Your Personal Bill of Rights

1. You have the right to be treated with respect.
2. You have the right not to take responsibility for anyone else's problems or bad behavior.
3. You have the right to get angry.
4. You have the right to say no.
5. You have the right to make mistakes.

6. You have the right to have your own feelings, opinions, and convictions.
7. You have the right to change your mind or to decide on a different course of action.
8. You have the right to negotiate for change.
9. You have the right to ask for emotional support or help.
10. You have the right to protest unfair treatment or criticism.

David Quam was born on a farm in North Dakota. A railroad line ran between his father's farm and adjoining farms. Many afternoons when David was either eight or ten years old, he led other farm boys to play a dangerous game. They would run in front of the five o'clock train. The boy who ran closest to the train was considered the hero and the boy who ran the farthest from the train was considered the coward. Usually, David won, but one afternoon he fell in front of the train and his right arm was severed at the shoulder.

David's parents never let him feel he was disabled. He could tie his shoestrings, milk a cow, saddle his horse, and do anything anyone else could do. In high school, he was all-state guard on the state championship football team. He was all-state forward on his basketball team. He played outfield on the baseball team—à la Pete Gray. Pete Gray played outfield for two years, 1944-1946, for the St. Louis Browns and had a batting average of .229. Pete had a stub of an arm. He would catch the ball in his glove, put the glove in the stub, and pull the ball out and throw in one motion.

David would catch the ball in the webbing, flip the glove, pull the ball out, and throw in one motion.

After high school, David moved to Minneapolis and started in the insurance business. He stayed at the YMCA. One night, about eleven o'clock, he was batting the ball off

---

Take a hard look at what you truly expect to get out of life, because that's what you'll get.

the walls in the handball court. The athletic director came by and said to David, "You can't play this game with one arm."

David went up to his room and cried himself to sleep. Were his feelings hurt? No, he was angry that someone told him he couldn't play handball.

Within two years David was Y champion. He moved a few blocks down the street and joined the Minneapolis Athletic Club, tougher competition. Within two years he was city champion and went on to become national champion and internationally rated. He was one of the first twelve inductees in the Handball Hall of Fame.

In 1945 Pres. Harry S. Truman called David to Washington and asked him to be a $1-a-year man and go into the veterans' hospitals and tell the guys who had lost arms and/or legs about his story.

David would take his two huge scrapbooks into a room and say, "I'm David Quam. When I was ten, I lost an arm I didn't need anyway, for I can do with one arm what anyone else can do with two." After questioning him, the veterans would say, "Get me up out of this bed and down to therapy."

For two years, he travelled all over the country to tell his story. He then returned to Minneapolis. My friend, Boo Buie, had recently returned to the city from Hawaii. He challenged David to a handball game. At the University of Minnesota, he had been National AAU Handball Champion. Now, his game was the best it had ever been.

David beat Boo 21—7. Over a cup of coffee afterward, Boo said, "David, I thought I could give you a good game. You swamped me." David replied, "Well, I had an advantage over you." Boo responded, "Advantage! You are 69 years of age, with one arm. I'm 38, at the best of my game, with two arms. What's the advantage?"

"It is not how much we have, but how much we enjoy that makes happiness."

Charles H. Spurgeon

With a bit of a grin, David said, "When the ball came to you, you had to decide which hand to use. I didn't have to decide." David Quam was a master of high self-esteem.

My friend, Bill Glass, played twelve of his thirteen years in the National Football League with the Cleveland Browns, nine of those years with the great Jim Brown, possibly the greatest running back in the history of the game.

Bill told me, "Seventy-two hours before every game, Jim shut out everybody and everything as he ran through his mind all the plays in the playbook, programming his mind for the players on the opposing team. Each of the 250 plays Jim played in his subconscious mind eleven times, each time for each of the opposing players. On an off-tackle slant, he anticipated how the outside linebacker would react and Jim programmed how he would respond. He did this for each player. He had a fraction-of-a-second advantage over his opponent. Rather than react, he anticipated. His mental power was as great or greater than his immense physical abilities."

Jim Brown's supreme self-confidence mentally and physically made him one of the greatest athletes of all time.

How to Improve Your Self-Esteem

1. Change is possible. Take control, decide, and act now.
2. Change takes time. Plan your work and work your plan.
3. Firmly give up low self-esteem. You can choose high self-esteem.
4. Take negative energy generated by low self-esteem and apply it with intensity to building high self-esteem.
5. You are not alone. Get involved in a caring network and help others build their high self-esteem.
6. Have compassion on yourself. You are loved, we are loved, they are loved.

Attitudes are habits of thinking. Remember:
First you form your habits, then they form you.

7. Make a commitment. Do everything you do with the best of your ability.

Self-Facing	vs.	**Self-Blaming**

1. Admits undeveloped areas
2. Admits mistakes
3. Resolves to overcome
4. Realizes need of friendships
5. Faces unkind actions with others
6. Commitment to achieve at work
7. Seeks goals to master time
8. Has long-range plans for success
9. Is at peace within

1. Blames self for failure
2. Condemns own mistakes
3. Quits in misery
4. Rejects friendships
5. Won't face hostility
6. Goofs off at work
7. Lets others control time
8. Has no plans for the future
9. Has no peace, only blame

Keys to High Self-Esteem

1. The secret to inner peace lies in self-affirmation. A quiet celebration.
2. You can't change others, but you can change your reaction to others.
3. The path to inner peace requires awareness, courage, decision, and action.
4. Form a positive personal belief system that values and celebrates yourself.
5. In your internal cast of characters, the troublemakers will be your "not OK" and "critical parent" tapes. They are hooked into the love of power. They try to manipulate, control, and win. Your nurturing adult and natural child

---

"The child wants simple things. It wants to be listened to.
It wants to be loved. It may not even know the words,
but it wants its rights protected and its self-respect
unviolated. It needs you to be there."

Ron Kuptz

are concerned with the power of love. They are the ones that work for the best interest of you and others.

6. To increase your self-worth, you do not need to change yourself. You need to change your "self-talk" and your negative beliefs about yourself. You can choose to become your own nurturing parent.

7. Change the words "should," "ought," "must," and "have to," to those of the nurturing parent—"wish," "prefer," "want," "choose," "feel," and "desire."

8. You can choose not to react to the judgments of others. You do this by giving space to blame, but refusing to take their bait.

9. Reasonable expectations are nurturing. Unreasonable ones cause pain.

10. When you are upset, check what expectations have gone unmet.

11. Your inner criticizer will ask for perfection in feelings, thoughts, and deeds. Give yourself permission to be less than perfect. Do not cling to past mistakes, but rather release them.

12. Give up the belief that things should always go as you want them to; that others should match your feelings, attitudes, and values; that life and others will always be fair; that others should know how you feel or what you want without being told.

13. Take time for meaningful leisure. Put balance into your life by doing those things that give you release from the pressures of daily work.

14. Improve your family, business, and friend relationships. We draw strength from the positive people around us. Release negative relationships that are destructive to your own feelings.

15. Write out goals for your life: career, family, personal,

Time is your most valuable personal resource.
Use it wisely because it can't be replaced.

and professional goals. If you fail to plan, you are planning to fail.
16. With subliminal videocassettes and audiotapes, condition yourself to positive self-talk. You alone are responsible for your feelings. Impact yourself with affirmations that give you the feelings and assurances of success.

Positive Statements

It takes both rain and sunshine to make a rainbow. A positive person understands that a little disappointment doesn't mean that it won't be a great day. Turn the "rain" into something beautiful. A positive person knows that if there weren't a challenge — there wouldn't be a champion.

If you feel down, keep a smile on your face and lift someone else's spirit. When they feel better, it reflects back to you. British Prime Minister Benjamin Disraeli said, "The secret of success is constancy of purpose." Everyone needs a direction in life, some goal he or she is pursuing. Set some good goals, make some plans, and then pursue them with all your might.

Ralph Waldo Emerson said, "Though we travel the world over to find the beautiful, we must carry it with us or we find it not." Real beauty lies within everyone.

Learn from each mistake. Each time you get a wrong answer, you know one answer that can be eliminated. Remember Edison and the light bulb.

A positive person is a good listener. Listening is a very important part of communication. Be willing to lend a listening ear to others, and in return, they lend a listening ear to you.

A positive person realizes that education alone does not guarantee success: only the application of education can do that.

"There is no security on earth. There is only opportunity."
Gen. Douglas MacArthur

Celebrate the uniqueness of yourself. Remember you are unique—there is no one else in the world like you, and there never will be another exactly like you. Be proud of yourself and your unique personality.

There is a saying, "It is better to light one candle than to curse the darkness." A positive person doesn't complain about unfavorable conditions or circumstances, but rather attempts to improve those conditions through positive actions.

Do not lower your goals to the level of your present abilities, but rather raise your abilities to the height of your goals.

If you make one person smile each day for forty years, you will have made 14,610 people happy.

"The best way to know life is to love many things." (Vincent Van Gogh)

Teachers devote their lives to helping young people acquire the knowledge and skills necessary to be successful in life. Teachers are very special people. Give your teachers a hug or a big "thank you" today.

If you are not perfect and you admit it, that's a perfect thing to say.

Remember that you are swapping a day of your life for what you do today. A day that cannot be replaced. Make it a good swap by having a positive and productive day.

Positive people say, "I can, I will, I'll try." Set a goal and then set out to accomplish it. And positive people make an effort to use positive words and phraseology in their daily language. Talk like a positive person and you will become a positive person. If you behave well and do not break rules, then other people will follow suit. Good behavior is a characteristic of a positive person.

"This is the day which the Lord hath made.
We will rejoice and be glad in it."

Ps. 118:24

"Habit is either the best of servants or the worst of masters," states Nathaniel Emmons. Develop positive, good habits and they will carry you far.

Some people worry so much about rainy days that they fail to enjoy the sunshine of today. Today is a special day—enjoy it.

"Let your hopes, not your hurts, set your goals." (Anonymous)

Smile today for someone in need—for tomorrow you may be the one in need.

Don't skip the first day of the rest of your life. Do your best.

A positive person knows that a healthy mind and body are priceless. Regular exercise and proper nutrition are the keys to keeping fit. Drugs will destroy your mind and body—the only mind and body you have. Be smart and say, "Nope to Dope."

Every action has a reaction. We cannot always control the actions in our lives; but we can control our reactions. Plan to react to all situations with a positive, optimistic attitude.

A positive person realizes that opportunities are available today, and every day. Have the courage and the confidence to seize the "opportunities of the day."

George Bernard Shaw said, "People are always blaming their circumstances for what they are. I don't believe in circumstances . . . look for the circumstances you want, and if you can't find them, make them."

Looking for the bad in life is easy because it's always there. Looking for the good in life is more challenging, because sometimes you have to dig deeper—but the good is there.

Chuck Norris, the karate expert and movie star, says, "Ability is not the major prerequisite in achieving any goal—determination and persistence will over come any obstacle."

"Two men look out through the same bars.
One sees the mud, and one the stars."

Frederick Langbridger

A positive person knows that the best of intentions are no good unless they are acted upon. To think nice thoughts and good deeds is OK, but to act out these thoughts and deeds is great. Arthur Schopenhauer noted, "We seldom think of what we have, but always of what we lack." Don't overlook the abundant blessings of which we all have many.

I have learned that success is to be measured not so much by the position that one has reached in life, as by the obstacles which he has overcome while trying to succeed.

Habits can be your best friend or your worst enemy. Develop good habits: the habits of success. And remember, bad habits can be replaced, it just takes desire, time, and persistence.

Summary

Psychologist Abraham Maslow says that every human needs:

1. A feeling of protection and safety learned in childhood and felt today
2. A sense of belonging to family, God, group, and to self
3. A feeling of love, affection, and acceptance from God, family, friends, and others
4. Respect, feeling of personal value, and self-esteem

People in whom all of these needs are met are self-actualizers and enjoy peak performances.

"Ask, and it shall be given you. Seek, and ye shall find. Knock, and it shall be opened unto you."

Matt. 7:7

CHAPTER 4

Taking Charge of Your Mind

Have you noticed that at the circus you may see a huge elephant with a small rope tied to his leg and to a small stake in the ground? He could pull that stake out with minimal effort. But he doesn't.

In training the elephant, they attach one end of a chain to his foreleg and the other end to a large tree. The elephant pulls time and again, but to no avail. Finally, the elephant quits pulling, surrendering to the rope rather than experience the pain. He has been mind-conditioned to the rope.

So have many people been mind-conditioned to failure. "The only thing in this world you may totally control is your own mind."

You must relearn that the mind is unlimited. If you don't believe that, then you must learn how to take charge of your mind.

Self-esteem is the reputation we have with ourselves.

Living in the Now	vs.	Living in the Pain
1. Thinking it out completely		1. Rejecting reasonable answers
2. Alert to every situation		2. Failing to be aware
3. Respecting others' opinions		3. Not willing to talk
4. Seeking truthful answers		4. Failing to seek truth
5. Clearly looking at all viewpoints		5. Muddled thinking

6. Willing to take responsible risks	6. Making no decision
7. Being honest and open	7. Not willing to face facts
8. Independently acting on facts	8. Depending on others only
9. Accepting responsibility	9. Blaming others
10. Confronting self with facts	10. Rejecting self with blame
11. Eager to correct mistakes	11. Unwilling to see or avoid mistakes
12. Reasoning everything out	12. Acting without reason

In an earlier chapter, I told you the story of David Quam. Boo Buie later moved to San Francisco, where he is the Dale Carnegie sponsor. At a downtown civic club, Boo told the David Quam story. Afterward, a tall, middle-aged man came up to Boo and said, "I'd like to tell you my story. When I was 19, my parents sneaked me out of Germany and sent me to Rotterdam to catch a boat for America. We are Jewish. Within six months after my leaving, my parents, brother and sister, and other relatives were taken by Hitler's SS troops to concentration camps. None of them survived.

"I arrived in New York and took a train to San Francisco, where my uncle was a real-estate broker. The first day here, I went with my uncle to his office. I observed agents calling people with German and French names. When they didn't get an appointment, they threw the slips in the wastebasket.

At the end of the day, I told my uncle, 'I want to start selling real estate tomorrow.' He said, 'You can't speak a word of English. I have enrolled you in a night course to learn English. A year from now, when you have mastered the language, I will train you in real estate. Meantime, I have you a job at a German restaurant as a busboy. Let's go home.' I said, 'You go on. I'll come home later.'

"When everyone had left the office, I picked up from the

Self-love comes from God's love.

wastebaskets the names of the people with German and French names. I could talk to them, because I spoke both languages. When they could not speak either language, I hung up. I got three appointments for the next day from these names.

"Then I took the telephone directory and started calling people with German and French names. By nine o'clock, I had seven appointments for the next day. The first month I sold thirty-three houses and led the state of California in real-estate sales. Still couldn't speak a sentence in English."

Dr. John T. Gates was pastor of the Riverside Church—John D. Rockefeller's church—in New York City many years ago. Dr. Gates suffered a heart attack at age fifty-two and had to retire. Mr. Rockefeller hired Dr. Gates as chaplain for his several companies.

One day, shortly after Dr. Gates joined the companies, Mr. Rockefeller came into his office and asked, "Dr. Gates, what are your plans for retirement?" Remember, this was before the days of social security and pension plans.

Dr. Gates replied, "I have $6,000 in savings and what I will be able to save during these next 13 years."

Mr. Rockefeller asked, "How would you like for me to take your $6,000 and invest it for you?" "Please do, Mr. Rockefeller, I consider you to be the greatest financial mind in the world." "All right, Dr. Gates, and I will give you a verbal annual report as to how well your investment is doing."

Annually, Mr. Rockefeller told Dr. Gates, "Your investment is doing well." Never anything about the amount.

When Dr. Gates came to retirement, the companies gave him a retirement banquet at the Waldorf-Astoria Hotel.

"The person who says it can't be done is liable to be interrupted by someone doing it."

Anonymous

There were the usual expressions of appreciation from a number of people, the watch, and a few other gifts.

Then Mr. Rockefeller came to the podium. He expressed his deep appreciation to Dr. Gates, then pulled from his pocket an envelope and said, "Thirteen years ago, Dr. Gates entrusted his life savings to me to invest for him. Here, Dr. Gates, is the return of your investment." Nothing was said about the amount invested nor the amount earned.

After the people had left, Mrs. Gates couldn't wait to find out how much the check was for. When Dr. Gates opened the envelope, he was dumbfounded. His $6,000 investment in thirteen years had grown to more than $6,000,000.

By taking control of your mind positively, there is no limitation on what you may achieve. Dr. Denis Waitley has stated this so well in the poem, "How to Be a Total Winner," on page 199 of his 1988 book, *Seeds of Greatness: The Ten Best Kept Secrets of Total Success*, published in New York by Picket.

The Chinese bamboo is the fastest-growing plant in the world. Yet, when you plant the seed, it takes five years before the stalk breaks the ground. But watch out. It grows at a rate of thirty-six inches each day, to a total height of 100 feet in just three months.

When you have taken positive control of your mind and have adjusted your conduct activity accordingly, you will win with high self-esteem. Here are the activities necessary for your success:

Goals. Nothing becomes dynamic until it first becomes specific. You must write out your goals, change your conduct activity to reach them, and you will. Personal growth goals, family goals, spiritual goals, career goals, financial goals, etc.

You are no bigger than what it takes to upset you.

As a nineteen-year-old, this young man moved from Wisconsin to Hollywood to pursue his career in show business as a pianist. He spent his last $100 on a piano to practice. He tuned and finished it himself. He went to the five-and-ten store and bought glitter that he sewed to his only blue serge suit until he looked like a rhinestone cowboy.

He went out to the Hollywood Bowl and asked the manager if he could come out some morning when the janitors were cleaning the huge bowl and practice a concert. The manager said, "I don't mind, but you can't use our piano." The young man said, "Thanks, I'll bring my own piano."

One morning, about half past ten, the manager's secretary came into his office and said, "Boss, you've got to hear this." The manager went out to the bowl, listened ten minutes and said to his secretary, "Close the office and invite all the people to come out and hear this. It's too good to miss." He turned to the janitors and said, "Sit down and enjoy the show, we'll pay you for your time."

After another two hours of beautiful music, anecdotes, and jokes, the thirty-five employees gave the young man a standing ovation. He thanked them and said, "I wanted to get the feel of how it will be when I pack this bowl with 17,500 people at $20 a head, and I'll do it within two years." He did and went on to earn more than $75,000,000 as he became the world's best-known pianist. His name was Liberace. He set his goal, put himself in the act of doing it, and did.

Audiotapes. By continually bombarding your mind with positive learning with audiotapes, you can salvage otherwise wasted time. For example, if you drive 10,000 miles a year, you have 400 hours of learning opportunity in your auto; 20,000 miles a year, 800 hours; 30,000 miles a year, 1,200

"The right man is the one who seizes the moment."

Goethe

hours; 40,000 miles a year, 1,600 hours. Four hundred hours is equal to one year's college education. So, you can get the same as a four-year college education each year that you drive 40,000 miles and listen to audiotapes. Convert this time for your success.

Subliminal tapes. Subliminal means *under the line.* The message is recorded and then masked with music and/or ocean waves, which makes learning so much fun. The message flows past the negative thoughts in your conscious mind, directly into the creative power of your subconscious mind.

Videocassette Tapes. When asked by an American research team why World War II ended earlier than expected, General von Rundstead, Chief of the German High Command, answered, "America's use of the 35-mm motion pictures." The Americans were amazed and asked, "What do you mean?" General von Rundstead replied, "We used motion pictures to train our military and industry [demonstrating the power of propaganda]." Germany had anticipated that it would take the United States at least five years to convert to a wartime economy. But the United States was able to accomplish this feat within two years. Rundstead said, "That's how you won the war."

Invest at least thirty minutes a day watching motivational, inspirational videocassette tapes to take charge of your mind.

Concert Learning. Some twenty-two years ago, in Sofia, Bulgaria, Dr. Georgi Lozonov took sixty professional and semiprofessionals and taught them French in one day. He spoke a Bulgarian word and another person stated the French word. None of these sixty people knew any French when they started. At the end of the day, having

---

"When you are through changing, you're through."
Bruce Barton

repeated 1,000 words, three times each, the group was tested. On average, they each learned 920 French words. Using this system, an entire new language can be learned in a week.

This concept, plus subliminal tape use, is primarily how the East Germans, a country of 16,000,000, have soundly beaten us in the last several Olympiads.

Here's how it works. Play largo music, symphonic recordings at about sixty beats a minute in a stereophonic sound system, and lower the volume so that the words can be heard over the music. What it does is remove the negative thoughts and limiting conditioning and creates a mesmerizing effect for learning.

You can do the same thing in your home. Set the music and play an audiotape with the message you want to learn. The mind you save may be your own.

Behavior That Expresses Self-Esteem

1. Your face, manner, way of talking, and moving project joy in being alive and a simple delight in the fact of being.
2. You are able to speak of accomplishments or shortcomings with directness and honesty.
3. You are comfortable in giving and receiving compliments, expressions of affection, appreciation, and the like.
4. You are open to criticism and comfortable about admitting mistakes.
5. Your words and movements have a quality of ease and spontaneity.
6. There is harmony between what you say and do, how you look, how you sound, and how you move.
7. You exhibit an attitude of openness to and curiosity

"Take time to deliberate: but when the time for action comes, go for it."
Pres. Andrew Jackson

about new ideas, new experiences, and new possibilities of life.

8. You are able to see and enjoy the numerous aspects of life, in self and in others.
9. You project an attitude of flexibility in responding to situations and challenges, a spirit of inventiveness, and even playfulness.
10. You are comfortable with assertive behavior.
11. You express a quality of harmony and dignity under conditions of stress.

Physical Signs of Genuine Self-Esteem

1. If you have alert, bright, and lively eyes.
2. If you have a relaxed face with natural color and good skin vibrancy.
3. If you hold your chin naturally in alignment with your body.
4. If your jaw is relaxed.
5. If you hold your shoulders relaxed, but erect.
6. If you keep your hands relaxed, graceful, and quiet.
7. If your arms hang in a relaxed, natural way.
8. If you maintain posture that is relaxed, erect, and well-balanced.
9. If you walk purposefully (without being aggressive or overbearing).
10. If you keep your voice modulated and maintain an intensity appropriate to the situation.

If these ten signs apply to you, then you have genuine self-esteem. This above list, which has been adapted from its original form, can be found on pages 17-18 of Nathaniel Branden's *Honoring the Self: Personal Integrity and the Heroic Potentials of Human Nature*, published in Los Angeles by J. P. Tarcher in 1984.

In his famous talk, "Acres of Diamonds," Dr. Russell Con-

If you look for the positive things in life, you'll find them.

well tells of a Persian farmer, who had for his guest one night a holy man. During the evening, the holy man noticed a piece of glassy rock on the farmer's mantle. He told him about diamonds and how they were formed and of their value. The farmer determined he would search the world over for diamonds. He sold his farm, turned his family over to relatives, and set out on his worldwide search. Many years later, having exhausted his search and now out of money, he walked into the ocean and drowned himself.

Within a few days of his death, the farmer who had bought his farm unearthed on that very farm a diamond mine. The glassy rock on the mantle was from that very field. That diamond mine was Golgonda, one of the richest diamond mines in the world. The searching farmer could have met his fondest dreams in his own backyard.

Your diamond mine is between your ears. By taking charge of your mind, you can achieve your greatest dream.

Positive Statements

Positive people know they will face disappointments, and that it will depend on the attitude with which one faces a disappointment that will determine whether you overcome the disappointment or whether it overcomes you.

Alexandre Dumas said, "A person who doubts himself is like a man who would enlist in the ranks of his enemies and bear arms against himself. He makes his failure certain by himself being the first person to be convinced of it."

When a road is being built, construction crews overcome obstacles such as mountains or rivers by building bridges or tunnels. Don't let obstacles stop you—find a way to overcome them.

---

*"And in every work that he began in the service of the
house of God, and in the law, and in the commandments,
to see his God, He did it with all his heart, and prospered."*
2 Chron. 31:21

A positive person knows that you can't get anywhere today if you are dwelling on the disappointments and misfortunes of yesterday. Every day is a golden opportunity to start anew and to achieve great things.

No one ever painted a masterpiece the first time he picked up a paintbrush. But, with practice and perseverance, masterpieces have been painted. It is the same with our daily lives. If you stick with your goals, you will achieve them.

On a football field, everyone knows the team's goal—to reach the goal line. The name goal line says it all. In life, everyone needs clear goals as well. Establish goals and put them in writing.

If you really want to be positive, you can be; just think positively, no matter what everyone else around you thinks. If you are positive, it will encourage others to be so, too. Before you know it, you'll have a positive attitude around you.

Enthusiasm is like fuel that keeps the fires of ambition burning. Without enthusiasm, the fire dies out. Get excited and enthusiastic about what you are doing and you will have all the necessary energy to carry you through.

Your attitude is a determining factor in the height of your day's success. Keep your attitude up and you're sure to have an "up" day.

Positive people believe that how you feel on the inside is reflected on the outside by how you dress. So always try to look your best.

Positive people believe it is more important to know where you are going than to see how fast you can get there.

Some people may have the grades and popularity, but they are not the best unless they have a positive attitude. Those with a positive attitude are the real winners.

A positive person knows that he is rich because of who and what he is; not what he has.

"Defeat never comes to any man until he admits it."
Joseph Daniels

Positive people know that the single most important cause of a person's success or failure has to do with the question of what he believes about himself. Believe in yourself.

There is a difference between loving oneself and being in love with oneself. The first example is called a healthy self-esteem; the second example is called self-centered.

It doesn't cost anything to think positively, but the cost of thinking negatively will surely bankrupt you of success.

Instead of spending time fixing blame when something is wrong, one should spend his time trying to fix what is wrong.

A positive person doesn't waste the sunshine of today by worrying about the rainy days that may come tomorrow.

Knute Rockne said, "When the going gets tough, the tough get going." When you are faced with a problem or adversity, don't despair or give up. Instead, be resolved to give it your best effort.

Live the best way you can—positively.

Throughout our lives, we are faced with a series of great opportunities brilliantly disguised as impossible situations. Remember, nothing is impossible to one who believes (Mark 9:23).

For most people, being negative is easy. These are the people who take the easy way out. Being positive takes work, and it's a challenge. Don't be lazy—accept the challenge.

"The best and most beautiful things in the world cannot be seen or even touched. They must be felt with the heart." (Helen Keller)

The secret of success is having goals and believing that you will achieve them. Anything the mind can conceive—if you believe, you will achieve.

Lee Burgland said, "Obstacles are the things we see when we lose sight of our goals." A positive person focuses on the

---

There is no limit to what you can do if you don't care who gets the credit.

goals he wants to achieve — not the obstacles that he may encounter on the way.

A happy person is not a person who is without any problems. A happy person is one who deals with problems in a positive manner: expecting the best out of all situations.

Wake up, look in the mirror, and say, "I like me," and your day will go great.

A positive person knows that when you always speak the truth, you never have to be concerned with your memory.

Helen Keller was one who did not allow her disabilities to control her life. Instead, she concentrated on her abilities and she became one of the greatest inspirations of all time. Make the most of what you have.

Just as the old wagon trails heading west became rutted to the point that they were unusable: by traveling the same path each day of your life, you too will find yourself stuck in a "rut." Take chances, explore new opportunities, and try something new today.

Learn to build bridges instead of walls. Believe the best, ignore the rest, and you've passed the test to find life's zest.

I am a positive person, as positive as can be. You can be one, too. Just follow me.

Your attitude now will reflect upon you later in life. So, if you want to look forward to a great life, start now by having a positive attitude.

Conclusion

Your subconscious mind is a vast reservoir of all your thoughts and experiences. We are the totality of what we have been through. Blot out of your mind those unpleasant experiences with the power of forgetfulness and recall all those pleasant experiences.

Take a joy inventory. Begin at the age of your earliest remembrance and write out all the joyful experiences you can

---

"An invincible determination can accomplish almost anything."
Thomas Fuller

remember. Continue to write for each age of your life. Ponder, recall, and delight in these experiences. Go over them again and again. Bombard your consciousness with these events. You will be amazed with the beautiful feelings that will follow.

Determine that the remaining years of your life will be invested in delightful experiences of joy and happiness. You then will have a life worth living.

"I will let no man control me by making me hate him."
Booker T. Washington

CHAPTER 5

How to Raise Your Children to Have High Self-Esteem

Isn't it strange that princes and kings, and clowns that caper in sawdust rings, and common people like you and me are builders for eternity?

To each is given a bag of tools, a shapeless mass, and a book of rules; and each must make ere life is flown, a stumbling block or a stepping stone.

R. L. Sharpe

The enabling parents. To *enable* means *to give sanction to.* Many enabling parents are unwittingly aiding their children to fail and have low self-esteem.

First we must define what every child needs. Every child needs to know:

I am loved. Love is not primarily an emotion. Love is a conduct. To love is to act in a manner so that the safety, security, satisfaction, and growth of another person is assured.

Love is a decision. It is a commitment to treat another person in his/her highest and best interest.

Love is unconditional. A child is to be loved because he/she exists. A child is a gift of God and must be treated as such. If you love your child only when he/she obeys, then you have put a condition on love.

You may love a child better when his/her conduct is correct. You certainly like a child when the conduct is correct.

You tell the child of your dislikes. You love a child with no conditions.

Love is forever. There are no time restraints, no limits, and no conditions. It is consistent and constant.

Love is a gift, based on the sense of worth. Because they are, they are loved. The greatest gift you grant your child is love with no strings.

Love affirms, not possesses. Love allows and develops independence.

Love is never having to say you're sorry you abused your child.

Love is never having to say you're sorry you blamed, condemned, and criticized.

Love is never having to say you're sorry you filled your child with guilt.

Love is never having to say you're sorry for destroying your child's imagination and creativity.

Love is never having to say you're sorry for driving your child away from the safety, security, and harmony of the home.

I am capable. This includes being capable to feel, able to meet his/her own needs; capable to feel independent as a person; capable to achieve excellence in grades, work skills, and play conduct; capable of owning good feelings of self-worth, self-value, and self-celebration; capable of warmly responding to parent's affection, hugs, and kisses; capable of having confidence to face life's opportunities and responsibilities.

I am able. A child needs to be able to relate effectively with other people, both children and adults; able to maintain his own inner-directed emotional support system; able to achieve his best in school, hobbies, sports, etc.; able to enjoy the beauties of nature and God's love and forgiveness.

"Nothing in this world is so powerful as an idea whose time has come."
Victor Hugo

Enabling parents do the following:

1. Excuse their children for bad grades by blaming the schools, TV, or other reasons.
2. Allow their children to stubbornly disobey their parents, teachers, and God's guidelines of conduct.
3. Fail to instill within their child self-discipline by not organizing a fair and firm code of conduct.
4. Allow their children to fight with other children, sass adults, and prove unmanageable with no recourse of action.

Parents must take intervention action. In other words, parents need to come in or between in order to stop, settle, or modify.

When the child's conduct is contrary to the laws of God, laws of the country, rules of schools, and rules of the home, a loving parent intervenes. Children want the acceptance and approval of their parents. When they do not get that, they will stoop to destructive behavior to receive attention. Intervening parents stop, control, and redirect that behavior that is not in the child's best interest.

In 1937, Lou Gehrig, the outstanding first baseman of the New York Yankees, was asked to go to the Children's Hospital in Chicago, while there to play the White Sox, and visit a boy with polio. Tim, ten years old, had refused to try therapy to get well. Lou was his hero and Tim's parents hoped that Lou would visit Tim and urge him to try the therapy.

Tim was amazed to meet his hero. Lou told Tim, "I want you to get well. Go to therapy and learn to walk again." Tim said, "Lou, if you will knock a home run for me today, I will learn to walk again." Lou promised.

All the way to the ball park, Lou felt a deep sense of

"To become what we are capable of becoming is the only end of life."
Spinoza

obligation and even apprehension that he would be able to deliver his promise that day. Lou didn't knock a home run that day. He had two.

Two years later, when Lou Gehrig was dying with the dreaded muscular disease that to this day bears his name, on July 4, 1939, they celebrated Lou Gehrig Day at Yankee Stadium. Eighty thousand fans, the governor, the mayor, and many other celebrities paid their respects. Lou was one of America's great heroes.

Just before the mike was turned over to Lou to respond, Tim, by this time twelve years old, walked out of the dugout, dropped his crutches, and with leg braces walked to home plate to hug Lou around the waist.

That's what Lou Gehrig meant when he exclaimed those immortal words: "Today I am the luckiest man on the face of the earth."

Lou Gehrig had intervened with Tim. He claimed and received a conduct favorable for Tim from Tim.

Guidelines for Building
Your Child's Self-Esteem

1. Parents set the standards. Never put the child down. Help him to learn the desired conduct and set the right example.
2. Other siblings must not be allowed to crush the confidence of the child.
3. Discount early social blunders and don't allow them to scar.
4. Magnify values and accomplishments so that money and things will not be out of proportion.
5. Any physical defects, such as bucked teeth, must be corrected or turned into a distinctive advantage.

"Have the daring to accept yourself as a bundle of possibilities and undertake the game of making the most of it."
Henry Emerson Foodick

6. Help your child to develop social skills so embarrassment will not follow.
7. Be constantly sensitive to your child's feelings and give him unconditional love and acceptance.
8. Don't allow time pressure to snuff out the essential time needed each day to give your child undivided personal attention.
9. Don't load your child with guilt and fear.
10. Teach your children the "no knock" attitude. Never allow them to put themselves down.
11. Help your children to compensate. The strongest drive of human nature is to compensate for a feeling of inferiority. Lead them to excel within themselves, to make up by their own conduct what they may first think of as a disadvantage.
12. Be constantly in touch with your child's teacher and be a partner in his growth and achievement.
13. Develop your child's sense of independence. Encourage your child to stand on his own two feet and to effectively grow away from parental dependence. Help him to take pride in himself and his achievements.

Typical Sources of Low Self-Esteem

Most low self-esteem stems from unfortunate childhood experiences. The greatest gift we, as parents, can give our children is sound self-esteem.

1. A parent's own low self-esteem is a model for the child.
2. A child's lack of recognition and appreciation by parents and others as an intrinsically valuable and important individual can mar his self-esteem. Phrases like "A child should be seen and not heard," "Mother knows best," etc., demonstrate that the child's needs,

---

*The people who succeed are those who have the
self-discipline to develop themselves.*

feelings, desires, and opinions not given due consideration.

3. If a child's parents, family, or friends make adverse comparisons with his peers or a favorite brother or sister—this, combined with child's own self-deprecating comparisons with those of his own age whom he admires for their strength and ability, their popularity, self-confidence, or achievements can overpower the child with a devastating sense of inferiority.

4. A child feels inadequate because he is not encouraged and motivated to be independent, to do what he can for himself—to take responsibility for his own needs and well-being to the greatest extent of his ability as he increases in age and experience. The child is not taught to think for himself.

5. The false concepts, values, and reactions of child's parents, teachers, and peers cause him to identify with his actions. For example, Johnny, whose mother has a severe migraine, is a "bad boy," because he slammed the door. Whereas, in reality, it was only his natural exuberance and lack of awareness that caused the act. This may load the child with self-condemnation, shame, guilt, and remorse.

6. Harsh and demanding parents set unreasonable standards, often raising them before the child has developed the ability to meet them. Parents may also subject their children to unreasonable, harsh criticism and undue and/or inconsistent punishment. Such actions cause early frustration, defeatism, and a destructive sense of inadequacy and inferiority.

7. A child being pushed beyond his capacity by the parents' vicarious need to achieve a sense of worth and importance through the child's achievements often causes

---

"To thine own self be true."

Shakespeare

a deep feeling of inadequacy and unworthiness in the child.

8. Rivalry and unsuccessful emulation of an extremely bright or gifted brother or sister, or of an exceptionally talented and prominent parent often generates a deep sense of hopelessness and inferiority.

9. A child's unflattering physical appearance and/or "odd" apparel, plus perhaps physical, mental, or emotional handicaps damage his sense of self-worth.

10. Child is raised on the basis of "reward and punishment," rather than being motivated through understanding and allowed to make his own mistakes and to accept and resolve, or suffer the consequences.

11. Adverse economic, social, cultural, or ethnic position of parents and family often invite depreciation and ridicule.

12. Overpossessiveness, overpermissiveness, and overcontrol exercised by one, or both parents, nurtures a feeling of unimportance and lack of esteem in the child.

13. A serious sense of guilt is frequently induced by one's material wealth or affluent background.

14. High values placed on money, achievement, and things rather than on the individual and his innate worth, can preclude or destroy one's self-esteem.

15. Repeated defeats and failures can destroy one's sense of self-worth and result in one or two extremes. The child may become a dropout from school or society, or he may become a compulsive overachiever in a desperate attempt to "prove himself."

16. Procrastination and lack of self-discipline, taking the path of least resistance, tend to demolish one's self-respect and sense of worth.

"Do one thing at a time, and do that thing as if your life depended upon it."

Eugene Grace

17. Lack of a sense of meaning and purpose in life, of clear goals and objectives, preclude sound self-esteem.

How to Build Great
Self-Esteem in Your Child

1. Be an example of self-value, self-love, and self-celebration.
2. Respect your child as a unique, never-to-be-repeated miracle of God.
3. Lead your child to feel loved, valued, and respected for his/her own self.
4. Make your child responsible for his/her actions and conduct.
5. Help your child to feel capable of accomplishing things on his/her own.
6. Show your child that each day is full of joys and wonderful experiences.
7. Give sincere praise and appreciation for every good experience.
8. Let your child find himself through your guidance. Don't make him a robot or rubber stamp of you.
9. Invest time and energy to help your child achieve greatness.
10. Lead your child to improve with each event, not compete with others who may be more beautiful, smarter, or wealthier. These are false standards of greatness and make one all but feel like a loser. The winner is the one who is doing his best for his own sake.
11. Be consistent in your discipline and lead your child to agree as to proper conduct.
12. Praise for good behavior and don't destroy the value of praise by taking away praise when improper conduct occurs.

"I always try to turn every disaster into an opportunity."
John D. Rockefeller

13. Teach children not to use self put-downs. Teach them how to give themselves self-support, self-value, and self-assurance.

When Don was born, the cord was wrapped twice around his neck. Forty-five minutes later, his face was still blue. The doctor hoped there would be no brain damage.

Don's three sisters progressed much faster than he did in most everything. Studying came easy for them, as well as good grades, while Don had to work so much harder for even *C*'s.

When he was eight, his parents had brain-wave tests made. The report was that he was a borderline learning-disabled child, would not be able to reach college, and probably couldn't finish high school.

His parents took him to Dr. Clyde Naramore's Clinic in Los Angeles where a full week was spent in testing. The result: yes, he did have a learning difficulty, but with parental tutoring, encouragement, praise, and especially travel, he could do college work. "Travel?" his parents asked. "Yes. Travel will open up the world to him and create his desire to discover and learn."

So, when Don was eleven, his parents took him and his older sister Claire to Europe and the Middle East. That boy must have asked a million questions.

He was thrilled when he returned to go into classrooms with his slides and tell of his experiences.

At age thirteen, he was taken back to Europe. At fourteen, he went on a trip around the world with his three sisters. At fourteen, also, he went on a trip with his dad to the Olympics in Mexico City. When he was sixteen, he and his sister Claire backpacked and stayed in hostels in Europe for two months. At seventeen, with his own savings

---

*"You must take responsibility for your own development.
Today a reader, tomorrow a leader."*

W. Fusselman

from working afternoons and weekends, he went to Europe, the Middle East, and worked on a kibbutz in Israel for a month. On that trip, he was gone a total of five months in all.

He enrolled in junior college, finished with good grades, went on to Georgia State University and graduated with a B.A. in marketing with a *B* average. He would stay up all night for two or three nights in a row preparing for exams. Then he went on to George Washington University, where he graduated with an *A* average in international marketing.

Today, Don is an executive with an international health organization, headquartered in Bangkok, Thailand. He is helping wipe out diseases in the Third World.

He is happily married and the father of two wonderful children. He has supreme self-esteem. Don is Donald Lamar Douglas, my son.

What did we do to help Don overcome learning difficulties that surely could have wracked him for life with low self-esteem?

1. His parents were always available to tutor, encourage, challenge, and praise his every achievement.
2. Every evening at dinner, we discussed the happy learning experiences at school that day.
3. He was not expected to take part in activities that he felt he was not talented in. For example, he went out for junior high school football, found he didn't excel in it, didn't care for it, and was encouraged to drop out rather than forced to stay in football.
4. Home was made into a happy place, a place where the gang was encouraged to gather and participate. We turned three double-car garages into game rooms, with a

---

"No man can really be big who does not read widely outside his own field."

Theodore N. Vail

pool table, stereo music system, etc. Most nights, the children were at home playing with their friends rather than having to find a place to "hang out."

5. Travel opened up the world and its opportunities.
6. Every achievement was praised and recognized. The children were rewarded with ten dollars when they received an *A*, and with five dollars for a *B*. They owed me five dollars for each *D* and ten dollars for each *F*. I believe we had one *D* in all of their school years. The forty or fifty dollars I invested each reporting time was the finest investment I ever made. All four are college graduates, and three have their master's degrees.

Live by the affirmations for the month. Take one each day, quote it with your children, and seek to live by it. The resulting good feelings your children experience will go a long way toward assuring them high self-esteem.

Affirmations for the Month

1. TODAY, I, _____ , was created with an unlimited capacity for love, joy, and fulfillment.
2. TODAY, I, _____ , accept the truth of this affirmation and live for growth and wholeness.
3. TODAY, I, _____ , release and remove all barriers of fear so I can receive all blessings.
4. TODAY, I, _____ , live in the positive truths of love, joy, peace, serenity, and prosperity.
5. TODAY, I, _____ , receive and give self-confidence, self-love, and self-celebration.
6. TODAY, I, _____ , reward myself for every accomplishment and every achievement.
7. TODAY, I, _____ , am learning to love myself more in every way as a gift of God's love.
8. TODAY, I, _____ , respect my own uniqueness, individuality, and personhood.

Make your life an unfolding greatness.

9. TODAY, I, _____ , meet my own emotional needs, because I will not be dependent on anyone.

10. TODAY, I, _____ , no longer am dependent on others to affirm me, because I do that myself.

11. TODAY, I, _____ , like, value, and please myself and renounce forever self-criticism.

12. TODAY, I, _____ , have unconditional warm feelings for myself, my friends, and all I meet.

13. TODAY, I, _____ , am 100-percent alive, alert, and excited, because I abound in unlimited enthusiasm.

14. TODAY, I, _____ , am unusual and confident, receiving an increasing amount of abundance.

15. TODAY, I, _____ , have replaced all negative thoughts with their opposite, positive thought.

16. TODAY, I, _____ , maintain control of my actions and emotions to achieve my greatness.

17. TODAY, I, _____ , live a life constantly enlarging as I seek beauty, joy, love, and peace.

18. TODAY, I, _____ , enjoy the beauty of fun, friendships, laughter, pleasure, and radiant joy.

19. TODAY, I, _____ , decide what thoughts will enter my mind and receive those I choose.

20. TODAY, I, _____ , release the true greatness within me as my self-appreciation expands.

21. TODAY, I, _____ , enrich my life as all of my activity and conduct is results-oriented.

22. TODAY, I, _____ , am moving on to a higher level of fulfillment as my life unfolds.

23. TODAY, I, _____ , am energized by newfound purpose, goals, dreams, and dynamic excitement.

24. TODAY, I, _____ , welcome the power of change and will ride the crest of opportunities.

25. TODAY, I, _____ , believe and receive the unlimited prosperity that surrounds me.

Everything is his who desires it.

26. TODAY, I, _____ , excitingly live this day in the beautiful unfolding of God's love.
27. TODAY, I, _____ , bless all mankind with my thoughts, prayers, and encouragement.
28. TODAY, I, _____ , look for, seek out, encourage, and recognize every sign of good in others.
29. TODAY, I, _____ , experience empathy, understanding, compassion, and love for all people.
30. TODAY, I, _____ , delight in the joyous feelings I receive and give to all my friends.
31. TODAY, I, _____ , love everyone unconditionally, as a conduct of my love for myself.

Conclusion

Nathaniel Branden, Virginia Satir, Haim Ginott, and Stanley Coopersmith have found that children who experienced being loved and accepted with assurance are able, capable, and have the formula for high self-esteem.

It's not family wealth, education, where we live, social class, parent's occupation, or always having a mother at home. These are not primary and may be of little value.

The four thought processes that every child needs:

1. I am loved, I am of value, I share strong feelings, I am able, and I am capable.
2. I have accepted clear, definite guidelines of conduct. I have freedom and security, confidence, and high standards.
3. I respect myself, my God, and all other human beings and I find within myself the motivation to do my best and to be myself.

"Progress results from persistence with purpose."

Frank Tyger

4. I received from my parents and other adult role models examples and experiences of genuine high self-esteem.

"Nothing is impossible to a willing heart."
John Heywood

CHAPTER 6

Build High Self-Esteem with Effective Work Production

Sigmund Freud said, "Man's link to reality is found in his work." We spend more time at work than any other thing we do except sleep. If you are unhappy on your job, you will be unhappy in everything else you do. Determine that you will love your job. Either change your attitude (for positive joy) about your job or change your job.

Work Values Questionnaire

Put a "check mark" by those values you personally believe in. Put an X by those you do not endorse. Put an O by those that are unimportant to you.

___ Career success

___ High individualism

___ Winning

___ My family's success

___ Providing well for my children

___ Keeping all commitments

___ Having balance in my life

___ Having a wide range of friends

___ Supervising other people well

___ Intellectual growth

___ Financial security

___ Personal attractiveness

___ Ability to influence others effectively

___ Eagerness to set a leading pace

___ Being a good team player

___ Awareness of my heritage

311

___ Developing many skills

___ Pride in my work production

___ Ability to get things done

___ Habits of thrift

___ Financial wealth

___ Self-sufficiency

___ Fame in my career

___ Being creative

___ Vital health and energy

___ Becoming an effective leader

___ Strong discipline

___ Projecting the right image

___ Marital harmony

___ Honoring my parents and family

___ Open-mindedness

___ Being loyal to my country

___ Being loyal to my God

___ Keeping good records

___ Orderly home life

___ Accuracy of work

Keys to Success on the Job

Never put yourself down. Never consider failure. You are able.

Take an accurate inventory of all of your strong points: talents, abilities, etc.

Take an accurate inventory of those undeveloped areas of your life. They are not weaknesses, but undeveloped areas. Areas you have not gotten around to develop yet. Improve on them one at a time.

Set your mind on succeeding in your work. Goethe said, "He who has a firm will molds the world to himself." Write out what great success in your work means to you. Spell it out. Make it definite. Nothing becomes dynamic unless it first becomes specific. Imagine yourself at the top of your career by the time you retire. Let nothing in the world keep you from achieving it.

Write out your goals. Long range goals are five years or longer; intermediate goals are from one to five years; and short range goals are monthly, weekly, daily, and even

---

"Do a little more each day than you think you possibly can."
Lowell Thomas

hourly. Ask yourself the question, "Am I doing the most important activity in this hour to reach my goals in life?"

There are many types of goals. Goals in your work could mean better production, greater human relationships, more effective customer service, or increased work production on the part of your associates.

Goals for your family could include better income, better grades for your children, more savings, a new car or home, and vacations.

Goals for your personal life may be to spend more time with your family, spiritual growth, and personal growth. Make goals in every area you would like to improve in.

Claim the fantastic power of the creative mind. When faced with a problem, incubate it in your past experience. Talk it over with others. You will soon come up with the correct answer. There is no problem bigger than you and God combined. Together, you form an unbeatable combination.

Start each day with positive plans and end the day with a positive review of your accomplishments. Live each day in day-tight compartments. Don't rehash worries from yesterday and don't anticipate worries for tomorrow. Remember Jesus's admonition: "Take therefore no thought for the morrow; for the morrow shall take thought for the things of itself. Sufficient unto the day is the evil thereof" (Matt. 6:34).

Every day, say to yourself several times, "This is the day that the Lord has made; I will rejoice and be glad in it" (from Ps. 118:24). Doing this will brighten each day and unleash the creative powers within you. The only limitations we have are those in our own minds. We were made for greatness. Claim yours this day and every day.

Practice and live with expectation and assurance of good things coming your way. Raises and promotions come to those who give more than they are paid for.

"Difficulties mastered are opportunities won."
Prime Minister Winston Churchill

Act enthusiastic and you'll be enthusiastic. Put excitement in everything you do. Benjamin Disraeli said, "Every production of genius must be the production of enthusiasm."

Olin T. Binkley was born and reared on a poor mountain farm in Western North Carolina. His parents, having only a grade school education, dreamed that their children would go to college. Olin learned high self-esteem from the love received in his home and the discipline of hard work that he applied to his studies. He led his class every year in school. Upon graduating from high school, he received a partial scholarship from Wake Forest University. That, with several hundred dollars he had earned working every odd job he could find, was all he had to start college.

He came home for the Christmas holiday the first year with his trunk. He told his parents he was out of money and would not go back to college until he had earned considerably more. His mother urged him to reconsider and made Olin promise not to unpack his trunk yet.

At breakfast on the morning he was to go back to school, he turned over his plate, after grace, and was shocked to discover fifty silver dollars. He looked at his father; he was eating; he knew nothing about the money. He looked at his mother. Tears were flowing down her cheeks, and love flowed from her eyes. The smile on her lips was a tremendous encouragement for him to go back to college.

Then he looked at her folded hands on her down-turned plate. They were stained black. Black from countless hours of staying up many a night, picking fifty dollars of black walnuts.

Olin went back to Wake Forest, took another part-time job and finished at the top of his classes. He went on to graduate school and earned his doctorate. He became a seminary professor and a seminary president. Olin was driven with

---

To know and not to do is really not to know.

high self-esteem by a poor mountain mother who had picked fifty dollars of black walnuts.

I had the privilege of teaching several Dale Carnegie leadership classes for the Fort Lauderdale, Florida, Police Department. The positive changes in these officers was amazing.

At the fifth session, on human relations, we challenged the officers to take one of the human relations rules and practice it with other people.

At the sixth session, reporting on the use of human relations, one officer, who worked the beach patrol, gave the following report:

"I have had no use for the 'hippies' I confront on the beach. I try to run in as many as I can. Then I decided to apply the human relation rule: 'Make the other person feel important.'

"I have been 'running in' this hippie for three years. I decided to try this rule. I asked him, 'Tell me more about yourself.' He said, 'I graduated from New York University of Architecture, was engaged to this lovely woman, and had set the date for our marriage the week after graduation. Then, I received this 'Dear John' letter. I fell apart, dropped out of school three weeks before I was to graduate, got on drugs, and came to Florida to hide.' "

"I replied, 'Man, if I was an architect, I would be building beautiful office buildings, hotels, churches, and homes to make people happy. Then you could look back on these and get real joy from the impact of your life.'

"I knew this impressed him, for he expressed it with a troubled look on his face. Each day this past week, I have

---

"Happiness comes of the capacity to feel deeply, to enjoy simply, to think freely, to risk life, to be needed."

Storm Jammeson

talked with him further, and maybe I'm getting across to him. I know I feel good about this rule."

The fourteenth session was graduation, when each officer told what he had received from the course.

When this beach officer came to give his talk, he said, "Do you folks remember the story I told you at the 6th session, how I changed my attitude about this 'Hippie' and his response?

"Last week, I was working the beach and this good-looking guy, with neat hair, clean-shaven, dressed in a three-piece suit, came up to me and said, 'You remember me?' I replied, 'No, I've never seen you before.' He answered, 'I'm the guy who was trained as an architect that you took a personal interest in. You really shook me up. I decided to get off drugs, went to a clinic, was allowed to take my exams, received my degree. Amazingly, my old girlfriend had not married that guy she dumped me for, and we are back together. And, I have a new job with the finest architecture company in Fort Lauderdale.'

"Last night, my wife and I went to dinner with that couple. They are here tonight and I want you to meet, in person, the results of the rule, 'Make the other person feel important.' " And he had them stand.

Chief of Police Parker, who was there, came up to me afterward and said, "Douglas, the expense of the entire course was worth it in the effect of this one life."

The architect discovered high self-esteem in the challenge of a police officer and the love of his lady.

Some Important Quotes on Work

The destiny of my life is up to me.

Belief in heroics makes heroes.

Vince Lombardi opened each training camp with this sort of speech:

Our only limitations are self-imposed.

Gentlemen, we are going to have a great football team. We are going to win games. Get that. You are going to learn to block. You are going to learn to tackle. You are going to outplay the teams that come against you. Get that. How is this to be done? You are to have confidence in me and enthusiasm for my system. The secret of the whole matter will be what goes on in your head. Hereafter, I want you to think of three things: your home, your religion, and the Green Bay Packers. In that order. Let enthusiasm take hold of you— beginning now.

"A man uses his work to define for himself who he is and what he will do with his life."   Dr. Harry Levinson

"Success, in the long run, is a measure of one's ability to turn task into adventure."   Dr. John Bjorksten

"The purest pleasure lies within the circle of useful occupation."   Henry Ward Beecher

"A man is a worker. If he is not that, then he is nothing."   Joseph Conrad

"An hour's industry will do more to produce cheerfulness than a month's mourning."   Barrows

"There is no development without effort and effort means work."   Pres. Calvin Coolidge

"All the geniuses I have encouraged have been the hardest workers and most indefatigable students I have known."   Archibald Henderson

"It is the man whose enthusiasm lasts for thirty years that becomes a leader."   Edward Burgess Butler

"If we all did the things we are capable of doing, we would literally astound ourselves."   Thomas A. Edison

---

"Without enthusiasm, there is no progress in the world."
Pres. Woodrow Wilson

"The world stands aside to let anyone pass who knows where he is going."   David Starr Jordon

"Without enthusiasm, there is no progress in the world."
                                        Pres. Woodrow Wilson

"A man can succeed at almost anything for which he has unlimited enthusiasm."   Charles Schwab

"When a man dies, if he can pass enthusiasm to his children, he has left them an estate of incalculable value."
                                        Thomas A. Edison

"I like a man who bubbles over with enthusiasm. Better be a geyser than a mud puddle."   John G. Sheed

"Every great and commanding moment in the annals of the world is the triumph of some enthusiasm."
                                        Ralph Waldo Emerson

"Face the thing that seems overwhelming and you will be surprised how your fear will melt away."   Dale Carnegie

"No man is worth his salt who is not ready at all times to risk his body, to risk his well-being, to risk his life, in a great cause."   Theodore Roosevelt

"Saints are sinners who believe in God and keep trying."
                                        Anonymous

"The harder I work, and the better I plan, the luckier I get."
                                        Anonymous

"I use all the brains I have, and all I can borrow."
                                        Pres. Woodrow Wilson

"Some people regard discipline as a chore. For me, it is a kind of order that sets me free to fly."   Julie Andrews

---

"A free society is one where it is safe to be unpopular."
Adlai Stevenson

"The greatest happiness comes from the greatest activity."

Bovee

"Life is too short to be little."   Benjamin Disraeli

"It is a funny thing about life. If you refuse to accept anything but the best, you will get it."   Somerset Maugham

"Happiness is a perfume you cannot pour on others without getting a few drops on yourself."   Ralph Waldo Emerson

"For a big job, find a busy man."   Anonymous

"No man stands as tall as he who makes other people more productive."   Anonymous

"If you work hard enough, and smart enough, success is sure to follow."   Anonymous

"Luck is where opportunity, preparation and dedication meet."   Anonymous

"The surest way to knock the chip off another fellow's shoulder is by patting him on the back."   Anonymous

"Success comes from mastering fundamentals, developing physical and mental toughness, hard work, and making the second effort."   Vince Lombardi

"The greatest discovery of my generation is that human beings can alter their lives by altering their attitudes of mind."

William James

"The ability to get along with and motivate people is life's greatest ability."   Dale Carnegie

"What makes a man great is the ability to decide what is important and to focus attention on it until it is done."

Anonymous

"The important thing in life is to have a great aim and to

"Do the thing you fear, and the death of fear is certain."
Ralph Waldo Emerson

possess the aptitude and perseverance to attain it."

Anonymous

"The person who says it can't be done is liable to be interrupted by someone doing it." Anonymous

"Every misfortune always carries the seed of an equal or greater benefit." Napoleon Hill

The only thing we totally control is our mental attitude.

Be a Good Listener

Reasons why listening will pay off for you:

1. To learn something
2. To understand better
3. To be entertained
4. To get information
5. To show respect for the other person
6. To be a team player
7. To ask intelligent questions
8. To discover other people's needs
9. To increase productivity
10. To be more effective
11. To make accurate evaluations
12. To make effective comparisons
13. To understand and be understood
14. To get the best value
15. To enhance relationships
16. To solve problems
17. To show you care and are involved
18. To make intelligent decisions
19. To prevent waste and loss
20. To make more money
21. To avoid being embarrassed
22. To stay out of trouble

"A wise man will make more opportunities than he finds."
Francis Bacon

23. To save time
24. To be a supportive friend
25. To be in "win-win" situations
26. To increase your concentration abilities
27. To build rapport with people
28. To settle disagreements
29. To improve my personality
30. To use the gift of hearing

Do you have a good listening attitude?

A Quiz to Help You Determine Your Listening Attitude

(Answer Yes or No.)

	Y	**N**
1. I am interested in many subjects and make an effort to not knowingly tune out dry-sounding information.	—	—
2. I listen carefully for a speaker's main ideas and points.	—	—
3. I take notes during meetings to keep a record of important information.	—	—
4. I am not often easily distracted.	—	—
5. I make an effort to keep my emotions under control.	—	—
6. I concentrate carefully and do not fake attention.	—	—
7. I wait for the speaker to finish speaking before I begin to evaluate what he has said.	—	—

The doors we open and close each day decide the lives we live.

8. I respond appropriately with a smile, a nod, or a word of acknowledgment (without disturbing other listeners) as a speaker is talking. __ __

9. I am aware of mannerisms that may distract a speaker and I try to keep mine under control. __ __

10. I am aware of and understand my biases and control them when I listen. __ __

11. I refrain from constantly interrupting. __ __

12. I value eye contact and maintain it most of the time. __ __

13. I often restate or paraphrase what the speaker said to make sure I have understood his intended meaning. __ __

14. I try to absorb the speaker's emotional meaning as well as subject matter content. __ __

15. I often ask questions for clarification. __ __

16. I do not finish other people's sentences unless I am asked to do so. __ __

17. When listening on the telephone, I keep one hand free to take notes. __ __

18. I attempt to set aside my ego and focus on the speaker and his message rather than on myself. __ __

"If you would like to be a power among man, cultivate enthusiasm."
Washington Irving

19. I make an effort to judge the message rather than the messenger. I understand that it's often easier to critize the information rather than to see how it may apply to me. — —

20. I make an effort to be a patient listener. — —

Scoring

1 — 5 *no*'s	You are an excellent listener.
6 — 10 *no*'s	You are a good listener, but can improve.
11 — 15 *no*'s	Through practice you can become a much more effective listener in your business and personal relationships.
16 — 20 *no*'s	Listen up!

This quiz has adapted from Diane Bone's *The Business of Listening*, published in Los Altos, California, by Crisp in 1988.

Working with Other People

Respect employees' feelings. Give yourself a *3* for always, a *2* for some of the time, a *1* for occasionally, a *0* for never.

__ I make an effort to greet each person pleasantly each day.

__ I take the time to manage by walking around, asking questions, chatting, and listening.

__ When I talk with employees, I make eye contact and speak respectfully and pleasantly.

__ I include others in as many decisions as possible.

__ I ask for others' advice on matters concerning their job, work area, etc.

"The heights by great men reached and kept, were not attained by sudden flight, but they, while their companions slept, were toiling upward in the night."
Henry Wadsworth Longfellow

___ I make an effort to treat everyone equally.

___ I do not knowingly withhold information from any team member or colleague.

___ I do not assign an overload without including essential employees in the decision-making process.

___ I emphasize team spirit and cooperation.

___ I do not assign special projects without carefully analyzing the growth needs of my employees and colleagues.

___ I praise in person when a job is well done.

___ I correct in private when a job is not well done.

___ I offer coaching and constructive suggestions to improve job performance and new skills.

___ I insist on high standards, exemplify those standards myself, and I communicate them respectfully.

___ Score.

This original version of this work quiz can be found in Twyla Dell's *An Honest Day's Work: Motivating Employees to Give Their Best*, published in Los Altos, California, by Crisp in 1988.

The Four-Step Management Meeting

Although they may have a job description and regular performance reviews, most workers unconsciously move away from the details they think their supervisors want them to do. Here is an effective plan that will correct this problem. Take a blank sheet of paper and complete the following exercises.

"To love is to believe, to hope to know,
it is a taste of heaven here below."

Waller

Five most important job functions:

1. _____

2. _____

3. _____

4. _____

5. _____

Write out your methods of achieving each of these job functions:

1. _____

2. _____

3. _____

4. _____

5. _____

Write out your goals to reach each of these job functions effectively:

1. _____

2. _____

3. _____

4. _____

5. _____

The happiest people are those with achieving
experiences of helping others.

Grade yourself as above average, average, or below average.
Now, ask your boss or that person reporting to you to do the same thing without seeing your sheet. Afterward, sit down together and compare notes with each other. You will find:

1. Unconsciously you have drifted apart. No one is at fault. It just happened.
2. You two can now take a third blank sheet and agree on your five most important job functions.
3. Have a checkup meeting once a month and stay on target.

The worker will feel better because he is on target with his boss. And the boss will be pleased because he will also know that the two of you are on target together.

In more than ninety-five percent of the cases, the boss rates the worker higher than the worker would rate him/herself. The reason: lack of supportive appreciation.

Team Building: Attitudes of an Effective Team Builder

By taking this quiz you can find your strengths and also your undeveloped areas in team building. On a scale of one to seven, circle the number that most closely corresponds to your evaluation of each question. Total the sum of the numbers when you have finished.

1. When I select employees, I choose those who can meet the job requirements and work well with others.

    7 6 5 4 3 2 1

2. I give employees a sense of ownership by involving them in goal-setting, problem-solving, and productivity-improvement activities.

    7 6 5 4 3 2 1

3. I try to provide team spirit by encouraging people to

"A happy family is but an earlier heaven."

Bowring

work together and to support one another on activities
that are related.

7 6 5 4 3 2 1

4. I talk with people openly and honestly and encourage
   the same kind of communication in return.

7 6 5 4 3 2 1

5. I keep agreements with my people because their trust is
   essential to my leadership.

7 6 5 4 3 2 1

6. I help team members get to know each other so they
   can learn to trust, respect, and appreciate individual
   talent and ability.

7 6 5 4 3 2 1

7. I insure employees have the required training to do
   their job and know how it is to be applied.

7 6 5 4 3 2 1

8. I understand that conflict within groups is normal, but
   I work to resolve it quickly and fairly before it can become destructive.

7 6 5 4 3 2 1

9. I believe people will perform as a team when they know
   what is expected and what benefits will accrue.

7 6 5 4 3 2 1

10. I am willing to replace members who cannot or will not
    meet reasonable standards after appropriate coaching.

7 6 5 4 3 2 1

Total _____

A score of 60—70 indicates a positive attitude toward people and the type of attitude needed to build and maintain a
strong team.

I've found that the way I treat others, determines the way they treat me.

A score of 40—59 is acceptable, and with reasonable effort, team building should be possible for you.

If you scored less than 40 points, you need to carefully examine your attitude in light of current management philosophy.

Listed here are thirty-one affirmations—one for each day of the month. Quote one each day, believe it, live it, and become it.

1. I accept myself totally and unconditionally.
2. I never devalue myself through destructive self-criticism.
3. I have warm, unconditional regard for myself and my friends.
4. I prove that I am alive by thinking, speaking, and acting with great enthusiasm.
5. I am completely self-determined about my future in my career.
6. I am an unusual, confident, achieving human being receiving an increasing flow of life's abundance.
7. I decide what thoughts will enter my mind.
8. I replace negative emotions with the opposite, positive emotions as the most effective way to take charge of my mind.
9. I keep only positive thoughts in my mind because they control what I will become.
10. I maintain complete control of my actions and emotions, thus sustaining my dynamic energies for worthwhile purposes.
11. My concept of life is constantly being enlarged as I seek beauty, health, wealth, joy, achievement, fulfillment, and happiness.
12. I enjoy all of life's experiences of fun, fellowship, laughter, and radiant joy.

Belief in heroics makes heroes.

13. Every day in every way, I am getting better and better.
14. My life is enriched since my activity is results-oriented.
15. I have true greatness still buried within me that is being released as my self-confidence, self-awareness, and self-appreciation expands.
16. I am the best friend I can have. I take myself out whenever I feel low. I alone am responsible for my feelings and I choose to feel beautiful.
17. I am a unique, never-to-be-repeated miracle of God. Therefore, today and every day, I celebrate myself.
18. Certainly I act differently, because I am different now that I control my thoughts.
19. I dwell on beautiful, powerful thoughts of self-affirmation.
20. I am forever free of negative thoughts such as doubt, fear, inferiority, hate, bitterness, strife, and hostility.
21. I live with the principle of unlimitedness. Abundance is mine because love, peace, joy, happiness, energy, health, and wealth have no boundaries.
22. I am energized by my newfound purpose, goals, dreams, and enthusiasm.
23. I welcome change and will ride the crest of new opportunities.
24. I am open, receptive, responsive, and obedient to life, love, joy, peace, energy, wealth, health, wisdom, and the beauty of wholeness.
25. I look for the good in all people.
26. I shall pass through this world but once. Any good, therefore, that I can do, or any kindness that I can show to any human being, let me do it now. Let me not defer or neglect it, because I shall not pass this way again.
27. A new friend is the best and most beautiful gift that I can give to myself.
28. I love other people unconditionally, as a result of my love for myself.

No one can make a fool of you unless you cooperate.

29. I will remember that the deepest urge of human nature is the desire to be important and I will sincerely and honestly seek to make every person I meet feel important.
30. The happiest people are those with achieving experiences of helping others.
31. I will give myself good feelings, diligent work, loyalty to my friends, and happy thoughts and I will thus assure myself high self-esteem.

Conclusion

My work is one of the finest expressions of who I am, therefore I will apply myself to the best of my ability to my work.

I will love my work. If I sincerely try and find myself not loving my work, I will seek other employment so that I can love what I do each and every day.

I will arrive at work excited and dedicated and will seek to produce more today than I did yesterday.

When I have felt depressed or discouraged,
it is because of the ways I let myself think and act.

CHAPTER 7

The Sacredness of Personhood

Originally, the word *guilt* came from a French word meaning *duty*. As with many other words, its usage has affected the meaning. Webster's now defines guilt as *fact of committing an offense, blameworthiness, feeling of responsibility for offense.*

Guilt may be used by controlling ministers, parents, or employers to make others feel bad. One of the worst things that we can do to ourselves is self-criticize and self-blame. This is done, so often, by negative, controlling words such as *ought*. By using *ought*, we are accepting others' control over us and our own self-blame.

How "oughts" often impact our lives:

I ought to be the perfect lover, friend, parent, or student.
I ought to be able to solve problems every time.
I ought to be able to handle any difficulty.
I ought never to feel bad, hurt, or negative.
I ought to be an outstanding achiever in everything I do.
I ought to anticipate every problem before it happens.
I ought never to feel anger, jealousy, or frustration.
I ought to love my children equally.
I ought to never make any mistakes.
I ought to be totally self-reliant at all times.
I ought never to have to ask anyone else how to do things.
I ought never to get tired or sick.
I ought never to be afraid.
I ought to be such an achiever that I will be wealthy.

I ought to be busy at all times and never take time out for myself.

I ought to be the best at my job.

I ought to be kind to all people even when I don't feel like being kind.

I ought to feel sexually excited about my mate at all times.

I ought to care about the poor and homeless.

I ought to be able to make enough money for my family to have all they need.

I ought to be able to protect my children from all fears and pain.

I ought to never take time for myself, but work always.

With these guilt-loaded thoughts, you have surrendered your control to fear, insecurity, and negative emotions.

Instead, take the positive approach by making your life a choice:

I choose to be the best lover, friend, parent, or student.

I choose to anticipate and solve all problems to the best of my ability.

I choose to handle all difficulties to the best of my abilities.

I choose to put my negative emotions and hurts into positive emotions.

I choose to be an outstanding achiever in all that I do.

I choose to feel anger, jealousy, or frustration when they are deserved.

I choose to love my children unconditionally and like them according to their conduct.

I choose to admit my mistakes and not blame myself for them, but learn from them.

I choose to be self-reliant to the best of my ability.

I choose to maintain good health, although sometimes I may get sick.

"If a child lives with approval, he learns to like himself."

Dorothy Law Nolte

I choose not to be overwhelmed by fear, but admit sometimes I have fears.

I choose to be the best at my job, because I like myself better when I do.

I choose to be kind to all people when I possibly can.

I choose to feel sexually excited about my mate whenever possible.

I choose to care for the poor and homeless and help them as I can.

I choose to make the money necessary to provide for my family.

I choose to protect my children from fear and pain as best I can.

I choose to work hard and enjoy my leisure equally as well.

Ought living is wrong, especially when it is employed with controlling, emotionally abusive conduct. To demand ought-motivated behavior as part of a person's conduct violates the sacredness of personhood. If you allow for *choice* conduct, individuals have the opportunity to freely make moral decisions regarding themselves and their actions.

Your Choice Inventory

I choose to maintain relationships: mate, children, parents, siblings, friends, etc.

I choose activities: cleaning, working, playing, cooking, hobbies, etc.

I choose recreational and social activities: dining out, vacations, weekends out-of-town, fishing, gardening, hunting, games, exercise, etc.

I choose good work habits: being on time, doing my best, loyalty to my company, learning, growing, improving, earning a raise, earning a promotion, etc.

"In all things we learn from those we love."

Goethe

I choose creative activities: church, clubs, reading, selective TV viewing, spirited discussions, traveling, etc.

I choose money and financial success: saving, investing, living on a budget, planning for retirement, etc.

I choose self-care: good appearance/dress, exercise, control intake of drugs, not smoking, careful eating habits, dieting when necessary, pride in myself, etc.

I choose ways of expression: anger, fear, love, affection, joy, sexual pleasure, controlling physical pain, etc.

In 1924, at the Olympics, Charles Pollock won a silver medal in the hundred-meter dash. In the early 1930s, Pollock was speaking at a high school in Cleveland. A skinny, fourteen-year-old boy came up to Pollock after his speech and said, "Mr. Pollock, I will do anything to win an Olympic medal." Pollock reached into his pocket and handed that boy an Olympic coin and said, "If you will pay the price of total commitment, you can win it. Take this coin as a sign of that commitment." In 1936, in Berlin, that boy, Jessie Owen, won four gold medals, including one for setting a world's record in the hundred-meter dash.

A few years later, speaking at East High in Cleveland, Jessie Owen was greeted after his talk by a tall, skinny boy. He said, "Mr. Owen, I will do anything to win a gold medal in the Olympics." Owen reached into his pocket and took out that same Olympic coin that Charles Pollock had given him some years before, and said, "Charles Pollock gave me this medal as my inspiration many years ago. I want you to have it with your commitment that you will pay the price of greatness." That boy, Harrison ("Bones") Dillard, won the high jump and a gold medal in the 1948 Olympics at London.

Three great athletes, all with high self-esteem, passed on the torch of greatness.

I am a unique, never-to-be-repeated miracle of God.
Therefore, today and everyday, I celebrate myself.

A professional speaker, a friend of mine, went to Silver City, New Mexico, to speak at a chamber of commerce banquet. During dinner, he turned to the man on his right and asked, "How is business?"

The man answered, "I am a real-estate broker with my own office. The two silver mines here have been out on strike for six months. I haven't sold a house in that time. If this strike lasts three months more, I will be broke. This is the worst time of my life," he complained.

The speaker turned to the woman on his left and asked her, "How's business?"

She excitedly replied, "I'm in real estate. This strike will be settled soon and all the workers for the mining companies will receive a good raise. Before the strike, the miners who work a lot of overtime haven't had the time to look for houses. Now they have plenty of time. I have sold more houses in the last six months than any three years in my life. I hope the strike ends soon, but if it lasts another three months, I will be set for life. Business is the best I have ever seen."

Here were two people, three feet apart. One, the woman, with high self-esteem, was making lemonade out of a lemon. The man was strangling on his lemon. He had low self-esteem.

What you believe about yourself makes all the difference in the world for you and those around you. We treat other people in the same way that we feel about ourselves. If you have genuine self-esteem, you can practice life's greatest ability: the ability to get along with people. Use these human relations rules:

Show genuine interest in the other person.
Smile. It spreads like a wildfire. You smile; others will also.
Be sure you get the other person's name. Use it, remember it,

---

There is more pleasure in loving than in being loved.

and recall it later. Dale Carnegie said, "The sweetest sound in any language is the sound of our own name."

Listen to all the other person says. Encourage him to talk about himself.

Talk about what he is interested in. Keep the ball in his court.

Make other people feel important. Make them feel you really care.

Give sincere compliments. Compliment people on things about their personalities, abilities, attitudes, etc. Everyone has something you can positively compliment him/her on. Look for good things people do and express your appreciation. They will rise up and call you blessed.

Never criticize. It puts others on the defensive and does no good. Use corrective suggestions for overcoming a mistake. Speak to someone privately. Call attention to some of your own mistakes, compliment a person on other achievements he has made and then ask, "Could this have been handled in some other way?" Together, you both can correct the mistake. He will feel good about it, will appreciate you on the way you have handled it, and will make a much better effort the next time.

Learn to accept compliments. Accept them, and thank the other person for them. Never reject the compliment. That offends the other person and makes you feel unworthy.

Talk little about yourself. Don't tell what *you* have done, etc.

Be pleasant. Enjoy what you are doing. If you don't like your job, either change your attitude or change your job. Don't say, "I have to go to work today." Instead, say, "I choose to go to work today, because I choose to pay my bills." Smell the roses.

As a guide on how to be assertive, not aggressive or recessive, the following lists may be helpful:

When love and skill work together, expect a masterpiece.

Assertive Behavior

Sensitive to feelings
Needs no threats
Force used only when and where necessary
Based on human rights
Firm but gentle, unyielding where appropriate
Negotiation a viable tactic
Leads to good feelings
Accepts workable outcomes

Aggressive Behavior

Insensitive to feelings
Attack-oriented
Use of force or threats of force
Leads to frustration and guilt
Either victory or defeat, no middle ground
Anger
Demands preconceived outcomes
Uses people

Recessive Behavior

Insensitive to needs and desires
Yields too often
Sacrifices basic human rights
Accepts unwanted outcomes
Leads to frustration, guilt, and bad feelings
Feel used and manipulated

Your Rights

Right to say "no" without feeling guilty
Right to make choices
Right to agree or disagree
Right to take care of yourself
Right to have your say

To love is to place our happiness in the care of another.

Right to ask for help
Right to reject
Right to change your mind

Positive Statements

"He who fails to prepare prepares to fail." Preparation is a key element in success. Preparation gives one the self-confidence that he/she is ready to meet a challenge.

Good things don't happen because one hopes for them. They happen because of positive actions.

A positive attitude is like an umbrella—it keeps you from getting all wet.

Technical knowledge becomes outdated every three years on the average, but positive attitudes will last you for a lifetime. Acquire the positive attitudes that can help you cope with change.

"Whatever you vividly imagine, ardently desire, sincerely believe and enthusiastically act upon—must inevitably come to pass." (Paul Meyer)

The best accessory you can add to any wardrobe is a smile.

To catch the big fish, you must be in the deep water; to accomplish great things you must be willing to leave the security of shallow water and venture where the water is deep and maybe where you have never been before.

A positive person realizes that in order for him to "win," someone else doesn't have to lose. In fact, the best way to win is to help someone else win.

Smile to let others know you are there. Smile to let them know you care. Soon there will be smiles everywhere.

The best attitude to have towards óne's daily work is a keep-at-it-tude.

A positive person knows that it is better to have done something imperfectly while giving 100-percent effort than to have done nothing perfectly while giving no effort.

"For as he thinketh in his heart, so is he. . . ."

Prov. 23:7

There should be no shame in admitting that you were wrong—instead be proud you are strong enough to admit a mistake, and be glad that you are wiser from having learned from your mistake or error.

Every man's work is a portrait of himself. Put your best effort into everything you do and your work will be a positive reflection of the kind of person you are.

A person who takes shortcuts usually finds himself on a dead-end street. Positive people know there are no shortcuts to success. It takes preparation, hard work, and dedication to be successful.

Keep in mind a positive thought. . . . attitudes are learned and can be taught.

You never fail unless you fail to learn from your mistakes.

You can try your best and make the best of everything.

A person is as young as his dreams—or as old as his doubts. Let your dreams rule your life—not your doubts.

Abraham Lincoln once said, "People are as happy as they make up their minds to be." Develop the habit of being happy.

Everyone has the potential to be a winner. The seeds of greatness are inside each of us.

Benjamin Franklin said, "If a man empties his purse into his head, no man can take it away from him. An investment in knowledge always pays the best interest."

Each new day is a new beginning. Claim your positive potential for greatness.

Be resolved to make this a positive year for yourself. Think positively, act positively, and become a positive person.

A positive person knows that great minds discuss events, small minds discuss people.

Smile, because as Sir Isaac Newton would say, "Every action has a reaction." If you smile, people will react positively.

Every goal has a beginning, a middle, and an end. So just by beginning to accomplish a goal, you are one-third of the way toward accomplishing your goal.

Home is a happy haven from harm.

Shakespeare said, "Our doubts are traitors and make us lose the good we oft might win by fearing to attempt." Don't let the fear of failure control your life. If you want something, go for it. Give it a 110-percent effort and you will have nothing to fear.

Thinking and looking negative will only bring you down. So put on a smile and get rid of your frown.

A positive person knows that not everything faced can be changed, but that nothing can be changed until it is faced. So face those things which interfere with your progress, or stand in the way of a goal you have, and try to change them.

All things work for the best for those who make the best of everything. You can become a positive person by thinking and acting positively each day.

An attitude is like a bread roll—when it goes stale and flat, it's not worth having around.

Enthusiasm is not reserved for only a fortunate few. Anyone and everyone can become an enthusiastic person by practicing being enthusiastic. It will become a good habit which will open many doors for you.

Pull the plug on negative thoughts and let them go down the drain.

Only in math does negative times negative equal positive.

Think not negative thoughts for they bring you lower in self-pride, but if you think positive thoughts they'll lift you higher than you imagine.

Be a positive person, go an extra mile.

Ten Commandments of the Lovable, Liberated Man

1. Thou shalt feel free to openly express your emotions honestly.
2. Thou shalt be open to honor and respect logical, practical, and intellectual viewpoints with thy mate.

We shall pass this way but once, so celebrate life to the fullest.

3. Thou shalt listen and value what is said both mentally and emotionally.
4. Thou shalt appreciate women as equals.
5. Thou shalt mutually share, experience, and explore the pleasures of sensuality.
6. Thou shalt recognize and encourage healthy ego growth equally with thy mate.
7. Thou shalt recognize thy partner as equal breadwinner to thyself if she so chooses.
8. Thou shalt share responsibility for housework with thy mate, especially if she works.
9. Thou shalt openly achieve vocational excellence that gives you personal satisfaction.
10. Thou shalt mutually seek the answer to problems of common interest.

What are some of the things men fear so much?

Men fear sexual failure. And when they are selfish in their lovemaking rather than sharing their total selves, they tend to have more problems with sexual achievement.

Men are afraid of aggressive women. This is because they don't know how to handle them. An aggressive woman should not be a threat, but this drive should be channeled into effective productivity that benefits everyone.

Men are afraid of a passive, nonresponsive woman. This is because they have not learned the art of arousing such a woman to her real potential.

Men are afraid of rejection. They are looking for someone else to meet their own emotional needs rather than learning to meet these needs within themselves.

Men are afraid of competing with a woman. Such a person is insecure, because competition should be a challenge to excellence.

Love people and use things, not love things and use people.

Men are afraid of female competence. They have been taught that women are basically inferior, which isn't true.

Men are afraid of failure. Often this is because they haven't developed genuine self-esteem.

Learning to Love

Becoming a lovable, liberated person. To become a lovable, liberated person, you must repudiate guilt, because most of it comes from things, which are not wrong as much as they are taught to be wrong by controlling, insecure parents and by fear-imposing, negative religion.

Looking at the ineffective roles we have been taught, we find:

The Limited Female

1. She has a poor self-image, either not developed in her home by her parents, or she has failed to develop her self-esteem because of a husband who puts her down, or just the role of male-superior vs. female-inferior syndrome.
2. She doesn't value her body, mind, and abilities.
3. She maintains a Puritanical attitude toward sex.
4. She is guilt-ridden.
5. She has an unreasonable fear of change.
6. She sits on her feelings, then explodes.
7. She has few hobbies, personal interests, or things that she enjoys doing.

The Limited Male

1. He has a poor self-image. He is unhappy in his work, dresses with poor taste, and is emotionally withdrawn.
2. He is filled with a fear of rejection.

---

*"Happy are the families where the government of
parents is the reign of affection."*

Francis Bacon

3. He has a low tolerance for others. He is frustrated and hates to wait for anyone.
4. He is loaded with guilt.
5. He holds strong prejudices.
6. He is selfish with his love. He can't say, "I love you."

Why can't men show their feelings—especially express their love to their wives and children?

1. Some have used love words to seduce women and therefore feel guilty in using them with ones close to them.
2. They never experienced such endearments in their homes from their parents and thus don't feel comfortable with them.
3. Some feel such expressions would mean they would be emotionally untrue to their mothers by telling other women they love them. These men fail to understand the paradox of love, for the more a man loves his mother, the greater capacity he has to love his children, and the greater capacity he has to love his wife.
   One man hadn't kissed his wife in twenty years, and then shot another man for doing it. He is the one who should have been shot.
4. Saying "I love you" is uncomfortable for some men, for they harbor an unconscious hostility towards women.
5. Others think that emotional expression is a final and complete letting go, and they don't know how to do so. You see, they aren't in control of their unused and unfamiliar emotions.
6. Some men think that loving is destructive to their sense of freedom and independence. Truly, such persons are in a prison of emotional constipation.
7. Some men think it isn't masculine to show emotions. Of course, such a person is more robotic than manly.

I can change my life by taking charge of my emotions.

8. If a man thinks sex is dirty, then he associates words of tenderness with vulgarity and obscenity.
9. And, finally, this type of man is afraid that tenderness is a total surrender of logic to emotion.

What is the answer? Let's look at the qualities of the lovable, liberated person.

The Lovable, Liberated Woman

1. She and her man come first in her life. Everyone knows she cares.
2. She is open, honest, and frank in conversation. She gets it out, forgives, and forgets. She never denies sex in revenge.
3. She initiates and lets him lead. She has the attitude, "If you ask me, I'll say yes." She is not fearful, but trusting.
4. She enjoys and encourages the beautiful pleasure of sex. She knows that most men have a limited knowledge of sexual matters; that the refusal of sex is a total rejection of a man; that a lack of femininity is an attack on his manhood; that her mate loves others to admire her as an extension of his personhood. He is saying, "Hey, look but don't touch." And she knows that men really respond to affection.
5. She realizes that men have a low tolerance for stress and frustration. She doesn't make him wait for an unreasonable length of time.
6. She accepts his interest in sports. She knows that "the difference between men and boys is the size of their toys."
7. She knows men detest being manipulated by guilt and martyrdom. She doesn't bitch.
8. She accepts his dedication to his work. She helps him

I live in the principle of unlimitedness. Abundance is mine for love, peace, joy, happiness, energy, health, wealth know no boundaries.

achieve balance by making his leisure time as exciting and meaningful as his work.

9. She knows that few people can resist emotional involvement with someone who really cares.
10. She loves herself, so out of the overflow of her self-celebration she abundantly loves him.
11. She has developed such genuine self-esteem through her work, social life, or other activity that she meets her own emotional needs, and thus isn't burdening him to meet her needs.

The Lovable, Liberated Man

1. He has genuine self-esteem and is not threatened by job loss, financial difficulties, family conflicts, or even the loss of love.
2. He is equally partnered to love his mate and children as much as his work.
3. He is a lifelong student of the art of love. He is curious about learning every way to help his mate enjoy their love life more. He is turned on by emotions, words, experiences, as well as his mate's appearance.
4. He is open and honest about his feelings. He loves to express his warmth and affection for her and does it without reason and as an act of his fullness.
5. He wants his mate to be mature and happy, and he is not threatened by her achievements.
6. He wants to regularly enjoy exciting leisure activities with his mate and children.
7. He can read and adjust to his mate's emotional wavelengths.
8. He is not a mama's boy in that he is controlled by his mother. He has equal love for his mother, his mate, and his children. He is his own man and will never let his mother separate him from his mate.

---

*The greatest use of life is to so live your life
that the use of your life outlives your life.*

9. He delights in his partner's freedom, personhood, happiness, and individuality.
10. He accepts and cultivates her leisure activity as important to her personhood, and thus their happiness.
11. He makes her financially secure so that she will never be threatened by the worry of financial destitution were she to lose him.

The Ideal Lovable, Liberated Person

1. He is assertive, assured, and confident.
2. He has willpower and is balanced emotionally and logically.
3. He is free to express himself emotionally and is able to laugh and cry.
4. He has genuine self-esteem, self-confidence, self-value, and self-celebration.
5. He is a loving, warm, tender, and sensuous person, because to live a life without sexual fulfillment is to accept punishment without cause.
6. He is strong, decisive, and in control of himself.
7. He is excited about life, people, and especially his mate and children.
8. He is cooperative and eager to build a relationship for a lifetime.
9. He puts himself first, so the overflow of joy will spill over on all who are touched.
10. He is a growing, searching, and fulfilled individual who is excited by life's fantastic opportunities.

Conclusion

In order to be whole yourself, you must go back and heal the harmful experiences you have had with others. Pray for those you

---

*"Success can only be measured by mastering
fundamentals, developing physical and mental toughness,
hard work, and making the second effort."*
Vince Lombardi

have injured. Then, after a time of conditioning your mind to harmony, go to those persons and offer your peace. Not everyone will not respond positively. Those that don't, forget them. You know in your heart that you have made your peace. You will be at peace within yourself. That's what counts. The ones who do respond positively will bring you a joy that will fill your heart.

Establish as a condition of life that you will never criticize another person. Look for the good in others. With kind words of praise and appreciation, you can bring out that good and both of you will enjoy warm feelings of good will.

Remember that life's greatest ability is the ability to get along well with other people. You do this by making them feel important. The greatest drive of every person is to feel important.

---

*"The deepest urge of human nature is the desire
to be and feel important."*

William James

Rewriting Your Tape: Why Did America's No. 1 Box Office Attraction Quit the Movies?

In 1965, at the height of her movie career, number one female box office star, Kim Novak, walked away from Hollywood and moved to the Big Sur, "running to my life."

Kim never felt that she was special as a child. "Oh, how I miss the fact that I never heard 'I love you' from [my parents]. It's something that I longed for, that keeps me always feeling that I never had enough love."

Her parents were strict Catholics and severe disciplinarians. They instilled in her the belief that she was very fragile and vulnerable. She felt she had to prove her worth; she sought her father's approval but never felt that she ever earned it, not matter how hard she worked for it.

"My father could never get in touch with his feelings or talk about them. He was remote, very private, a loner, raised in a family of farmers who believed in hard, physical work."

Her father, Joseph Novak, worked for the Chicago-Milwaukee Railroad and raised Kim and her sister in a tough, working-class district of Chicago where she was a shy, often frightened child with few friends.

Kim worked with a lot of powerful men in Hollywood—Harry Cohn, Otto Preminger, and Alfred Hitchcock. They were like her father, for she felt that she could never gain their approval.

"Yes, I felt like I was coming home." Kim was named the most popular star in the world in 1956, only two years after the release of her first movie. Kim was asked what went wrong. Why did she leave such an exalted position?

She felt she was sinking. "All I wanted was for them to tell me that I was doing something right, to let me find some way that I could be good." She tells how when she first went into show business, she had a pact with God, that she wanted to serve him and to do something meaningful. She says she had never really wanted to be an actor until it happened. "I thought, 'God thinks enough of me to let me communicate to the whole world.' I took it very seriously, and then as time went on, it [her life] seemed to be slipping through my fingers."

And what happened after she withdrew from the Hollywood scene? "I made nature my parents, my teachers. My teachers became the animals, the plants, the sea."

In 1974, nine years after leaving Hollywood, Kim met Dr. Robert Malloy, a veterinarian. Now they have been happily married for twenty years. Kim became her own self-nurturing parent. She discovered her self-value, her self-esteem.

If your parents did not raise you to have high self-esteem, then you must become your own self-nurturing parent and discover your own sense of importance. That's the way to wholeness.

How to Rate Your Self-Esteem
(Answer True or False.)

____ 1. I usually feel inferior to other people.

____ 2. I feel that I am a warm, loving and happy person.

"A relationship is a loving thing. It needs and benefits
from the same attention an artist lavishes on his art."
David Viscott

_____ 3. When things go wrong, I usually say, "Just my luck."

_____ 4. I feel life is wonderful and I can make it.

_____ 5. I have a strong drive to prove myself.

_____ 6. I am free of guilt, fear, and negative emotions.

_____ 7. I have a strong desire for recognition and approval.

_____ 8. I don't need to correct other people's mistakes.

_____ 9. When things don't work out right, I feel like a loser.

_____ 10. I look forward to new opportunities with enthusiasm.

_____ 11. I feel I must correct other people when they go wrong.

_____ 12. I do my own thinking and make my own decisions.

_____ 13. I tend to be critical and belittling of other people.

_____ 14. I am confident in meeting my own needs and reaching my goals.

_____ 15. I tend to sell my talents, abilities, and accomplishments short.

_____ 16. I am usually poised and confident around strangers.

_____ 17. I am vulnerable to the opinions and criticism of others.

_____ 18. I bear no prejudice toward people of other races or ethnic backgrounds.

_____ 19. I am fearful of revealing who I really am.

Two or more minds agreed in perfect harmony create a super mind, greater than the totality of the individual minds.

___ 20. I feel comfortable with myself and enjoy times of being alone.

___ 21. I am a compulsive "perfectionist."

___ 22. I accept compliments graciously and with appreciation.

___ 23. I am often compulsive in eating, talking, and drinking.

___ 24. I am appreciative of other people's accomplishments and talents.

___ 25. I don't like new experiences because I feel I will fail.

___ 26. I easily make new friends and keep old friends.

___ 27. I feel uneasy making new friends, because many people are not sincere.

___ 28. I easily admit my mistakes, because I learn from them.

___ 29. It is very important to me that people approve of me.

___ 30. I accept my responsibility to meet my own emotional needs.

___ 31. I often am embarrassed by the actions of some of my friends.

___ 32. I can accept someone's "put-down" without taking offense.

___ 33. It is very important to me for my boss to give me compliments.

"Flaming enthusiasm, backed up by horse sense and persistence, is the quality that most frequently makes for success."
Dale Carnegie

____ 34. I judge my self-worth by comparing myself to others.

Scoring

15—17 *true* answers to the odd statements and 15—17 *false* answers to the even statements mean you have very low self-esteem.

10—14 *true* answers to the odd statements and 10—14 *false* answers to the even statements mean you have low self-esteem.

5—9 *true* answers to the odd statements and 5—9 *false* answers to the even statements mean you have average self-esteem.

10—14 *false* answers to the odd statements and 10—14 *true* answers to the even statements mean you have high self-esteem.

15—17 *false* answers to the odd statements and 15—17 *true* answers to the even statements mean you have very high self-esteem.

My Childhood Role Models

	Father	Mother	Sister	Brother	Other
1. Attitude toward myself	____	____	____	____	____
2. Attitude toward men	____	____	____	____	____
3. Attitude toward women	____	____	____	____	____
4. Attitude about work	____	____	____	____	____
5. Attitude about emotions	____	____	____	____	____
6. Who played criticizer?	____	____	____	____	____
7. Who played victim?	____	____	____	____	____
8. Who played goof-off?	____	____	____	____	____
9. Who played irresponsible?	____	____	____	____	____
10. Who played peacemaker?	____	____	____	____	____

If you work hard enough, and smart enough, success is sure to follow.

11. Who played pessimist? _____ _____ _____ _____ _____
12. Who held the power? _____ _____ _____ _____ _____
13. Who played optimist? _____ _____ _____ _____ _____
14. Who played official
    worrier? _____ _____ _____ _____ _____
15. Who played achiever? _____ _____ _____ _____ _____
16. Who played the clown? _____ _____ _____ _____ _____
17. Who played out of sorts? _____ _____ _____ _____ _____
18. Who was the "heavy"? _____ _____ _____ _____ _____
19. Who manipulated whom? _____ _____ _____ _____ _____
20. Who was scared most of
    the time? _____ _____ _____ _____ _____
21. Who was happy? _____ _____ _____ _____ _____
22. Whose values
    predominated? _____ _____ _____ _____ _____
23. Whom did you pattern
    after? _____ _____ _____ _____ _____
24. Whom did you reject? _____ _____ _____ _____ _____

In re-evaluating this role model, you can determine who influenced your life the most and choose to relate to the ones whose positive models you choose.

Remember, self-esteem is that package of beliefs about yourself that you carry around inside, and which you take for granted is the real truth about yourself, whether it is or not.

If you rated low on the self-esteem test, you must rewrite your script, or tape, so that you can develop genuine self-esteem.

You can also view self-esteem as the self-accepted reputation you have with yourself, but a reputation and the real truth are often different.

People with low self-esteem are the ones who are both the victor and the victim in the *fatal attraction* syndrome. There are three stages of this kind of romantic love:

Stage I: The Fantasy Stage. The emotion is loneliness, the

The destiny of my life is up to me.

dynamic is hope. The fantasy is to find someone to meet my needs. Since I am incomplete without love, then I will be complete when I have met the ideal love of my life. There is a fantastic attraction when two people, both desperate for love, meet. Each one's own desperate chemistry hooks into the desperate chemistry of the other person.

The infatuation is a match with the mental role model I so desperately need. The energy is powerful. The sex is overwhelming. It is an infantile, unfulfilled need that craves satisfaction. The script is to find someone to "feel bad" with. The next day, or in a few days, the questions come: "If this love is so great, when am I going to feel better? Why isn't this person meeting my needs?" The truth is, the other person can't meet your needs, for the other person can't meet his own needs. And you don't know what your own needs are. Manipulation follows. You must force this person to meet your needs. So you start controlling the other person. Criticism and conflict follow.

The symptoms are as follows:

1. Primarily physical
2. Strong sex appeal
3. Little or no rational involvement
4. You hurt deeply when you are away from him/her
5. Lots of argument, frustration, and conflict when you are together
6. Your children and friends often can't understand what you see in this person
7. Usually you together have few value relationships
8. Both have probably been through a number of such experiences
9. Very little mental control

This affair will most likely break up in a short time. Most do. Then you feel hurt, cheated, that you are a failure,

---

Definiteness of purpose is the starting point of all achievement.

angry, and resentful toward the other person. As often as eight hundred times a day, thoughts of the other person flood your memory. This is the time when one may kill the other. The reason is not just anger toward the other person, but anger toward life. For a part of yourself, the incomplete, troubled, desperate self is even more fractured than before. *When the other person left, he took a part of you.* After all, Hollywood and the great music themes have promised that love is the answer to all needs. This lie has become truth to a great number of desperate people.

Get into counseling. Stay away from the other person. Throw yourself into your work and other constructive activities. The other person is not the reason. Don't blame him. He is just as hurt as you.

Stage II: The Anxiety Stage. The emotion is pain. The dynamic is power. You feel if you could force the other person to fulfill his obligation to you, it would work out. This whole problem comes from the script you have been living with.

A bad script comes with these feelings:

1. I am not wanted.
2. I blame myself, my parents, others, etc.
3. It's all my fault.
4. I'm not enough.
5. I'm powerless.
6. I'm not good enough.
7. I'm a failure because I wouldn't please my parents, others, etc.
8. I can be perfect.

Usually this bad script comes from a home where the

"Enthusiasm is the mother of effort and without it nothing great was ever accomplished.".
Ralph Waldo Emerson

parents and other adults, by their criticism, had contributed to your low self-esteem. So, you live an illusion.

Signs of an illusion include:

1. You are looking for a perfect mate.
2. You feel unlovable and unworthy.
3. You want to be loved more than to love.
4. You fear if you find love it won't be enough.
5. You want to be loved before you will give any love back.
6. You believe there is only one person in the world to meet your needs.
7. You look for someone to trust you before you will open up.
8. You continually fantasize with false expectations.
9. You are looking for someone to care about you, but you are unable to care back.
10. You believe love will solve all problems including loneliness.
11. You keep searching for someone to love rather than becoming a loving person.
12. You blame yourself for being alone.
13. You don't realize that affection is shared in many ways.
14. You feel you have never been loved by your parents.
15. You think that love is only an emotion.

How to get over this stage and become a real person:

1. You must determine the script and change it. Usually must have counseling. Few people can find their own bad scripts and change them.
2. You must rewrite the bad script into a good script. This is healing.
3. You must develop high self-esteem. Must learn to accept yourself, value yourself, and learn to love yourself.

You can change your life by changing your attitudes or mind.

4. You must develop own pathway to growth and pursue it as a lifelong journey.
5. You must work through to reality.

You must realize that love is not an emotion, or an energy. Love is a learned response. Love is a decision to act in a loving, caring manner. Love is a commitment to your own growth and happiness and a commitment to the safety, satisfaction, security, and happiness of the person loved. Love is a decision not to criticize the other person. Love is a pattern to live your life in harmony, happiness, unity, and sharing life's great moments. Love is a commitment to grow to become the kind of person you always have wanted to become. Love is encouraging the one loved to become all he/she can become.

How do you know when you are in reality? When you can positively write out ten things about yourself you want to improve, can sit down and discuss this openly with another person, and honestly agree on a plan of action to grow.

Stage III: Real Love. The emotion is serenity, the dynamic is sharing love. Now you can share love rationally as a fact. You can share love emotionally as a feeling and behaviorally as an act. You are a totally self-accepting individual. You are living in the truth of your healthy selfhood. You are the supplier of your own emotional needs. You have decided to love yourself.

Keys to Genuine Self-Esteem

The secret to inner peace lies in self-affirmation, a quiet celebration.

You can't change others, but you can change your reactions to others.

"There is no man, no woman, so small but that they cannot make their life great by high endeavor."
Thomas Carlyle

The path to inner peace requires awareness, courage, decision, and action.

Form a positive personal belief system that values and celebrates yourself.

In your internal cast of characters, the troublemakers will be your "not OK" and "critical parent" tapes. They are hooked into the love of power. They try to manipulate, control, and win. Your nurturing adult and natural child are concerned with the power of love. They are the ones that work for the best interest of you and others.

To increase your self-worth, you do not need to change yourself. You need to change your "self-talk" and your negative beliefs about yourself. You can choose to become your own nurturing parent.

Change the words "should," ought," "must," "have to," to those of the nurturing parent—"wish," "prefer," "want," "choose," "feel," and "desire."

You can choose not to react to the judgments of others. You do this by giving space to blame but refusing to take their bait.

Reasonable expectations are nurturing. Unreasonable ones cause pain.

When you are upset, check what expectations have gone unmet.

Your inner criticizer will ask for perfection in feelings, thoughts, and deeds. Give yourself permission to be less than perfect. Do not cling to past mistakes, but rather release them.

Give up the belief that things should always go as you want them to. Others don't have to match your feelings, attitudes, and values. Life and others are not expected to know how you feel or what you want without being told.

Take time for meaningful pleasure. Put balance into your life by doing those things that give you release from the pressures of daily work.

"Some people regard discipline as a chore.
For me it is a kind of order that sets me free to fly."
Julie Andrews

Improve your family, business, and friend relationships. We draw strength from the positive people around us. Release negative relationships that are destructive to your own feelings.

Write out goals for your life—career, family, personal, and professional goals. If you fail to plan, you are planning to fail.

With subliminal videocassettes and audiotapes, condition yourself to positive self-talk. You alone are responsible for your feelings. Impact yourself with affirmations that give you the feelings and assurances of success.

After Ty Cobb retired from baseball, he became a scout for the Detroit Tigers. He was sent to Memphis to check out a twenty-one-year-old first baseman. He returned after three days to Detroit and said, "Forget him. He's as clumsy as an ox in the field and he can't hit curve balls."

Three years later, that player, Lou Gehrig, was the first baseman for the New York Yankees. The Detroit management said to Cobb, "Ty, you missed that one."

"No," said Ty. Somewhere within those three years, Gehrig decided to pay the *price of greatness.* Lou Gehrig had high self-esteem.

Andy Strasberg is the director of marketing for the San Diego Padres. He says, "I went to my first baseball game as an 8-year-old. My dad took me to the Giants-Phillies game. I fell in love with baseball.

"In 1960, Roger Maris came to the Yankees from Kansas City. That year, Roger won the most valuable player award. He became my idol. In 1961, the entire country was wrapped up in the home run race between Maris and Mickey Mantle and Babe Ruth's ghost. I cut out every single article on Roger and eight years later, had them bound in an eleven-volume scrapbook.

"We work to become, not to acquire."

Elbert Hubbard

"I always sat in Section 31, Row 162-A, Seat 1 in Yankee Stadium. Right field. I would watch Maris park his car and told him what a big fan I was. After awhile, he began to notice me. He threw me a baseball in batting practice. I was so excited, I couldn't lift my arms to catch it. Someone else got it. I yelled to Roger that I didn't get it, so he stopped and gave me another one.

"My friends kept pushing me to ask Roger for one of his bats. He said, 'Sure, next time I break the bat.' That was 1965. When the team was in Los Angeles, I heard on the radio that Roger had broken his bat.

"When the team returned to New York, during batting practice, Roger came over to me and gave me his bat and said, 'I've got this bat for you.'

"I said, 'Oh, my God, I can't thank you enough.' He knew who I was. He had brought that bat back from L.A.

"I brought that bat home and told my friends. They said, 'Now that you have the bat, why not ask him for one of his home run balls.'

"I asked Roger for one. He said, 'You're gonna have to catch one 'cause I don't have any.'

"Maris was traded to St. Louis on December 8, 1966. In 1967, while in school at the University of Akron in Ohio, one day six of us drove to Pittsburgh to see Roger play the Pirates. I saw Roger as he was entering the stadium. I went up to him and said, 'Roger.'

"He turned and said, 'Andy Strasberg, what the hell are you doing here in Pittsburgh?' That was the first time I knew that Roger knew my name.

"I replied, 'Well, I'm here with some guys from college and we wanted to say hello.'

"I introduced my friends to Roger. Roger said, 'Wait a minute, I want to give you an autographed National League ball.' I felt like a million dollars.

You get the best out of others when you give the best of yourself.

"That day, I sat in Row 9, Seat 9 out in right field. In the third inning, Roger hit a home run off Woodie Fryman. I caught the ball. The most amazing thing in the world had happened to me. Tears were rolling down my face. When Roger came to right field he looked up at me and said, 'I can't believe it.'

"I said, 'You can't, I can't.'

"Back at school, I was afraid I was going to lose that baseball, so I went down to the Akron Dime National Bank and put it in a safety deposit box. Later, when I was back in New York, Roger came to Shea Stadium and Roger signed that ball. In 1968, Roger played his last game in St. Louis. I flew out to see him play. I was seated behind the dugout. When Roger came into the dugout, he stopped, saw me in the stands and winked at me. A reporter for *Sporting News* saw that and interviewed me. When he found out I had flown out from New York to see Roger's last game, the reporter asked Roger about me and Roger said, 'Andy Strasberg was my most loyal fan.'

"Roger and I started exchanging Christmas cards and the relationship continued. When I got the job with the Padres, Roger wrote me a letter of congratulations. When I got married in 1976, Rog and his wife, Pat, sent us a wedding gift, and we talked on the phone several times a year. In 1980, when Roger and Pat were in Los Angeles for the All-Star Game, we (my wife, Patti; my dad; Roger and Pat) went out to dinner.

"Roger passed away in December 1985. I made arrangements to go to Fargo, North Dakota, for the services. After the services, I went up to Pat. She hugged me, introduced me to their six children and said, 'I want to introduce you to someone really special, kids; this is Andy Strasberg.'

"I have yet to find the man, however exalted his station,
who did not do better work and put forth greater effort
under a spirit of approval, than under a spirit of criticism."
Charles Schwab

"Roger Maris, Jr. said, 'You're dad's number one fan.'

"Now I go back to Fargo every year for a charity golf tournament and auction held in Roger's name for the Hospice of the Red River Valley. One year I asked for the opportunity to address the 700 people present. I said, 'You've heard from Roger's family, Roger's friends, his teammates, but there is another side, and that is Roger's fans, and this video tells it all.'

"The lights went down and on came a 3½ minute video I had put together with a friend—pictures of Maris, of Maris and me together, with Lou Rawls singing in the background: 'Did you know that you're my hero? You are the wind beneath my wings.' It gave me the opportunity to tell everyone about Roger Maris, the man."

Roger Maris and Andy Strasberg both had high self-esteem.

How to Become an Assertive Person

Assertive behavior is the middle ground between aggressive and passive behavior. To be assertive, one must modify five facets of his behavior: eye contact, body language, voice tone and pitch, body posture, and place and timing of action.

Aggressive: Expressing your emotions openly by using threatening behavior toward a person or object, which violates another's rights.

Passive: Hiding your emotions so that others do not know how you feel; not standing up for your rights.

Assertive: Expressing your emotions honestly and standing up for your rights without hurting others.

Aggressive Behavior Description

1. Eye Contact: Constant eye contact, glaring, staring

I learn something and useful from every positive-minded person I meet.

2. Facial Expression: Frown, tight-lipped, jaw set, no smile, mouthing words, threatening
3. Body Position: Feet wide apart, standing
4. Gestures: Shaking arm, fist, or finger; waving arms threateningly
5. Personal Space: Very close to person or thing addressed
6. Voice: Harsh, threatening tone
7. Volume: Loud, or low and threatening

Understanding Aggressive Behavior

Aggressive behavior lets us express our feelings, but hurts others. It is appropriate only in life-threatening situations or contact sports like football. We act aggressively both verbally and nonverbally. Verbally, we scream. Nonverbally, we threaten others with our arms, fists, and bodies by hitting, shoving, or shaking our fists. Most importantly, aggressive behavior in inappropriate places may let us say how we feel, but it usually results in a negative consequence (being hit back, detention in school, suspension from work, etc.).

Passive Behavior Description

1. Eye Contact: Little or none, often looking down, doesn't meet others' eyes
2. Facial Expression: Little or no emotion, slight smile
3. Gestures: Arms folded limply or close to side; little or no motion with arms or hands
4. Posture: Feet together, head down, shoulders slumped, does not stand close to others
5. Voice: Soft
6. Volume: Mumbles; inaudible, soft voice

Understanding Passive Behavior

Passive people let others take advantage of them because their behavior doesn't allow them to express their feelings and

---

No man stands as tall as he who makes other people more productive.

prevents them from standing up for themselves. Nonverbal passive behaviors include looking at the floor or away from others and standing with head down and shoulders slumped. Verbal passive behavior is speaking softly, sometimes so that people can't hear. Often passive people are often ignored by others.

Assertive Behavior Description

1. Eye Contact: Intermittently looking directly at other person
2. Facial Expressions: Showing emotion, pleasant, smiling, questioning
3. Posture: Relaxed, shoulders back, head up, facing the other person, feet a comfortable distance apart
4. Gestures: Nods head, uses hands and arms to show feelings and thoughts (in a nonthreatening manner)
5. Voice: Normal tone, easily heard, polite

Understanding Assertive Behavior

Assertive behavior lets us express how we feel about something or stand up for our rights without hurting others. Assertive nonverbal behaviors include good eye contact; gesturing to emphasize what we are saying; using smiles, interested expressions, laughter, or questioning looks as facial expressions; standing with head and shoulders back and comfortably near the person to whom we are speaking. Assertive verbal behaviors include a normal speaking voice that is loud enough for others to hear. This behavior lets us say what we feel or think; but we should realize we may not always get what we want.

How to Live in the Joy of High Self-Esteem

1. See yourself as a positive, enthusiastic, growing, and achieving person with genuine self-esteem.

"I use all the brains I have, and all I can borrow."
Pres. Woodrow Wilson

2. Rid yourself of all negative emotions and learn to meet your own emotional needs.

3. Learn the values of relating to people—your children, friends, and the people you date. Trust yourself to grow.

4. Remember where you were and acknowledge where you are now. Then you have the confidence to become what you want to be. Don't consider marriage until you can give of the overflow of your wholeness.

5. Be sure you have reevaluated your values and rejected those that are unworthy of you. For example, it is more important to value people and use things than to use people and value things. You must be in a position of caring, sharing, and giving, rather than demanding.

6. You must have come through the process of being in charge of your life. No one else will or should do for you the things you can do for yourself. You are neither dependent nor independent, but interdependent.

7. It is necessary to respect the personhood of each individual. You no longer fit people into confining grooves, but realize the uniqueness of every person.

8. You no longer make snap judgments of people. You trust yourself, so you now can trust others, expect the best, and look for the good in others.

9. Now you can face and handle your own problems rather than look for a rescuer to solve problems for you. You have the well-deserved confidence that you can overcome most any adversity.

10. You are now a unique, self-celebrating person of value. You control your own mind with positive thoughts; you

---

*"By virtue of being born to humanity, every human being
has a right to the development and fulfillment of his
potentialities as a human being."*
Ashley Montagu

control your own emotions by relating only to those people you choose to relate to.

11. You are free to be you. Now, if the right people come into your life, you can choose to relate to them. You are on your way to a meaningful, purposeful, and fulfilling life.

Quotes

"The success in life is for a man to be ready for his opportunity when it comes."

British Prime Minister Benjamin Disraeli

"It is a funny thing about life. If you refuse to accept anything but the best, you often get it."   Somerset Maugham

"Always behave like a duck. Keep calm and unruffled on the surface but paddle like the devil underneath."

Anonymous

"The three really great things in the world are a mountain, the ocean, and an earnest man at his work. The potentialities of each are beyond human calculation."

Edward W. Bok

"Genius is one percent inspiration and ninety-nine perspiration."   Thomas Edison

"If you are a self-made man, you are working on a job that will never be finished."   Anonymous

"Far better it is to dare mighty things to win glorious triumphs, even though checkered by failure, than to take rank with those poor spirits who neither enjoy much nor suffer much, because they live in the gray twilight that knows not victory, only defeat."   Pres. Theodore Roosevelt

---

"He who is firm and resolute in will molds the world to himself."
Goethe

"Success is like a good movie: It is only exciting when you have someone to share it with." Anonymous

"If you have built castles in the air, your work need not be lost: That is where they should be. Now put foundations under them." Henry David Thoreau

"The world stands aside to let anyone pass who knows where he is going." David Starr Jordan

"No man can be happy unless he feels his life is in some way important." Bertrand Russell

"One person with a belief is equal to a force of 99 who have interests." John Stuart Mill

"Always do right. This will gratify some people and astonish the rest." Mark Twain

"There is no security on this earth. There is only opportunity." Gen. Douglas MacArthur

"You cannot climb the ladder of success with your hands in your pockets." Anonymous

"There are those who are so scrupulously afraid of doing wrong that they seldom venture to do anything."

Anonymous

"There are no great men, only great challenges that ordinary men are forced by circumstances to meet."

Adm. William F. Bull Halsey

"Our greatest joy is not in never falling, but rising every time we fail." Confucius

"The really happy man is the one who can enjoy the scenery when he has to take a detour." Anonymous

---

I can control the way I feel about others for I choose not to yield my good thoughts and feelings to negative and destructive thoughts and feelings.

"You can have anything out of life you want, if you help enough people get what they want."   Zig Ziglar

"We are forever on the verge of all that is great: trust in yourself, claim your share of the greatness of life: surrender yourself to the power within you: dare to become the master of your own fate."   Ralph Waldo Emerson

How to Develop Genuine Self-Esteem

1. Fact: God wants you to love yourself. Nineteen times in the Bible we are commanded to love ourselves.
2. Desire to change your life. Decide what more you want out of life and do it.
3. Put yourself first. Then out of your self, love overflows; others will benefit.
4. Perform the program of change. Write out your goals, commit yourself to them, and achieve them.
5. Get in touch with yourself, with your feelings, your mind, your will, and become a whole person.
6. Practice the policy of benefiting others. Enjoy the positive power of giving sunshine to others.
7. Enjoy meaningful work production. Give more than you expect to receive and the law of compensation will pay off for you.
8. Improve your physical health. Get in shape and stay in shape. Fatigue makes cowards of us all.
9. Improve your mental health. Enjoy spirited conversation, read challenging books, and stretch your mind.
10. Improve your social health. Give yourself the greatest gift of good friends. Enjoy theater, music, travel, nature, dining, and and other good social experiences.
11. Improve your spiritual health. Rid yourself of unhealthy guilt feelings. Learn to accept God's love.
12. Increase your pleasure activity. Decide and enjoy pleasure free of regret.

The harder I work, and the better I plan, the luckier I get.

13. Feed yourself good strokes. Learn to meet your own emotional needs.
14. Plan an achieving life. You pass through this life but once. Make it a great life. The only thing you and I can totally control are our own minds.

Self-esteem comes from
1. Meaningful work production
2. Good human relations
3. God-love, romantic love, family love, and self-love.
4. Enjoyable recreation
5. Music, worship, nature, and other values

Self-love, self-esteem, self-confidence, self-value, and self-celebration are yours. Live it up. You are of value, you are important, and you are beautiful.

Self-Esteem

1. I am the best friend to myself. I take me out whenever I feel low. I alone am responsible for my feelings and I choose to feel beautiful.
2. I am a unique, never-to-be-repeated miracle of God. Therefore, today, and every day, I celebrate myself.
3. I live in the principle of unlimitedness. Abundance is mine for love, peace, joy, happiness, energy, health, and wealth know no boundaries.
4. I am open, receptive, responsive and obedient to life, love, joy, peace, energy, wealth, health, wisdom, and the beauty of wholeness.
5. A new friend is a beautiful gift I give myself.
6. No one can make me stoop so low as to hate him.
7. I draw people to me by the power of my love for them.

"Love cures people. Both the ones who give it,
and the ones who receive it."
Dr. Karl Menninger

8. I will not be an emotional cripple controlled by negative attitudes.

9. I relate to positive-minded people and choose not to expose my sensitive emotions to negative-minded people, for such thoughts are destructive.

10. I dwell on beautiful, powerful thoughts of self-affirmation.

11. My personality is the outward expression of the inward person. I want that person to be fulfilling and whole, so I will love myself and be loved by others.

12. The happiest people are those with experience in helping others.

13. I will remember that the deepest urge in human nature is the desire to be important, and I will sincerely and honestly seek to make every person I meet feel important.

14. I can develop the skill of getting along with people.

15. I can cure many of my ills by helping friends cure theirs.

16. I can control the way I feel about others, because I choose not to yield my good thoughts and feelings for negative and destructive thoughts and feelings.

17. I believe in the redeeming power of God's love.

18. "For as he thinketh in his heart, so is he. . . ." (Prov. 23:7).

19. God is my instant, constant, abundant source of energy, love, and peace.

20. "And all things, whatsoever ye shall ask in prayer, believing, ye shall receive." (Matt. 21:22).

21. The love of God lives in me, the peace of God lives as me, the power of God flows through me; wherever I am God is, and all is well.

22. I have faith in the power of the human body to heal through nutrition.

Not failure, but low aim, is the real crime in life.

23. From my healthy body and my healthy thoughts, I live an abundant life.

Conclusion

Regardless of what you have suffered from the past of poor self-esteem, only you can change these feelings. Determine your script, erase the bad feelings, and replace them with the positive self-affirmations to become the person God intended you to be. Only when you have bombarded your subconscious mind with more positive self-talk than the total of negative self-talk will you become a positive person.

Realize you and you alone must be responsible for who you are. Become your own self-nurturing parent.

This is a lifelong journey toward wholeness and happiness. You are not alone. There are many others available to help you. Your public library is full of self-help books.

A friend is someone who loves and cares.

CHAPTER 9

Self-Esteem in Relationships: How to Enjoy Real Love

In order to appreciate and share love as an adult, children must grow through the following steps and have the various needs met, as originally theorized by psychologist Abraham Maslow:

1. Physical Needs—food, lodging, and a sense that physical needs will be adequately provided for.
2. Safety Needs—freedom from fear, worry, abuse, and hostility, so that one feels safe and secure.
3. Social Needs—a warm feeling and satisfaction of belonging to parents, other family members, peer groups, church, school, and God.
4. Love Needs—unquestioned acceptance of God's love, parents' love, family love, friends' love, and self-love.
5. Self-Actualization—exciting growth toward fullness, wholeness, and completeness; a strong assurance that one can achieve any goal desired.
6. Peak-Experiencing—beautiful mental and emotional overflowing feelings of God's blessing, goal-seeking, strong assurance of direction, warm satisfaction, and self-celebration. Directly proportionate to this achievement is the adult able to give and receive real love.

One is growing in real love when one is more dedicated to the satisfaction, security, growth, happiness, and self-esteem of the one loved than for one's self.

Love is not an emotion. Emotions such as passion, greed, jealousy, ambition, strife, etc. are uncontrolled feelings that fluctuate like a yo-yo.

Love is an activity. It is growing in, not "falling in." Love is the activity of giving, sharing, communicating, experiencing, and becoming.

Real love has feelings as a result of this activity— overflowing, alive, joyful, and exciting feelings built on the firm foundation of assured and proven conduct instead of the insecurity of an uncontrolled passion.

Love is a decision. It is a commitment to love based on common values and compatibility in spiritual, mental, financial, character, family, vocation, happiness, and openness beliefs.

Love is unconditional. You do not turn off your love when another irritates you. You love without reservation. You like or dislike conduct.

Love is forever. Without this intent, you do not give love your best.

Love is a decision to grow, to love, to be fulfilled, and to achieve happiness.

Love affirms, not possesses. Love doesn't smother, but sets free. If you love someone, set him free. If he comes back to you, he is yours forever. If he doesn't, he never was yours in the first place.

How to Give Real Love Worksheet

On a scale of one to ten, rate yourself on these steps of self-actualization:

____ 1. *Physical Needs.* I am free of concern for my physical needs such as food, lodging and financial pressure.

Today and every day, I look for people who want to share my journey toward greatness.

____ 2. *Safety Needs.* I feel safe where I live and feel secure from fear, worry, hostility, and negative emotions.

____ 3. *Social Needs.* I have a strong feeling of belonging to my parents, family, church, friends, and to God.

____ 4. *Love Needs.* I really love myself and am able to give and receive love from God, parents, other relatives, friends of the same sex, and friends of the opposite sex.

____ 5. *Self-Actualization.* I enjoy my journey toward fullness, wholeness, completeness, and achievement.

____ 6. Peak-Experiencing. On occasion, I experience a peak of wonderful feelings of emotional overflowing.

____ 7. Now I am able to give security, satisfaction, self-esteem, and happiness to the one I love.

____ 8. I have made a decision of emotions, mind, and the will to commit my love. I give this wonderful gift as the highest expression of my personhood.

____ 9. I give my love unconditionally, as I appreciate and chose my mate for her/his values and character.

____ 10. I commit my love forever. I hold no reservation, because I intend this experience to last a lifetime.

____ 11. I am open to growth and communication in every area with my intended.

____ 12. My love empowers my mate to love her/himself.

____ 13. I affirm my mate and will not possess her/him.

____ Total

"Happiness is a perfume that you cannot pour on someone else without getting a few drops on yourself."
Ralph Waldo Emerson

Scoring

100—130   You are a strong, emotionally mature, actual-izing person able to give genuine, real love.

80—99   You are growing toward self-acceptance and desire an achieving life.

60—79   You have areas in your life that need facing so you can proceed on your journey toward full-ness.

40—59   Work through your emotions in order to ac-cept yourself. Only then will you be able to give love to another.

Getting to Know Yourself

I like myself better when _____

_____

I feel bad when _____

_____

I am at my best when _____

_____

I feel good when _____

_____

My greatest asset is _____

My most important need is _____

My greatest accomplishment is _____

_____

_____

"You make more friends in two months by becoming
interested in other people than you can in two years
by trying to get other people interested in you."

Dale Carnegie

My intellectual hero is _____

My spiritual hero is _____

My political hero is _____

If I could change one thing in my life _____

_____

The best time of my life was _____

_____

The worst time of my life was _____

_____

Check up on your relationships. Separately, sit down and grade your mate (or a friend) on a scale of 1-10 on each of these areas:

1. Shared goals ___

2. Values ___

3. Communication ___

4. Spiritual unity ___

5. Social satisfaction ___

6. Touching, affection ___

7. Positive method of conflict ___

8. Male/female identity ___

9. Sexual fulfillment ___

10. Compatibility with friends ___

11. Food and drink experiences ___

12. Individual growth ___

It pays to share. The more you pass on to others, the more you get to have for yourself.

377

13. Decision making ___

14. Fun and play time ___

15. Intimate talk time ___

16. Freedom and independence ___

17. Parenting ___

18. Recreation fulfillment ___

19. Vacation and travel ___

20. Financial agreement ___

Total ___

Scoring

Less than 100   poor relationship
101 — 125   fair relationship
176 — 200   great relationship

Any area where the rating was less than 5 is the area you need to work on. Here is where you have problems. Talk this over with your mate (or friend). Encourage him (or her) to communicate openly. Work on your relationship.

Living the Spirit of Cooperation

Plentifulness. With openness, discussion, good communication, and fulfilling mutual experiences, each person can have all the strokes, values, joys, achievements, and self-celebration he or she may desire. The more love you share, the more you have. There is no limitedness in love.

Equal Partners. Each verbalizes what he/she wants, can give and contract for strokes, financial security, work responsibility, love-sharing, and every mutual experience.

What makes men great is their ability to decide what is important, and to then focus their attention to it.

Lovingly, call the other on power plays. Since there can be no losers in a cooperation, and no tyranny, you openly and lovingly call the other's hand when winner-versus-loser power plays are consciously or subconsciously expressed. Only then can preconceived roles be discontinued.

Ask for what you want 100 percent of the time. No one can meet your needs if you yourself don't know what they are. Hold no secrets from the other, but let it all hang out. With each request, there may be a compromise response. Then contract for what you want.

Don't rescue, but help when agreed upon. To rescue means there must be a victim. The rescuer says, "I know what you need and I'll give it to you whether or not you want it." The helper says, "I can give you 'warm fuzzies' or emotional affirmations if you want me to."

The rules:

You don't help unless you contract to do so.
Your mate is able to help himself/herself.
You help your mate to achieve fullness.
You do no more than fifty percent of the process.
Do only what you want to do.

These principles also should apply to parent-child, boss-employee, and friend-friend relationships.

Creating Ecstasy in Your Relationships

1. Are you willing for your relationship to work?
2. Do you really want satisfaction in your relationships?
3. Do you desire completion in your relationships?
4. Do you strongly desire aliveness and vitality in your relationships?
5. Do you want certainty and constancy in your relationships?

The only way to have a friend is to be one.

6. Do you give completeness and commitment in your relationships?
7. Do you know what you want in your relationships (family, friends, romance)?
8. Can you pinpoint what has happened to end other relationships?
9. Do you remain friendly with others when the relationship is over?
10. Can you look back and appreciate what you learned and experienced in other relationships?
11. Can you honestly evaluate how you contributed to the failure of former relationships?
12. How much of the failure of former relationships was due to relating to the wrong person for you?
13. Do you need to be more careful in choosing your relationships?
14. Have you tended to hold back and not give your best effort in a relationship?
15. Do you clearly know what you want in a relationship?
16. Do you openly and honestly tell the other person what you want?
17. Do you tend to get too involved too soon in a romantic relationship?
18. Are you looking for someone to meet your needs in a romantic relationship?
19. Do you know how to heal a troubled relationship?
20. How would you like to have a recreational relationship?
21. Are you willing to take the time to let the relationship develop naturally?
22. Do you tend to become too possessive in a relationship?

"You can cure your ills by helping a friend cure his."
Dale Carnegie

23. Do you know how to give "space" in a relationship?
24. Are you capable of giving more to a relationship than you take from it?
25. Who is the source of love in a relationship?
26. In a relationship of two others close to you, who is the source of love?
27. Who do you need in order to experience love?
28. If love is scarce in your relationship, who isn't creating love?
29. Have you learned how to love a person into loving you?
30. From whom do we draw out love?
31. Do you know how to create love and how to do it consistently?

Ecstasy. A state of feeling of overpowering joy.

Relationship. Understanding and awareness of another person's way of being. Living as the other person. Thinking and acting as the other person.

Involvement. Making life intricate, full of puzzles, full of elaborate detail, entangled, endangered, and difficult to catch so that escape is nearly impossible.

Completeness. To make whole, full, perfect; inclusion of all that is needed for wholeness. No need for something else, no sense of being difficult. No sense it could be better, no sense of inadequacy. Perfect and accepted as is.

Create. To cause to come into existence, to make, to originate, to bring about, to cause, to give rise to.

Space. The boundless expanse within which all things are contained, room for self, personhood, soul, being, an interval of time.

> "This is the true joy in life: that being used for a purpose recognized by yourself as a mighty one, being a force of nature, rather than a feverish, selfish little clod

---

My personality is the outward expression of the inward person and I want that person to be fulfilling and whole so I will love myself and be loved by others.

of ailments and grievances, complaining that the world will not devote itself to making me happy. . . . Life is no brief candle to me, but a sort of splendid torch which I've got a hold of for the moment and I want to make it burn as brightly as possible before handing it on to future generations."

George Bernard Shaw

We Relate to People We Admire and Respect

Sydney Smith said, "Life is to be fortified by many friendships. To love and be loved, is the greatest happiness of existence." Quit trying to get along with people you don't admire and respect. You have a relationship problem with these people. Cultivate the relationship with time, energy, activity, concern, and love. For this is the only basis of a real relationship.

Look back on failed relationships, marriages, courtships, etc. Wasn't this the reason for its dissolution?

What are the values that you admire and respect? List as many as you can.

1. _____   4. _____

2. _____   5. _____

3. _____   6. _____

Now, look back on experiences that didn't work out—a parent, brother or sister, mate or friend. Do you see why? Don't feel guilty. You have a right to be you and have your own values. Anyone who doesn't measure up to them isn't to be blamed. That's the way life works.

Draw people to you by the power of your love for them.

Creating Space

Rainer Maria Rilke said, "Love consists in this, that two solitudes protect and touch and greet each other."

Space is personhood—the sacredness of the human soul; the preciousness of the individual personality; the priceless dignity of an eternal person. No one has the right to injure, hurt, hinder, harass, limit, embarrass, or damage someone's personhood.

Think back and recall some times when you were so damaged. List them:

1. _____   3. _____

2. _____   4. _____

Think back and recall some ways you have violated the personhood of another.

1. _____   3. _____

2. _____   4. _____

Space is privacy. In what ways has your privacy been denied? In what ways have you violated the privacy of another person?

1. _____   3. _____

2. _____   4. _____

Space is values. List some of your values others have violated:

1. _____   3. _____

2. _____   4. _____

---

*"I have found that if I have faith in myself and
in the idea I am tinkering with, I usually win out."*
Charles F. Kettering

Space is time. How do you feel others are violating your time?

1. _____   3. _____

2. _____   4. _____

Living the "No Wrong" Life

Eleanor Roosevelt said, "No one can make you feel inferior without your consent." You and I do not have the right to make others feel that they are wrong. We are not God. They do not have to answer to us. And you violate any opportunity to bring about change or to influence other people when you make them feel wrong. List some ways others have made you feel wrong:

1. _____   3. _____

2. _____   4. _____

Now list some ways you have unwittingly made another person feel wrong.

1. _____   3. _____

2. _____   4. _____

We are carrying on our backs a load of garbage or a load of gold. Don't dump garbage on others. Instead, shower them with gold dust, or even a nugget or two.

Goal-Seeking

Anyone can set a goal. The realization of goals is dependent on two other factors: a change of attitude in that you act as if your goal is now yours, and conduct of activity

---

"Every great and commanding moment in the annals of the world is the triumph of some enthusiasm."
Ralph Waldo Emerson

that assures the achievement of your goal. Nothing becomes dynamic until it becomes specific. Write out your goals as clearly and concisely as possible. Let this stimulate you:

What problems in the relationship do you want resolved?

_____

What are you now doing in the relationship that you want to stop doing?

_____

_____

What are you not doing in the relationship that you want to start doing?

_____

_____

What fantasy or desire do you want fulfilled?

_____

_____

What do you feel needs to be done to make the relationship more complete?

_____

_____

What travels, possessions, or experiences do you want to experience in the relationship?

_____

_____

---

*Build a reservoir of good will by placing the
interest of others above your own.*

Growing the Relationship

Walter Winchell said, "A friend is one who walks in when others walk out."

Put energy into it. Assign priority to it. Friendship is as important as eating, sleeping, and working. Satisfaction is followed by dissatisfaction.

The strongest of life's desires is to feel important. With this is the desire to reveal our innermost self. With your trusted friend, really open up as to who you are, what you want, and what you want to become.

Enjoy touching. "There is one temple in the universe— the human body. We touch heaven when we touch the human body." (Thomas Carlyle) More than a million sensory fibers flow from the skin through the spinal cord to the brain. Our skin is the most powerful organ in the body. Reveal your love, your warmth, and your wholeness by touching.

Constantly affirm. Never let the other person doubt your support, love, concern, assurance, and availability. Spoken and written words are so important. Pablo Casals said, "As long as one can admire and love, then one is young forever."

Loyalty. Nothing will ever be allowed to sever or weaken the relationship. This loyalty can bring back from disaster a person to renewed ecstasy.

Creating ecstasy. There are two states of being:

1. Planned achievement. This comes as the result of a process. Maslow's six steps to self-actualization is an example. Learning is a process.

2. Instant achievement. This is the statement of a desired truth. The human mind, at least the subconscious part, is very vague. The conscious mind gives clear-cut commands and the subconscious mind instantly obeys. You can create a miracle by the decision to do so.

"Love and you shall be loved."

Ralph Waldo Emerson

There is a four-thought pattern toward this accomplishment:

1. *Desire.* Strong enough to be willing to change.
2. *Expectancy.* By faith accepting it as truth.
3. *Behaving as fact.* From this moment on, it is a fact and nothing will change it.
4. *Reinforcement.* With affirmations, attitude control, and conduct response, you can continue to reinforce the decision. You must never look back.

Whatever you tell yourself and believe, it is then truth for you and you behave accordingly. *You have now created ecstasy. You live the truth of overpowering joy.*

How to Communicate with Your Mate

1. What is the funniest thing that ever happened to you?
2. Where did you spend the most delicious weekend of your life?
3. What is your favorite movie? Favorite book? Favorite food? Favorite music?
4. Who was your hero as a child? As an adult?
5. On a scale of one to ten, rate yourself as a loving, caring person.
6. Rate yourself as to your openness, your honesty, and your friendliness.
7. Rate yourself as to your being fun to be with.
8. Rate yourself as to your sensuousness. Rate your ambition. Rate your happiness.
9. If you had but one year to live, what would you do?
10. If you had one year to live, *and money were no object*, what would you do?
11. What member of your family are you closest to? Who is your closest friend?
12. If you had an overwhelming problem, to whom would you go?

To be a free person is life's greatest achievement.

13. What parent are you closest to? What child? What brother or sister?
14. Who is your best friend of the same sex? Nonromantic friend of opposite sex?
15. Who is your most spiritual friend? Most emotionally mature friend?
16. What do you want most in a friend? In a mate?
17. Name an activity you hate to do. Name an activity your mate hates to do.
18. If you had but one word to describe yourself, what would it be?
19. If you had but one word to describe your mate, what would it be?
20. What do you like most about your mate?
21. What do you like least about your mate?
22. What is the best value you add to your mate's life?
23. What is the best value your mate adds to your life?
24. What is the greatest thing you have received from this relationship?
25. What do you want most from this relationship?
26. What have you learned from this relationship?
27. What would you like to contribute most to this relationship?
28. What in life is the most important to you? To your mate?
29. What is the most important for you and your mate to share?
30. What would you like to change in the way your mate acts toward you?
31. What should you change in the way you act toward your mate?
32. Close your eyes. What was the happiest expression ever on your mate's face?

---

*I choose not to be an emotional cripple controlled
by the negative attitudes of others.*

33. What was the most pained expression you have ever seen on your mate's face?
34. What do you feel when your mate looks lovingly at you?
35. What do you feel when your mate lovingly touches you?
36. What do you feel when your mate says he/she loves you?
37. Is there anything you would like your mate to tell you that he/she hasn't?
38. Is there anything you would like to tell your mate that you haven't?
39. How do you feel when you are alone and you think about your mate?
40. Does your mate ever make you feel sad? Was it your activity that caused it?
41. Do you ever make your mate feel sad? Why? By accident or with intent?
42. What first attracted you to your mate? What continues to attract you?
43. If you could go anywhere in the world with your mate, where would it be?
44. Do you think you spend too much time with your mate? Too little time?
45. What physical feature of your mate do you like the most?
46. What physical feature of your mate do you like the least?
47. What emotional feature of your mate do you like the most?
48. What emotional feature of your mate do you like the least?
49. What spiritual feature of your mate do you like the most?

---

*God will not bestow blessings on you if there is no
room in your heart to receive them.*

50. What spiritual feature of your mate do you like the least?
51. What habit of your mate do you like the least?
52. When you are away from your mate, what do you miss the most?
53. What do you need most from your mate? What does your mate need most from you?
54. What do you need to contribute most to your mate?
55. What do you want your mate to contribute most to you?
56. What do you lack most that your mate has not fulfilled?
57. What are you most emotional about?
58. When are you most in tune with God?
59. Do you ever pretend to be something you are not? Does your mate?
60. Do you ever dream about your mate?
61. Do you ever try to control or manipulate your mate? Does your mate ever try to control or manipulate you?
62. Do you ever feel smothered in this relationship? Do you ever smother?
63. When he/she came into your life, were you a happy person?
64. Are you a much happier person now? Are you more in touch with yourself now?
65. Have you grown spiritually since you have been in this relationship?
66. Have you grown mentally since you have been in this relationship? Emotionally?
67. What do you think you mean to your mate? What does your mate mean to you?
68. When was the closest you have ever felt with your mate?
69. What does your mate say that makes you feel good?

"Children who are not loved in their very beingness do not know how to love themselves. As adults, they learn to nourish, to mother their lost child."

Marion Woodman

70. What do you say that makes your mate feel good?
71. When do you enjoy your mate the most, when alone or in a group?
72. What is the greatest experience you and your mate have enjoyed?
73. You were happiest when _____
74. What is the most important wish you have for this relationship?
75. Are you willing to continue to open up and share what you feel with your mate?

Lee Iocacca is one of the most achieving people in America. He performed a miracle at Chrysler Corporation. In his book, *Talking Straight*, he describes his relationship with his family. Here are some of the highlights:

He never let his money or fame go to his head. His daughter, Lia, was asked one day in kindergarten what her father did. She answered, "I'm not sure. I think he washes cars."

He never sat and lectured the kids by saying, "Here's the way I want you to grow up." He gave them simple guidelines: that they come talk to him whenever there was a problem, not to keep it inside; never lie; never get into debt; if they ever borrowed from a friend, never forget to repay the debt; never make a promise they couldn't keep. He said, "If the kids did not make super grades, I didn't go crazy about it." He kept after them if they did below average in their classes, but if they kept with the work and kept their grades up, he was satisfied.

He placed his family first on his schedule. He spent every weekend with his family, every vacation. "Kathi was on the swim team for seven years and I never missed a meet. . . . I was afraid that if I missed one, Kathi might finish first or

---

"If we can stop one heart from breaking, we shall not live in vain. If we can ease one life from aching, or cool one pain, or help one feinting robin into its nest again, we shall not live in vain."

Emily Dickinson

finish last, and I would hear about it second hand and not be there to congratulate—or console her."

He tells how his daughter Lia, when she was six, had just gotten into the Potawatami Tribe at Brownie Camp. She had wanted to join the "Nava-Joes," but didn't make it. He recalls that they were both excited, regardless. "Funny thing, I missed an important meeting that day, but for the life of me, I have no recollection of what it was."

He showed love to his family. "I've always been affectionate with my kids. . . . [they] were always what mattered most . . . I love them" (*Talking Straight*, 288-89).

That is high self-esteem. Lee loved them out of the overflow of his life. If one of the busiest men in America can schedule the time to go to swim meets and plays with his children, so can you. Don't sacrifice your family on the altar of commerce.

How to Build a Better Marriage

1. Enjoy effective communication.

Cliche. This is as far as communication goes for some. Move on.

Activity. Still not enough. Sure, discuss what you both have done that day, but life is more than activity.

Attitudes and opinions. Find out how the other feels and thinks.

At the gut level. Never pass judgment on the other. Withhold moral opinions. Don't blame. Emotions must be integrated into intellect and conduct. And emotions must be reported at the time.

Peak-blending relationship. You think, feel, and act as one.

2. Develop individual self-esteem.

"Every part of your body responds to your emotions."
Robert E. Decker

He develops self-esteem in his profession, and/or her profession, family, romance, and recreation.

She develops self-esteem in her profession, and/or his profession, family, romance, and recreation.

Each encourages the other's independence, creativity, self-esteem, financial security, cultural, and aesthetic interest.

Self-esteem overflow radiates to others.

3. Participate in an equal partnership.
   Openness in feelings
   Nonpossessiveness
   Partnership in home responsibility
   Respect for privacy and individuality
   Freedom to grow and encouragement of the other to grow
   Annual contract of intent, not control

4. Become the ideal loving mate.
   Assertive and self-confident
   Rational and emotional balance and openness
   Capacity and practice of sharing deepest feelings
   Sincere empathy for the other's happiness
   Well-defined plan for growth
   Creative leisure sharing experiences
   Tender, warm and achieving sensuality

Quotes on Love

"To love one who loves you, to admire one who admires you, in a word: to be the idol of one's idol is exceeding the limit of human joy: it is stealing fire from heaven."

Madame de Girardin

"Mature love is union under the condition of preserving one's integrity, one's individuality. In love, the paradox

---

You must take responsibility for your own development.

occurs that two beings become one and yet remain two."

Erich Fromm

"Love casts our fear; but, conversely, fear casts out love."

Aldous Huxley

Loneliness is the pain a person who doesn't love himself suffers. Solitude is the joy a person who loves himself experiences.

"To love is to stop comparing."   Anonymous

"The risks of love are higher than most investments. The rewards are greater than winning a sweepstakes."

Anonymous

"Forgiveness is the fragrance the violet sheds on the heel that has crushed it."   Anonymous

"Jealousy is a way of getting rid of everything you are afraid of losing."   Anonymous

"The worst sin towards our fellow creatures is not to hate them; but to be indifferent to them; that's the essence of inhumanity."   George Bernard Shaw

"It is not fair to ask of others what you are not willing to do yourself."   Eleanor Roosevelt

"Loneliness is never more cruel than when it is felt in close propinquity with someone who has ceased to communicate."   Germaine Greer

"The great secret of a successful marriage is to treat all disasters as incidents and none of the incidents as disasters."

Harold Nicolson

"True friendship comes when silence between two people is comfortable."   Dave Gentry

---

I'm Alive. . . . I'm Alert. . . . I'm Excited.

"Shared joys make a friend, not shared sufferings."

Nietzsche

"Those who love deeply never grow old. They may die of old age, but they die young." Anonymous

"The only way to have a friend is to be one."

Ralph Waldo Emerson

"There is a destiny that makes us brothers, none goes his way alone. All that we send into the lives of others comes back into our own." Edwin Markham

"The greatest discovery of my generation is that human beings can alter their lives by altering their attitudes or mine."

S. M. James

"Just remember that what you are going to be tomorrow you are becoming today." Anonymous

"Behavior is a mirror in which everyone shows his image."

Goethe

"The outward behavior of a man is at once the sign and proof of the inner self." Mahatma Gandhi

"You had better live your best, think your best and do your best today—for today will soon be tomorrow and tomorrow will soon be forever." Goethe

"The best things in life are never rationed. Friendship, love, loyalty do not require coupons." G. T. Hewill

"The doors we open and close each day decide the lives we live." Flora Whitmore

"I have yet to find the man, however exalted his station, who did not do better work and put forth greater effort under a spirit of approval, than under a spirit of criticism."

Charles Schwab

"No one can make you feel inferior without your consent."
Eleanor Roosevelt

"Our doubts are traitors and make us lose the good we oft might win by fearing to attempt."　　　Shakespeare

"A man is no greater than his dream, his ideal, his hope, and his plan. Man dreams the dream—and, fulfilling it, it's the dream that makes the man."　　　Anonymous

"If you would love me you must be on higher ground."
　　　Ralph Waldo Emerson

"We may elevate ourselves, but we should never reach so high that we would ever forget those who helped us get there."　　　Will Rogers

"No man is free who cannot command himself."
　　　Pythagoras

"In life we get what we order."　　　Anonymous

"Kindness is the golden chain by which society is bound together."　　　Goethe

"To be what we are, and to become what we are capable of becoming, is the only end of life."　　　Spinoza

"We have committed the golden rule to memory, let us now commit it to our lives."　　　Edwin Markham

"Our life is what our thoughts make it."
　　　Marcus Aurelius

"If we take people as we find them, we may make them worse; but if we treat them as though they are what they should be, we help them to become what they are capable of becoming."　　　Goethe

Conclusion

Dr. Karl Mennenger said, "The purpose of life is to delete the misery of people."

We become what the people with whom we surround ourselves are.

Our life is what our thoughts make us.

Commit yourself to giving happiness and high self-esteem to your mate, and especially to your children.

Invest time and energy in joyful daily family experiences. Sigmund Freud said, "The three most important factors in life are (1) the quality of marital and sexual relationships, (2) meaningful occupation, and (3) the quality of friends and social life."

You deserve valued and loving feedback from your family. You will receive from them only a part of what you give to them. If you want love, you must give love.

"Self-confidence is the first requisite to great undertakings."
Dale Carnegie

CHAPTER 10

Controlling Your Conduct

To control your conduct, you must have positive self-expectancy. Here's how:

Begin the day with positive self-affirmations. Take charge of your mind. The only thing in the world you can totally control is your own mind.

Invest time in positive relationships. A good friend is the best gift you give yourself.

Turn every problem into an opportunity. Ask yourself, "In what way can we . . . ?"

Control your stress. Learn to relax and enjoy the luxury of leisure.

Improve your health with powerful exercise.

Use only positive statements with others. Accentuate your strengths.

Invest valuable time in improved family relationships.

Look for and expect the best in others. Challenge others to achieve their best.

Choose to associate with positive-minded people. We become whatever the crowd we run with is.

Expect each day to be a happy experience. Say to yourself:

> I'm going to be happy today,
> Though the skies may be cloudy and gray;
> No matter what may come my way,
> I'm going to be happy today.

The Power of Mind

Reader's Digest told the story of a high school class that proved the power of the mind. People with equal ability were divided into three groups. Group I was told not to practice shooting free throws for a month. Group II practiced shooting 100 free throws each day for a month. Group III was told to imagine they were shooting 100 free throws each day for a month.

Group I, with no practice for a month, slipped from a 39% to a 37% free-throw average.

Group II, who practiced in the gym, increased from a 39% to a 41% free-throw average.

Group III, who practiced in their imaginations, went from a 39% to a 42.5% free-throw average.

On January 16, 1973, I attended the Super Bowl in the Los Angeles Coliseum when the Miami Dolphins completed their perfect 17-0 season with a win over the Washington Redskins, 14-7.

During the half, Andy Williams was singing in the field with the entire playing field covered by bands, cheerleaders, and others. Foster Brooks, the comedian, was seated just behind me. While Andy was singing, Foster stood up and called out to two guys some ten rows ahead of us who had just thrown a couple of oranges on the field, one hitting a cheerleader in the back. Foster said, "You two guys throwing oranges, my friends and I are very disappointed in you, aren't we, friends?" And he turned to all the fans around us and said, "Nod your heads, friends, if you are disappointed in these two guys throwing oranges." And we all nodded. Then Foster said, "I want you two guys—Hey! Look here, you two guys. I and all my friends want you to

---

"If one man can enhance his position in life by self-proclamation, then why not?"

Joe Theismann

promise us you won't throw any more oranges. Do you agree? Nod your heads." And they did.

When he sat down, I told Foster, "That was the best use of crowd psychology I have ever seen."

He answered, "I've worked clubs for many years. You have to learn how to handle the guy who is drunk and wants to take over the act. You use the crowd against him. You make him the victim and you become the hero. The crowd will always side with the innocent party."

We learn to take charge of our conduct by controlling our minds. It's not easy, but anything that's as important as handling our emotions is worth the effort.

Suggestions for Emotional Well-Being

1. Make an effort to love yourself as well as everyone else.
2. Make an effort to do things that provide you with a sense of fulfillment, joy, and purpose.
3. You can choose to nourish, support, and encourage yourself.
4. Be sure to express all of your feelings, because once they are out, they lose their power to control you, to tie you up in knots.
5. You can choose to record your feelings and dreams in a daily journal.
6. If you hold pictures in your mind of what you truly want in life, you have an idea of what your goals are and how to achieve them.
7. View everything in your life, every circumstance, as an opportunity for growth and learning.
8. You can join a support group of people with similar problems and interests; this may enable you to recognize other ways to deal with things. And the support group can show you that you're never alone in your problems.

The difference between what I am and what I become is what I do.

The above list is adapted from Bernie Siegel's *Love, Medicine and Miracles*, published in New York by HarperCollins in 1986.

Finding and Meeting the Needs of Others

Basic needs:

1. To give love out of the wholeness of self-love and then to love others
2. Food, home, and safety from harm
3. A sense of self-worth
4. Financial security
5. Living a life that is needed by others and useful to others
6. Assurance of life after death
7. Fellowship with family and friends
8. Reasonable good health and activity that produces happiness
9. Belonging, enjoying meaningful fellowship with others, and being in harmony with God
10. A life that works

"There is no value judgment more important to man than the estimate he passes on himself."

Nathaniel Branden

Stanley Coopersmith, author of *Antecedents of Self-Esteem*, defines self-esteem as *the evaluation which the individual makes and customarily maintains with regard to himself; it expresses an attitude of approval or disapproval and indicates the extent to which the individual believes himself to be capable, significant, successful, and worthy.* Self-esteem is learned, not genetically acquired.

Experienced teachers have come to know, and research

I reveal the way I feel by the things I think and do.
When I change the things I think and do, I change my feelings, too.

supports, Norman Vincent Peale's observation: "There is a deep tendency in human nature to become precisely what we imagine or picture ourselves to be. We ourselves determine either self-limitation or unlimited growth potential."

A negative thinker engages in a self-destructive process, activating the world around him by sending out negative thoughts and drawing negative thoughts back to himself. The positive thinker constantly sends out positive messages that activate the world around him positively, thus drawing to himself positive results.

Four Sources of High Self-Esteem

1. Amount of respectful, accepting and concerned treatment the individual receives from the significant others in his life. We value ourselves as we are valued.
2. Successes and the status and position we hold in the world. Successes bring recognition and are thereby related to our status. Successes are the building blocks of self-esteem.
3. Living up to aspirations that the individual regards as personally significant.
4. Responding to devaluation. Demeaning actions by others (assuming that these actions do not include those by parents and teachers) is a fact of life. The ability to cope successfully with these put-downs is the key to healthy self-esteem.

Additional Sources of Self-Esteem

Power. The ability to influence and control others and the environment in which we live.

Importance. The acceptance, attention, and affection of others. The more frequent and the more varied the sources

---

"The truest wisdom, in general, is a resolute determination."
Napoleon

of appreciation and approval, the more positive will be the self-approval and self-esteem.

Competence. Successful performance in meeting the demands for achievement. In whatever area it may be, competence, resulting in the recognition and approval of others, is very important in developing self-esteem.

Value. Adherence to a code of moral, ethical, and religious principles. Our moral beliefs are a vital part of the framework that makes us responsible people. When our conduct is in agreement with our moral beliefs, we feel good within ourselves. When we violate our moral beliefs, we feel rotten, especially when we have hurt or damaged another person.

What we put back into our world should be more than what we have taken out as a reasonable payment for our right to live in this world. When we influence other people for their good, when our achievement results in approval and appreciation of others, when our effectiveness in life measures up to our own desire for excellence, when our values benefit mankind and leave a better place for our having been here, we will enjoy high self-esteem.

The key to controlling your conduct is to never take the bait others offer you. If you yield to their emotions, they have taken control of your life. You are out of control. Remember, your emotions are in your control.

Some years ago, I was driving from Atlanta, Georgia, to South Florida. I stopped in Orlando, late at night, to sleep. I called a friend of mine, Jim, and suggested we meet for breakfast the next morning.

We met in the motel lobby at 7 A.M. and waited for the dining room to open. The waitresses were seated, having their

---

"Jesus said unto him, 'If thou canst believe, all things are possible to him that believeth.'"

Mark 9:23

coffee, but had not opened the room for guests. At 7:20 I asked if we could come in and have coffee.

One of the waitresses answered in a gruff voice, "Sit anywhere you want to; I don't care." After Jim and I had seated ourselves, she came over and said, "Well, what do you birds want?"

I greeted her with a smile, called her Rosa from the name tag on her dress and said, "I'd like a cup of coffee, bacon, scrambled eggs, orange juice, and a glass of water." Jim gave his order, and with a scowl, Rosa left.

Jim said, "We don't have to take this. Let's go somewhere else to eat."

I replied, "Jim, how many people are you going to see today?"

He replied, "Maybe thirty."

I said, "And I will see about thirty also. If we let her make us mad, then you and I will emotionally contaminate sixty people today. That sixty will contaminate sixty each tomorrow for a total of 360, that group will do the same the next day, by the end of the week, the entire state of Florida will be at each other's throats. Let's see if we can change Rosa."

When Rosa returned with our coffee, I said to her, "Rosa, I was in a restaurant the other day and I said to the waitress, 'Do you serve crabs?' She said, '"Sit down, we'll serve anybody.'"

Rosa smiled. The next time she came with our water, I said, "Rosa, I asked that waitress for a piece of raisin pie. She shook her head and said, 'That isn't raisin, that's coconut.'" Rosa really laughed.

When she came to bring us a coffee refill, I said, "Rosa, the epitaph of the waitress is, 'The Lord finally caught her eye.'" Rosa roared.

When she brought us our checks, she asked, "Are you guys coming back for lunch today?"

In life, we get what we order.

Jim said, "No." I promised to come back the first time I was back in Orlando.

Then Rosa said, "Last night I had the worst night of my life. If I had had a pistol, I would have killed myself. I came to work today feeling the worst of my life. With your jokes and interest in me, I can make it. Thank you." Tears cascaded down her cheeks.

By controlling our emotions and conduct, we were able to turn Rosa around.

By living the following affirmations, you too can take charge of your emotions and conduct. Repeat the affirmation of the day over and over and seek to live the truth expressed.

Affirmations for the Month

1. TODAY, I , _____ , was created with an unlimited capacity for love, joy, and fulfillment.
2. TODAY, I , _____ , accept the truth of this affirmation and live for growth and wholeness.
3. TODAY, I , _____ , release and remove all barriers of fear so I can receive all blessings.
4. TODAY, I , _____ , live in the positive truths of love, joy, peace, serenity, and prosperity.
5. TODAY, I , _____ , receive and give self-confidence, self-love, and self-celebration.
6. TODAY, I , _____ , reward myself for every accomplishment and every achievement.
7. TODAY, I , _____ , am learning to love myself more in every way as a gift of God's love.
8. TODAY, I , _____ , respect my own uniqueness, individuality, and personhood.
9. TODAY, I , _____ , meet my own emotional needs because I will not be dependent on anyone else.

I choose not to be an emotional cripple, controlled by
the negative attitudes of others.

10. TODAY, I , _____ , no longer am dependent on others to affirm me, because I do that myself.

11. TODAY, I , _____ , like, value, and please myself, and renounce forever self-criticism.

12. TODAY, I , _____ , have unconditional warm feelings for myself, my friends, and all I meet.

13. TODAY, I , _____ , am 100-percent alive, alert, and excited, because I abound in unlimited enthusiasm.

14. TODAY, I , _____ , am unusually confident, receiving an increasing amount of abundance.

15. TODAY, I , _____ , have replaced all negative thoughts with their opposite, positive thought.

16. TODAY, I , _____ , maintain control of my actions and emotions to achieve my greatness.

17. TODAY, I , _____ , live a life constantly enlarging as I seek beauty, joy, love, and peace.

18. TODAY, I , _____ , enjoy the beauty of fun, friendships, laughter, pleasure, and radiant joy.

19. TODAY, I , _____ , decide what thoughts will enter my mind and receive those I choose.

20. TODAY, I , _____ , release the true greatness within me as my self-appreciation expands.

21. TODAY, I , _____ , enrich my life as all my activity and conduct is results-oriented.

22. TODAY, I , _____ , am moving on to a higher level of fulfillment as my life unfolds.

23. TODAY, I , _____ , am energized by newfound purpose, goals, dreams, and dynamic excitement.

24. TODAY, I , _____ , believe and receive the unlimited prosperity that surrounds me.

25. TODAY, I , _____ , welcome the power of change and will ride the crest of opportunity.

26. TODAY, I , _____ , excitedly live this day in the beautiful unfolding of God's love.

No man can be happy unless he feels his life is in some way important.

27. TODAY, I , _____ , bless all mankind with my thoughts, prayers, and encouragement.
28. TODAY, I , _____ , look for, seek out, encourage, and recognize every sign of good in others.
29. TODAY, I , _____ , experience empathy, under-standing, compassion, and love for all people.
30. TODAY, I , _____ , delight in the joyous feelings I receive and give to all my friends.
31. TODAY, I , _____ , love everyone unconditionally as a conduct of my love for myself.

Self-esteem is the package of beliefs you carry around in your head that you have accepted to be the truth about you whether it is or not.

The single greatest assurance that you have genuine self-esteem is, *Can you take total control of your mind?*

Pres. Abraham Lincoln's wife, Mary Todd, had deep-seated emotional problems. She spent money to excess, buying clothes she would never wear. Her greatest emotional outbursts were against the president. One night, she instructed President Lincoln to go to the grocery store the next morning to pick up some items. President Lincoln forgot and was conducting a Cabinet meeting at nine the next morning, when Mrs. Lincoln burst into the Cabinet room and cursed, blamed, and condemned the president because he didn't go to the grocery store, her punishment for him. He smilingly nodded his head during some fifteen minutes of her out-of-control tirade. When she ran down, he hugged her and said, "You are right, Mrs. Lincoln, you told me to go and I forgot it. I deserve what you have said." He turned to his secretary and asked her to send someone else to the store. He hugged Mrs. Lincoln again and ushered her out the door.

"Our greatest glory is not in never falling,
but in rising every time we fall."

Confucius

Then he returned to his seat at the head of the conference table, smiled and said that he was glad she had done that.

Secretary of War Steward asked President Lincoln what he meant by that, to which the president responded, "Why, Mr. Steward, she feels better now."

When you can take a tirade like that, overlook it, and forgive the person doing it, you are in control of your life and reveal your high self-esteem.

Causes of Low Self-Esteem

1. Negative body image
2. Critical blow-ups
3. Critical tapes; feelings of self-criticism you have accepted from others about yourself
4. Chronic comparisons to others that placed you in a lesser light
5. Demands of perfection imposed by others who also felt less than perfect
6. A sense of hopelessness
7. Inability to accept a compliment or to believe anything good can happen to you

Playing the If-Then Game

1. If I am nice, then people will like me.
2. If I am beautiful, then I will never be alone.
3. If I am smart, then I will be valued.
4. If I make people laugh, then no one will be angry with me.
5. If I am super-competent, then I will have many career opportunities.
6. If I lose weight, then everything in life will be fine.

"Losing isn't fatal and winning isn't final."

Don Shula

Sources of High Self-Esteem
(originally listed in chapter 2)

Parental approval. A child needs this from the first days of life and always after. This includes his own sense of personhood, his own sense of proven ability, his own sense of individuality, his own sense of realistic achievements, and meaningful values.

Other adult models. Relatives and friends of parents, as well as teachers, clergy, etc.

Siblings and peers. We become what the crowd we run with is.

Educational achievements.

Skills mastery. This includes mastery in sports, music, hobbies, games, etc.

Learning to feed ourselves good strokes.

Affirming romantic experiences. Being in love may be life's most exciting experience.

Receiving God's love. Religion that unloads guilt, fear, and blame without God's forgiveness may do serious damage to people's feelings about themselves.

Career expertise.

Root-value transfer. This necessary to receive strong feelings of belonging, respect, and the ability to identify with our forefathers.

What Every Human Being Needs

1. To belong, to be meaningfully involved in something that really counts.
2. To feel success in some achievement which he regards as his own thing.
3. To feel compassion, freedom, and discovery.
4. To be able to use his life to make a difference in his own world.

An affirmation is a positive thought that you consciously choose to immerse in your consciousness to produce a desired result.

5. To live comfortably in the face of constant anxiety.
6. To cope with threats against his identity—both real and imagined.
7. To feel genuine control over his own destiny, to create his own future.
8. To be responsible for his own behavior, to know the consequences of it, and to face the consequences with total acceptance.
9. To own a self-concept that is real, relevant, appropriate, and respected.
10. To have a number of chances to become a better person than he is right now and the freedom to want to.
11. To develop a capacity for sharing strong feelings of affection with at least one other person.
12. To be open to change and personal growth. To become an agent of constructive change in the world and to value the outcome, the process, and the traditions.
13. To have an ideology he can value and share.
14. To have a chance to learn as much as he can, as well as he can, and as fast as he can about what is true in the universe.
15. To have a will to try and a reason to want to.

We must build into every person the resources to face anything, not just to fill his tank, but to give him the techniques for manufacturing his own fuel, handling his own repairs, and perhaps building his own vehicle from his own resources in his own world—and then to make it in our shared world.

All human beings have the same basic needs. We strive in many ways to meet those needs and to satisfy our desires. Show people how they can achieve their own wants, needs, desires, and purposes through what you are doing.

You are the source of your own self-loving energy.
You now have an internal self-support system. You have
built a constructive program of self-care and self-nurturing.

411

Positive Quotes

Errors are evidence that you are human—and what's wrong with being human?—or better yet, a human becoming.

Good things usually begin with a difficulty, but great things invariably begin with an impossibility. Welcome the impossible as the messenger of impending greatness.

Most people allow their lives to be controlled by "they" and "luck." Why hand over your life to excuses or the whims of fortune? Remember: "they" is us, and "luck" is when preparation meets opportunity.

Are you playing it too safe? Success will come to you in direct proportion to the number of times you are willing to risk failure.

What do you stand for? What do you want your children to tell their children about you?

"The difference between perseverance and obstinacy is that one often comes from a strong will, and the other comes from a strong won't." Henry Ward Beecher

You are completely responsible for all your responses to other persons and events. You control your response—and therein lies your freedom.

"Once your mind is stretched by a new idea, it will never again return to its original size." Oliver Wendell Holmes

One definition of integrity: being on the "inside" what you profess to be the "outside."

You can't leave footprints in the sand of time by sitting on your butt, and who wants to leave buttprints in the sands of time?

"You think me the child of circumstances: I make my circumstances."
Ralph Waldo Emerson

God's easiest task is to make us humble, but his most difficult task is to make us positive.

Why not give teamwork a try? Put two people with a common goal together and suddenly, one plus one is more than two.

Whenever you undertake a new project, attempt to make as many mistakes as rapidly as possible in order to learn as much as you can in a short period of time.

Two weeks before he died, a young boy who had lived in a plastic bubble because of a rare disease, left that bubble for the very first time. He was able to kiss his mother . . . sleep on a real bed . . . walk barefoot on real grass. These simple things, which are all around us, gave him great joy.

The smallest goal achieved stands taller than the grandest intention. Do whatever your heart leads you to do—but do it. Don't beat up on yourself. Some of the worst "demotivators" in the English language are the words, "I should have . . . I would have . . . I could have." Why not make a conscious effort to strike them from your vocabulary? Instead, say to yourself, "Next time, I'll . . ."

You may occasionally give out, but never give up.

Purpose is the engine that powers your life.

"You will never find time for anything. If you want time, you must make it."   Charles Buxton

Gossip has no place in the thoughts or conversation of the successful person. It is just as harmful to the gossiper as it is to the person being gossiped about.

"Self-examination, if it is thorough enough, is nearly always the first step towards change—no one who learns to know

---

"Treat people as if they were what they ought to be and you help them to become what they are capable of being."
Goethe

413

himself remains just what he was before."

Thomas Mann

The energy derived from setting goals comes in large part from the focus it brings to our lives. It's like igniting a fire by channeling the gentle rays of the sun to a single spot through a magnifying glass.

Losers always have an excuse. Winners always have an idea.

Seen on a bumper sticker: "God loves you—whether you like it or not."

"No airplane was designed to taxi down the runway. They were all designed to fly high in the sky, above the clouds, above the storms. How many people do you know who spend their lives taxiing down the runways of life, revving their engines, but afraid to take off? We were all designed to fly."

Dr. H. Paul Jacobi

By intentionally raising your own expectations of yourself, you will create a gap between where you are and where you wish to be. Having created this gap for yourself, everything about you will automatically begin working on your behalf to close it. This explains why goal-setters enjoy boundless energy. Losers say, "Why don't they do something?" Winners say, "Here's something to do."

Most organizations are looking for ways to help people become better employees. High-performance organizations recognize that the key is finding ways to help employees become better people.

Though the road you're walking may be well-traveled, that does not necessarily mean it is leading to your destination.

"Each of us is connected to all living things whether we are aware of this beautiful fact or not. And, should you ever

---

"Enthusiasm is self-confidence in action."

Franklin Field

begin to feel that you are becoming separated from the world, you are simply self-deceived, for you could no more do this than a wave could separate itself from the ocean and still be a wave." Gerald Jampolsky

In the Auschwitz death camp, a group of inmates told Victor Frankl that they no longer expected anything from life, but Frankl responded that they had it backward: "Life expects something of you, and it is up to every individual to discover what it should be."

You can never be completely successful as a whole person until you learn to be considerate of every person with whom you come into contact.

"One machine can do the work of fifty ordinary people. No machine can do the work of one extraordinary person." Elbert Hubbard

"With ordinary talent and extraordinary perseverance, all things are attainable." Thomas F. Buxton

Personality can open many doors, but only character will keep them open.

If you don't feel good, act like you do, and you will almost immediately feel like you do. That's the way it works. Researchers have now determined that a smile—even if forced—triggers an intricate series of responses throughout the body, all of which conspire to make you feel good.

"A loss of courage may be the most striking feature which an outside observer notices in the West today." Alexander Solzhenitzyn

Historically, a decline in courage has signaled the beginning of the end. You are history in motion; your greatest power is your power to choose. Choose courageously.

Bad start? No sweat. It's the finish, not the start that counts.

I am a unique person reaching forth toward the fulfillment I deserve.

415

"No person was ever honored for what he received. Honor has been the reward for what he gave."

Pres. Calvin Coolidge

"Life is like playing the violin in public and learning the instrument as you go along." Samuel Butler

Rather than acknowledge a mistake, nations have gone to war, families have separated, and individuals have sacrificed everything dear to them. Admitting that you have been wrong is just another way of saying that you are wiser today than yesterday. All meaningful and lasting change starts in the imagination and works its way down. Therefore, dream often . . . and dream big.

"Virtually all new ideas which have resulted in change in our society were at one time scorned (or illegal). . . . People ridiculed the Edisons, Henry Fords, Einsteins, and Wright Brothers—until they were successful." Dr. Wayne Dyer

Predict another good day for yourself. Expect something great to happen.

Conclusion

Any time a negative thought enters your mind, contradict it with its opposite, positive thought.

Plan every day so that the conduct of that day's activity is under your mental and emotional control.

Saturate your thoughts with positive affirmations so that the conduct is obedient to the positive thought. Dr. Brach Waynbaum discovered in 1907, "Facial expression takes place before the brain acts to express that facial emotion." The thought precedes the emotion. Decide you will be happy, smile, and the brain responds accordingly. The smile sends an oxygen explosion to the brain.

"The secret of success is constancy of purpose."
Prime Minister Benjamin Disraeli

Look for every opportunity to serve other people. Dr. Albert A. Schweitzer once commented, "I don't know what your destiny will be, but I do know the only ones among you who will be truly happy will be those who have sought and found how to serve."

I am the best friend to myself. I take me out whenever I feel low. I alone am responsible for my feelings and I chose to feel beautiful.

CHAPTER 11

Guidelines for a Self-Celebrating Life

Retired Vice Adm. James Stockdale received our nation's highest medal for valor, the congressional Medal of Honor, for more than 200 combat missions and his leadership while a POW for eight years in North Vietnam. Now, professor of philosophy at Stanford University and author of several books, his own life provides a formula for others to live a courageous life:

1. Don't worry about things you don't control. People with high self-esteem take life's battles and problems without flinching and make the most out of each situation.
2. Courage is endurance in the presence of fear. Fear is a coward and flees the moment we face it.
3. You *are* your brother's keeper. No man is totally free while other men are enslaved. When we love and value ourselves, we love and value others.
4. Hatred and all other negative emotions are self-defeating. We replace negative emotions with their opposite, positive emotions.

Self-acceptance. People with high self-esteem honestly acknowledge all of their strengths and accept that any so-called weaknesses are areas that we haven't found time to confront and win over. Pride is "I have." Self-esteem is "I can."

Self-acceptance is self-value, self-commitment, and

self-confidence to face the fact that we are not perfect, but are growing, experiencing, and becoming all we desire to be. Self-acceptance is unconditional in that we admit our imperfections as areas we are improving. As we do grow, develop, and overcome, we develop more and more self-esteem.

People that do not now experience overwhelming self-esteem may be assured that they can do so by accepting themselves as of value, capable, worthy, and victorious. To accept ourselves means that this is where we are now, not where we are going to be. Life is a journey, not a destination. Because we are and have been achieving, we will continue on this adventure as long as we live and pursue self-esteem. The human brain, except for chemical imbalance or disease, is the only part of man that continues to defy age and senility. It expands and develops as long as we live.

We can develop self-acceptance by discarding the garbage and renewing the emotions. Try this exercise:

I discard fear and replace it with courage.
I discard ineptness and replace it with achievement.
I discard laziness and replace it with goals and life control.
I discard negative emotions and replace them with their opposite, positive emotions.
I discard guilt and replace it with good feelings about my personhood.
I discard depression and replace it with enthusiasm.
I discard inaction and replace it with controlled conduct.
I discard hatred and replace it with compassion.

Now discard other feelings and replace them.

_____

_____

_____

"Freedom is the one thing you can't have unless you give it to others."
William Allen White

Self-interest vs. selfishness: do I exist for myself, for God, or for others? Auguste Comte, the nineteenth-century advocate of collectivism, coined a term, "altruism." Altruism holds that a human being must make the welfare of others his primary moral concern, placing their interests above his or her own sake.

Beneto Mussolini said, "Fascism . . . a life in which the individual, through the denial of himself, through the sacrifice of his own private interests, through death itself, realizes that complete spiritual existence in which his value as a man lies."

According to Joseph Goebbels, in *Escape From Freedom* by Erich Fromm: "To be a socialist is to submit the 'I' to the 'thou.'" Socialism is the sacrifice of the individual to the whole.

But the Bible teaches otherwise. As mentioned earlier, nineteen times in the Bible we are commanded to love ourselves. Paul writes, "So ought men to love their wives as their own bodies. He that loveth his wife loveth himself." (Eph. 5:28) And in explaining the two greatest commandments, Jesus says of the second: "And the second is like, namely this, 'Thou shalt love thy neighbour as thyself.' There is none other commandment greater than these." (Mark 12:31) In Matthew 5:13-16, Jesus tells his disciples:

> Ye are the salt of the earth: but if the salt have lost its savour, wherewith shall it be salted? It is thenceforth good for nothing, but to be cast out, and to be trodden under foot of men.

"It is a funny thing about life. If you refuse to accept anything but the best, you will get it."
Somerset Maugham

421

> Ye are the light of the world. A city that is set on a hill cannot be hid. Neither do men light a candle, and put it under a bushel, but on a candlestick; and it giveth light unto all that are in the house. Let your light so shine before men, that they may see your good works, and glorify your Father which is in heaven.

The Christian principle, then, is to be of value, salt so others may be saved. Salt keeps food from spoiling, and brings out the flavor, the best in it. Light is to shine to bring hope and to illuminate the darkness. It is not to burn out, but to continue to burn constantly and consistently for others to benefit from and find safe passage to safety.

Selfishness is "I'll get mine first and to hell with everyone else." Self-interest is "I will become whole, a light, a saving influence from degradation, from ruin so that others may also find the way to wholeness." Self-interest is primary. We can't help someone else if we are unable. We can't pull others from the deep waters if our own feet are not safely on shore. We can't love others if we don't love ourselves. We can't train and inspire others if we haven't been there ourselves. We can't show others how to cross the dangerous stream if we haven't discovered the safe rocks to step on. So, self-esteem is self-interest, so that the wholeness of our experiences can spill over and be shared with others coming our way.

Positive self-talk. You must be your own self-nurturing parent. If you are waiting for someone else to affirm you, and he doesn't, then you fall apart. Develop the interdependent attitude that you and you alone will affirm your self-worth.

Benjamin Franklin had a wonderful program of self-growth. Each year he wrote out the thirteen areas of his life that he wanted to improve, for example: saving, creativity,

---

*"If you have your heart fixed on what you want,
there is nothing I can do to stop you from getting it."*
Andrew Carnegie

human relations, industry, etc. Then he spent a full week on each of these. At the end of the first quarter he started over again. At the end of the year he had invested four weeks, a quarter apart, working on achieving these areas in his life. At the end of the year he started over again. If there was any conduct he felt he had not mastered, then he included that conduct in the next year. In this way, he took charge of his life and was one of the best informed, achieving people of his day or any day.

Now try this program for yourself. Remember, the only thing you control is your own mind. Do not surrender your mind, your emotions to others—only to God and yourself.

Begin each day with thoughtful meditation. Arise a half-hour early and invest this precious time in yourself. Read good books, the Bible, poetry, inspiring thoughts, and affirmations. When you dress, realize that you have ten coats in your closet. They are numbered from one to ten. One is the lowest, the despair coat. Ten is the highest, the self-esteem, the high-excitement coat. Decide which coat you are going to wear today. If you chose a "ten" coat, you will be in charge of your emotions all day. You will relate to other ten's and they will relate to you. The six's and seven's will climb higher by having experienced your ten conduct.

On entering your car, turn on your motivational audiotapes and play them all the way to the office and upon your return home. Turn your auto into a university. Play the tapes while you are dressing and before you go to sleep at night. Let every day be a growth day, a fulfilling day, and a learning day.

Live the twenty-one-day, goal-achieving experience. Find a quiet time, best early in the morning. Write out all the things you want to develop in your life: family achievement, personal growth, business success, spiritual fulfillment, etc. Then the next day, go over the previous day's goals and

---

Where there is hope, there are people. Where there are people, there is God. And where there is God, there is nothing missing.

write out goals for this day. Do this every day for twenty-one days and you will be amazed how effectively you have taken charge of your life.

Visualization: Jack Nicklaus, the greatest golfer of all time, sees, in his mind, the ball going exactly where he wants it to go. Then his muscles obey his mind. Visualize what you want to become. See your children (as I did) crossing the stage to receive their graduate degrees. See yourself accepting the awards of your associates, see yourself and your name on the door, as president of your company. See yourself accepting God's blessing, approval, and reward.

Self-Expectancy. The perfectionist is under a compulsive drive to do, but with no satisfaction. The person with low self-esteem has no expectancy because he/she has had all expectancy destroyed by criticism, fear, and self-doubt. The person with high self-esteem is the only one capable of defining and achieving self-expectancy and this will vary greatly.

Twenty-seven percent of the people in the nation expect something for nothing.

David McClellan, professor of psychology at Harvard University, reported after a thirty-five-year study that only sixty percent are just making it through.

Ten percent have goals to do, to accomplish. They are winners. They expect good things for themselves.

Three percent have goals to be. They are the super-winners. They 1) love problems to solve, 2) take reasonable risks, and 3) are committed to become all they are capable of becoming.

So it is with readers of this book:

Twenty percent will buy the book and never read it or finish it.

"Reading is to the mind what excellence is to the body."
Sir Richard Steele

Sixty percent will read it, find some inspiration from it, and get a general understanding of what high self-esteem is.

Twenty percent will read it, love it, read it again and again (you must read a book six times to get fifty percent of the value, and twenty times to get ninety percent of the value of a book), fill out the outlines, fill in the blanks, continue to get and stay excited, draw inspiration from it, and make a commitment to themselves to become all they are capable of becoming. *That's the best definition of self-expectancy.*

The Plan of Action for My Life

What

I want approval from _____ .
I want approval for _____ .
I want deeper bonding with my mate.
I want friends to listen and understand me better.
I want better-defined goals for myself, my team members at work, and my family members.
I want recognition for my achievement, promotions at work, and at home.
I want satisfying sexual experiences.
I want exhilarating peak experiences, emotionally, mentally, and spiritually.
I want variety, travel, exciting vacations and weekends, and renewing leisure.
I want forgiveness, guilt-free feelings, and a personal relationship with God.
I want time to play, have fun, to rest, to renew, and to be constantly growing.
I want _____ .
I want _____ .
I want _____ .
I want _____ .

Just as the constant dripping of water will wear away the hardest granite, so continued effort will overcome every obstacle.

I want _____ .

Who

I want approval, acceptance, and understanding from my parents.

I want approval, acceptance, and understanding from my mate and children.

I want approval, acceptance, and understanding from my team members and contemporaries.

I want approval, acceptance, and understanding from my clients and/or business associates.

I want approval, acceptance, and understanding from God and religious leaders.

I want approval, acceptance, and understanding from ____
_____ .

I want approval, acceptance, and understanding from ____
_____ .

I want approval, acceptance, and understanding from ____
_____ .

Myself

I want to really know all I can know about myself.

I want to understand how I have effectively dealt with the troubled past in my life.

I want to clearly plot my journey for a satisfying, achieving life.

I want to become all I can be.

I want _____ .

I want _____ .

I want _____ .

I want _____ .

Bucky Wertz was a 5-foot, 6-inch "walk-on" as a linebacker for the football team at Ohio State University in the fall of

The length of my life is influenced by how I take care of myself.

1946. The coach was shocked. He was too small. They would kill him, and he told Bucky so. At the end of practice, he told Bucky he couldn't play. The next day, Bucky was back in uniform. Coach called him over and said, "I told you I had cut you from the squad. You are too small; these guys will kill you." With a firm, committed voice, Bucky said, "Coach, with due respect, you nor no one else can prevent me from playing football for my school." The coach was shocked. He allowed Bucky to stay on the squad.

Bucky was the best tackler on the squad. Fast as lightning, sure on his feet, he would burst through the line and hit the ballcarrier before he could get started. Still, he was too small, the coaches agreed.

In the third game of the season, after the game was "in the bag," the coach sent Bucky in. He made every tackle the rest of the game. He started every game for the rest of the season and led the team in tackles.

The next season, Bucky was 5-feet, 8-inches, weighed in at 168 pounds, and led the team in tackles. Every season, junior and senior years, was the same.

On January 1, 1950, Ohio State played USC in the Rose Bowl. USC had an all-American fullback, weighing 240 pounds, who was the finest running back in the nation. Bucky was assigned to "rover" this fullback. The fullback never gained a yard. Bucky hit him behind the line every time he had the ball. Ohio State won in a shocking upset. Bucky Wertz had high self-esteem.

Now, test your own self-esteem (choose A or B):

1. A. I feel hurt when people disapprove of me.
   B. When criticized, I feel compassion for that person.

2. A. I control myself, my feelings, and my conduct.

"The quality of a person's life is directly proportionate to his/her commitment to excellence."

Vince Lombardi

B. When I feel out of control of myself and of others, I feel I'm "out of it."

3. A. I believe that I am no better or worse than other people.
   B. Since I'm an achiever, I feel I'm better than those who are not.

4. A. How I look at others is very important for I want to be admired.
   B. How I look is important, for it reflects how I feel about myself. I stay in shape always.

5. A. I don't pick arguments, but when they occur, I apply the win-win principle . . .
   B. I dislike arguments and seek to avoid them whenever I can.

6. A. It's very difficult for me to turn down an opportunity to help someone.
   B. I help others when I can, but not at my own expense; I can say no when it's wise.

7. A. I do my best always, because I enjoy life that way.
   B. It pains me when I don't do my best, because that is what everyone should do.

8. A. I detest making mistakes and avoid them whenever I can.
   B. I don't enjoy making mistakes, but they don't bother me. I learn from them.

9. A. Whenever I need help, I ask for it from whoever can help me.

"Enthusiasm is not merely an outward expression.
It works from within. Enthusiasm is born of genuine liking
for some phase of what you are doing."

Anonymous

   B. I do not like to ask for help. I should be able to do it myself.

10. A. When others do things wrong, I tell them so. Then I feel better.
   B. I am not critical of others. They don't learn from criticism; they learn from examples.

11. A. When others differ with me, I listen; that's their right, and I learn.
   B. When others differ with me, I set them straight. I like to help people do it right.

12. A. I don't like to be praised. It makes me feel uneasy.
   B. When I receive praise, that's nice, but I don't have to have it.

13. A. If people like me, that's nice, but not necessary. I like myself.
   B. I like to make new friends. They are very important and meaningful to me.

14. A. Achieving my best is very important to me, and I want it.
   B. Success, wealth, and recognition come to me as a net result of my own high self-esteem.

15. A. Life is so enjoyable and fulfilling that I seldom take time to look back.
   B. I tell others about my successes because that makes me feel good and may help them.

16. A. When mistakes occur, it usually is the fault of someone else.
   B. I take full responsibility for my mistakes. Blaming others does no good.

17. A. My achievement is the result of who I am, not the

"The best effect of any book is that it excites the reader to self activity."
Thomas Carlyle

goals I have set.

   B. I set goals and strive to reach them. Then I know someday I will have it all.

18. A. I can be outspoken when necessary. Others need to get things right.

   B. My happiness means I can speak my opinions without being harsh to others.

19. A. Others do what is in their best interests, right or wrong.

   B. I really get upset when people are treated unfairly and let others know it.

20. A. I watch carefully what I say, because I don't want to be hurt back.

   B. I will not let others' words hurt me. It's what I say to myself that counts.

Answers are at the end of the chapter.

Affirmations

1. Every day, in every way, I am getting better.
2. I am constantly moving onto a higher level of fulfillment and consciousness as my life unfolds.
3. I delight in the joyous feelings I share with dear friends.
4. No one can make me stoop so low as to hate him.
5. I learn something useful and meaningful from every person I meet.
6. I share, love, trust, support, and encourage all people, especially my children.
7. I am patient, tender, and understanding in dealing with all people.
8. Since I accept myself unconditionally, I find others accept me the same.

Talent is God's gift to you. What you do with it is your gift to God.

9. People will respond positively to me, because my personality is controlled by my positive mental attitude.

10. I seek to become more charming, persuasive, and popular every day I live.

11. I draw people to me by the power of my love for them.

12. I will not be an emotional cripple controlled by negative attitudes.

13. I relate to positive-minded people and choose not to expose my sensitive emotions to negative-minded people, because such thoughts are destructive.

14. I dwell on beautiful, powerful thoughts of self-affirmation.

15. My personality is the outward expression of the inward person, and I want that person to be fulfilling and whole so I will be well-received.

16. The happiest people are those with achieving experiences of helping others.

17. I can develop the skill of getting along with people.

18. I can cure many of my own ills by helping a friend cure his.

19. "If thou canst believe, all things are possible to them that believeth." (Mark 9:23)

20. "For as he thinketh in his heart, so is he. . . ." (Prov. 23:7)

21. God is my instant, constant, and abundant source of energy, love, and peace.

22. "And all things, whatsoever ye shall ask in prayer, believing, ye shall receive." (Matt. 21:22)

23. The love of God lives in me, the peace of God lives as me, the power of God flows through me; wherever I am, God is, and all is well.

24. Success is the persistent achievement of a worthy, challenging goal.

"Most people are about as happy as they make up their mind to be."
Pres. Abraham Lincoln

25. Success is the reward you give yourself for having the courage to do with your life what you want to do and doing it well.
26. The greatest use of life is to so live your life that the use of your life outlives your life.
27. Every misfortune always carries the seed of an equal or greater benefit.
28. Not failure, but low aim is the real crime in life.
29. Our life is what our thoughts make us.
30. I can change my life by changing my attitudes or my mind.
31. When I have felt depressed or discouraged, it is because of the ways I have let myself think and act.

In 1968, I was in Belem, Brazil, on the Amazon River. A friend, Glen Goble, arranged to take me to visit the national leper colony, some twenty miles from the city.

Some eight hundred lepers from all over the nation live there, families in their own cottages, raising their children, the vast majority never contaminated by the disease. Upon finishing high school in the colony, they are sent forth to work or college, leaving their parents in the colony. The mayor, Jose, is also pastor of the Baptist church in the colony. He took us on a tour of the colony, visiting the hospital where those in the final stages of this dread disease live out their final days under medication and care.

Then we went to Jose's modest two-bedroom home. We met Maria, a beautiful, lovely lady, now nearly fifty years old, giving a piano lesson to a twelve-year-old girl. Maria had a cloth covering her arms, because her hands had dropped off with leprosy.

At thirteen years of age, Maria had gone with her mother

"If one advances confidently in the direction of his dreams and endeavors, to live the life which he has imagined, he will meet with success unexpected in common people."
Henry D. Thoreau

to Paris, France, to study ballet and the organ. She was the most outstanding ballerina and organist in all of Brazil. For three years, she studied in Paris and was the rage of Europe in both dance and music.

Then she returned to Brazil for the summer. She came down with leprosy. The disease was no respecter of her talents, or the fact that her father was one of the wealthiest men in Brazil. The law required that she be placed in a leper colony. Can you imagine a more shocking experience? Jose, a poor worker's son, had been sent to the colony at age eighteen. He fell in love with Maria, and she responded to this handsome and kind man.

At age nineteen, Jose's leprosy was arrested, and he was released from the colony. He spent a year away, pining for Maria. Then, he went back to the colony as a government employee, to invest his life there with Maria. They were married, he free of the disease, she not. He studied to become the pastor, and at age forty, became the mayor and chief government employee in the colony.

Maria taught hundreds of children piano, organ, and ballet. She sent forth some of the most talented students in all Brazil, filled with the love and dedication Maria gave them.

I have never experienced such love, devotion, and such a happy home like Maria and Jose shared. They both have high self-esteem, giving their lives for others. Some years later, Maria died of leprosy, leaving Jose to carry on and leaving a heritage of love and devotion seldom seen.

Answers to Self-Esteem Test: 1-A, 2-B, 3-A, 4-B, 5-A, 6-B, 7-A, 8-B, 9-A, 10-B, 11-A, 12-B, 13-A, 14-B, 15-A, 16-B, 17-A, 18-B, 19-A, 20-B.

If you had 16—20 right, you have an outstanding sense of high self-esteem.

Share success, love, appreciation, and unconditional love and acceptance with all members of your family.

12—15 means you are on your way to having high self-esteem.

If you scored lower than this, you need a lot of work!

Conclusion

The only thing you and I totally control is our own minds. Determine that you will never surrender your high self-esteem to other people's negative thoughts about you.

Live in a day-by-day high of self-celebration.

Plan your joy time and luxuriate in it.

Be the best friend to yourself. Take yourself out to experience meaningful, free-from-regret pleasures that enhance your self.

Make your job a joyous, achieving event every day.

Give more of yourself in personal and family relationships than you expect to receive.

Live the ideal of "I will live my life so that the use of my life will outlive my life."

Blackie was from the Hell's Kitchen section of New York City. He carried a heavy load of self-hate that reflected itself in his spending several months in the brig.

Blackie was the worst marine in training I ever saw. Blackie was the greatest marine in combat I ever saw. He was so outstanding that our colonel said this to a new lieutenant just assigned to the platoon Blackie was in during combat in Okinawa: "Lieutenant, if I had the power, I would place you under the command of this private, Blackie. He's the most brilliant combat marine I've ever seen. Listen to him. He'll keep you alive."

Two days later, Blackie was dead. I helped bring his body in. He had been hit on the left wrist, shattering the bone, penetrating his watch and going into his chest. The doctor

---

"Pray as if everything depended upon God and work as if everything depended upon man."
Cardinal Francis J. Spellman

said, "Look at this." He picked the bullet out of Blackie's chest with this fingers. It had barely punctured his skin, not even entering the muscle or bone. "These hits are not life-threatening. He died of shock. He expected to die. It was self-induced."

In 1961, I was driving a new Chrysler on a two-lane highway in Mississippi when a car came out from my left, failed to see me, and hit my car on the side, flipping me. I was traveling seventy-five miles an hour and had no time to avoid being hit. My car turned over ten times in a water-filled canal before coming to a stop, upside down, some distance down the road. The top of the car was level with the dashboard, all four wheels were gone. I touched my seat belts, opened the door (other doors had to be opened later with a blow torch), and swam to shore. I couldn't see out of my left eye, and my face was covered with blood. I walked back some distance to the road where I was hit, having covered my left eye with my handkerchief. A Mr. Bell met me there, removed my handkerchief, and said, "Your eye is not injured, you have a cut on your forehead. I'll take you to the hospital."

We got into his pickup truck and started into town. I began to use self-hypnosis on myself to control the pain in my head. By the time we had driven the four miles into town, I felt no pain. I had a considerable cut on my head that took a number of stitches.

The doctor said, "Why aren't you in shock? I've seen people die of shock with less injuries than you."

I told him about Blackie and said, "My high self-esteem has given me the confidence to overcome problems, not to be overcome by problems."

The three most important words in communication:
"You are important."

Blackie died because of low self-esteem. I lived because of high self-esteem.

The California Task Force found self-esteem was "appreciating my own worth and importance and having the character to be accountable for myself and to act responsibly toward others." Dr. John Talbert, professor and chairman of the department of psychiatry at the University of Maryland School of Medicine, says that self-esteem is often the result of a combination of factors: early childhood events, genetics, and personality. "It's the sum total of experiences, thoughts, fears, and fantasies that come together in a composite impression of how we are."

Martin E. Ford, a developmental and educational psychologist at Stanford University who has studied self-esteem for more than a decade, believes "it's an evaluation that things are going well with you."

So, there is no short cut to high self-esteem. If you were bestowed self-esteem by your parents, teachers, and life experiences, consider yourself fortunate. If you were not so blessed, then determine that for the rest of your life you will pursue this highest of life's values, believing in yourself. Take charge of your life by using this workbook to certify your importance, to achieve high self-esteem.

"The greatest discovery of my generation is that human beings can alter their lives by altering their attitudes of mind."
William James

Bibliography

BOOKS

Albert, Dora. *You Are Better Than You Think*. Englewood Cliffs, N.J.: Prentice-Hall, Inc., 1957.

Allen, Mel and Graham, Frank, Jr. *It Takes Heart*. New York: Harper, 1959.

The Amplified Bible. Grand Rapids, Mich.: Zondervan Publishing House, 1965.

Baker, Samm Sinclair. *Your Key to Creative Thinking*. New York: Harper, 1962.

Battista, O. A. *The Power To Influence People*. Englewood Cliffs, N.J.: Prentice-Hall, Inc., 1959.

Benson, Herbert, and Klipper, Miriam Z. *The Relaxation Response*. New York: Avon, 1976.

Bettger, Frank. *Benjamin Franklin's Secret of Success and What It Did for Me*. Englewood Cliffs, N.J.: Prentice-Hall, Inc., 1960.

———, *How I Multiplied My Income and Happiness in Selling*. Englewood Cliffs, N.J.: Prentice-Hall, Inc., 1954.

———. *How I Raised Myself From Failure to Success in Selling*. Englewood Cliffs, N.J.: Prentice-Hall, Inc., 1958.

Bone, Diane. *The Business of Listening*. Los Altos, CA: Crisp, 1988.

Brande, Dorothea. *Wake Up and Live!* New York: Pocket Books, Inc., 1939.

Branden, Nathaniel. *Honoring the Self: Personal Integrity and the Heroic Potentials of Human Nature*. Los Angeles: J. P. Tarcher, 1984.

———. *How to Raise Your Self-Esteem*. New York: Bantam, 1988.

———. *The Psychology of Self-Esteem*. New York: Bantam, 1971.

Briggs, Dorothy C. *Your Child's Self-Esteem: The Key to His Life*. New York: Doubleday, 1975.

Bristol, Claude M. *The Magic of Believing*. Englewood Cliffs, N.J.: Prentice-Hall, Inc., 1957.

Bristol, Claude M. and Sherman, Harold. *TNT: The Power Within You*. Englewood Cliffs, N.J.: Prentice-Hall, Inc., 1954.

Bryant, Al. *1,000 New Illustrations*. Grand Rapids, Mich.: Zondervan Publishing House, 1957.

Carnegie, Dale. *How to Stop Worrying and Start Living*. New York: Simon and Schuster, Inc., 1948.

———. *How To Win Friends and Influence People*. New York: Simon and Schuster, Inc., 1936.

Carnegie, Dorothy, ed. *Dale Carnegie's Scrapbook*. New York: Simon and Schuster, Inc., 1959.

Cousins, Norman. *Anatomy of an Illness As Perceived by the Patient*. New York: Bantam, 1983.

————. *The Healing Heart.* New York: Avon, 1984.

Custer, Dan. *The Miracle of Mind Power.* Englewood Cliffs, N.J.: Prentice-Hall, Inc., 1960.

Davidson, Clinton. *How I Discovered the Secret of Success in the Bible.* Westwood, N.J.: Fleming H. Revell Co., 1961.

Dell, Twyla. *An Honest Day's Work: Motivating Employees to Give Their Best.* Los Altos, CA: Crisp, 1988.

Doan, Eleanor. *The Speaker's Sourcebook of 4,000.* Grand Rapids, Mich.: Zondervan Publishing House, 1960.

Douglas, Mack R. *Freedom Unlimited.* West Palm Beach, FL: Easy Read Publishing Co., 1983.

————. *How to Give Your Child Self-Esteem.* West Palm Beach, FL: Easy Read Publishing Co., 1986.

————. *How to Make a Habit of Succeeding.* Grand Rapids, MI: Zondervan, 1987.

————. *How to Raise Drug-Free Children.* West Palm Beach, FL: Easy Read Publishing Co., 1986.

Edwards, Tryon, ed. *The New Dictionary of Thoughts.* New York: Standard Book Company, 1957.

Ely, Virginia, ed. *1 Quote.* Westwood, N.J.: Fleming H. Revell Co., 1963.

Farrell, Warren. *The Liberated Man.* New York: Random House, 1974.

Felleman, Hazel, ed., *Best Loved Poems of the American People.* New York: Doubleday, 1936.

Flesch, Rudolf. *The Book of Unusual Quotations.* New York: Harper, 1957.

Gabriel, H. W. *Twenty Steps to Power, Influence, and Control Over People.* Englewood Cliffs, N.J.: Prentice-Hall, Inc., 1962.

Garn, Roy. *The Magic Power of Emotional Appeal.* Englewood Cliffs, N.J.: Prentice-Hall, Inc., 1960.

Germain, Walter M. *The Magic Power of Your Mind.* rev. ed. New York: Hawthorne Books, Inc., 1956.

Giblin, L. T. *How To Have Confidence and Power in Dealing With People.* Englewood Cliffs, N.J.: Prentice-Hall, Inc., 1956.

Giniger, Kenneth S., ed. *The Compact Treasury of Inspiration.* rev. ed. New York: Hawthorne Books, Inc., 1964.

Gorman, Mike. *Every Other Bed.* Cleveland: The World Publishing Co., 1956.

Haggai, John Edmund. *How To Win Over Worry.* Grand Rapids, Mich.: Zondervan Publishing House, 1959.

Hanson, Peter G. *The Joy of Stress.* New York: Doubleday, 1985.

————. *Stress for Success.* New York: Ballantine, 1990.

Hart, Hornell. *Autoconditioning.* Englewood Cliffs, N.J.: Prentice-Hall, Inc., 1956.

Hart, Louise. *The Winning Family: Increasing Self-Esteem in Your Children and Yourself.* New York: Lifeskills Press, 1989.

Hegarty, Edward J. *How To Build Job Enthusiasm.* New York: McGraw-Hill Book Company, Inc., 1960.

———. *Showmanship in Public Speaking.* New York: McGraw-Hill Book Company, Inc., 1952.

Henry, Louis C. *Five Thousand Quotations for All Occasions.* Garden City, N.Y.: Garden City Books, 1956.

Hill, Napoleon. *How To Sell Your Way Through Life.* Cleveland: Ralston Publishing Company, 1958.

———. *The Master-key to Riches.* Los Angeles: Willing Publishing Company, 1945.

———. *Think and Grow Rich.* rev. ed. Greenwich, Conn.: Fawcett Publications, Inc., 1960.

Hovey, E. Paul. *The Treasury for Special Days and Occasions.* Westwood, N.J. Fleming H. Revell Co., 1961.

Howard, Vernon. *Success Through the Magic of Personal Power.* Englewood Cliffs, N. J.: Prentice-Hall, Inc., 1961.

Iocacca, Lee. *Talking Straight.* New York: Bantam, 1984.

Laird, Donald A. and Eleanor C. *Tired Feelings and How to Master Them.* New York: McGraw-Hill Book Company, Inc., 1960.

Lincoln, James F. *Incentive Management.* Cleveland: Lincoln Electric Company, 1951.

Lozanov, Georgi. *Suggestology and Outlines of Suggestopedy.* New York: Gordon & Breach, 1978.

McCay, James T. *The Management of Time.* Englewood Cliffs, N.J.: Prentice-Hall, Inc., 1959.

McFarland, Kenneth. *Eloquence in Public Speaking.*Englewood Cliffs, N.J.: Prentice-Hall, Inc., 1961.

Maltz, Maxwell. *Psycho-cybernetics.* Englewood Cliffs, N.J.: Prentice-Hall, Inc., 1960.

Martin, Clement G. *How To Live To Be A Hundred.* New York: Frederick Fell, Inc., 1963.

Milt, H. and Stevenson, G. *Master Your Tensions and Enjoy Living Again.* Englewood Cliffs, N.J.: Prentice-Hall, Inc., 1959.

Murphy, Joseph. *The Power of Your Subconscious Mind.* Englewood Cliffs, N.J.: Prentice-Hall, Inc., 1963.

Narramore, Clyde M. *Improving Your Self-Confidence.* Grand Rapids, Mich.: Zondervan Publishing House, 1961.

———. *This Way to Happiness.* Grand Rapids, Mich.: Zondervan Publishing House, 1958.

Peale, Norman Vincent. *The Power of Positive Thinking.* Englewood Cliffs, N.J.: Prentice-Hall, Inc., 1954

Porat, Freida. *Self-Esteem: The Key to Success in Work and Love.* Saratoga, CA: R & E Publishers, 1982.

Price, Eugenia. *What Is God Like?* Grand Rapids, Mich.: Zondervan Publishing House, 1960.

Prochnow, Herbert V. *The Public Speaker's Treasure Chest.* rev. Ed. New York: Harper, 1964.

Prochnow, Herbert V. and Herbert V., Jr. *A Dictionary of Wit, Wisdom, and Satire*. New York: Harper, 1962.

Ray, Sondra. *I Deserve Love*. Berkeley, CA: Celestial Arts, 1987.

Roth, Charles B. *My Lifetime Encyclopedia of Selling Ideas*. Englewood Cliffs, N.J.: Prentice-Hall, Inc., 1963.

———. *Winning Personal Recognition*. Englewood Cliffs, N.J.: Prentice-Hall, Inc., 1954.

Sadhu, Mouni. *Concentration*. New York: Harper, 1959.

Satir, Virginia. *Self-Esteem*. Berkeley, CA: Celestial Arts, 1975.

Schindler, John *How To Live 365 Days a Year*. Englewood Cliffs, N.J.: Prentice-Hall, Inc., 1955.

Schleh, Edward C. *Successful Executive Action: A Practical Course in Getting Executive Results*. Englewood Cliffs, N.J.: Prentice-Hall, Inc., 1956.

Schwartz, David J. *The Magic of Thinking Big*. Englewood Cliffs, N.J.: Prentice-Hall, Inc., 1959.

Sherman, Harold. *How To Turn Failure Into Success*. Englewood Cliffs, N.J.: Prentice-Hall, Inc., 1958.

Siegel, Bernie. *Love, Medicine and Miracles*. New York: HarperCollins, 1986.

Starch, Daniel, *How To Develop Your Executive Ability*. New York: Harper, 1943.

Stone, W. Clement. *The Success System That Never Fails. Englewood Cliffs, N.J.: Prentice-Hall, Inc., 1962.*

Sweetland, Ben. Grow Rich While You Sleep. Englewood Cliffs, N.J.: Prentice-Hall, Inc. 1962.

———. *I Can, The Key to Life's Golden Secrets*. New York: Cadillac Publishing Company, 1953.

———. *I Will!* Englewood Cliffs, N.J.: Prentice-Hall, Inc., 1960.

Uris, Auren. *How To Be a Successful Leader*. New York: McGraw-Hill Book Company, 1953.

Walker, Harold Blake. *Power To Manage Yourself*. New York: Harper, 1955.

Whiting, Percy H. *The Five Great Rules of Selling*. rev. Ed. New York: McGraw-Hill Book Company, 1957.

Waitley, Denis. *The Double Win*. New York: Berkley, 1986.

———. *The Psychology of Winning*. New York: Berkley, 1984.

———. *The Seeds of Greatness: The Ten Best Kept Secrets of Total Success*. New York: Picket, 1988.

———. *The Winner's Edge*. New York: Berkley, 1984.

Waitley, Denis, and Witt, Reni. *The Joy of Working: The Thirty Day System to Success, Wealth and Happiness on the Job*. New York: Ballantine, 1986.

RECORDS

Bennett, Millard. *The Power of Inspired Salesmanship*. Waco, Texas: Success Motivation Institute, Inc.

Brown, Ralph R. *The Power Within You*. St. Louis, Mo.: Sales Success Unlimited.

Bibliography

Clasen, George F. *The Richest Man in Babylon.* Waco, Texas: Success Motivation Institute, Inc.

Conklin, Bob. *The Key to Motivation.* Minneapolis, Minn.: Midwest Audio-Visual Company.

Conwell, Russell. *Acres of Diamonds.* Waco, Texas: Success Motivation Institute, Inc.

Kohe, J. Martin. *How To Overcome Discouragement.* Waco, Texas: Success Motivation Institute, Inc.

Leterman, Elmer G. *Personal Powers to Creative Selling.* Waco, Texas: Success Motivation Institute, Inc.

Ling, Mona. *How To Get Appointments by Telephone.* Waco, Texas: Success Motivation Institute, Inc.

Meyer, Paul J. *Who Motivates the Motivator?* Waco, Texas: Success Motivation Institute, Inc.

Nightingale, Earl, *Lead the Field.* Chicago, Nightingale-Conant, Inc.

———. *The Strangest Secret.* St. Louis, Sales Success Unlimited.

———. *The Top Five Percent. Chicago,*Nightingale-Conant, Inc.

Steincrohn, Peter J. *Mr. Executive: Keep Well—Live Longer.* Waco, Texas: Success Motivation Institute, Inc.

Sweetland, Ben. *I Can.* Waco, Texas: Success Motivation Institute, Inc.

Wardlaw, Jack. *Thought Plus Action.* Waco, Texas: Success Motivation Institute, Inc.